Foundations of Law

Pearson

At Pearson, we have a simple mission: to help people make more of their lives through learning.

We combine innovative learning technology with trusted content and educational expertise to provide engaging and effective learning experience that serve people wherever and whenever they are learning.

We enable our customers to access a wide and expanding range of market-leading content from world-renowned authors and develop their own tailor-made book. From classroom to boardroom, our curriculum materials, digital learning tools and testing programmes help to educate millions of people worldwide — more than any other private enterprise.

Every day our work helps learning flourish, and wherever learning flourishes, so do people.

To learn more, please visit us at: www.pearson.com/uk

Foundations of Law

Selected chapters from:

Elliott and Quinn's English Legal System
Nineteenth Edition
Emily Allbon and Sanmeet Kaur Dua

Harlow, England • London • New York • Boston • San Francisco • Toronto • Sydney • Dubai • Singapore • Hong Kong
Tokyo • Seoul • Taipei • New Dehli • Cape Town • São Paulo • Mexico City • Madrid • Amsterdam • Munich • Paris • Milan

Pearson
KAO Two
KAO Park
Harlow
Essex CM17 9NA

And associated companies throughout the world

Visit us on the World Wide Web at:
www.pearson.com/uk

Compiled from:

Elliott and Quinn's English Legal System
Nineteenth Edition
Emily Allbon and Sanmeet Kaur Dua
ISBN 978-1-292-20851-0
© Pearson Education Limited 2012, 2013, 2014, 2015, 2016, 2017, 2018 (print and electronic)

ISBN 978-1-787-26888-3

Printed and bound in Great Britain by CPI Group.

CONTENTS

1

Case law

This chapter contains:

- an introduction to judicial precedent;

- a description of the hierarchy of the courts and judicial precedent;

- an analysis of how judicial precedent works in practice;

- a discussion of whether judges actually make the law, rather than simply declaring the law;

- consideration of whether judges should be allowed to make law; and

- an overview of the advantages and disadvantages of binding precedent.

Historical background

Before the Norman Conquest, different areas of England were governed by different systems of law, often adapted from those of the various invaders who had settled there; roughly speaking, Dane law applied in the north, Mercian law around the midlands and Wessex law in the south and west. Each was based largely on local custom and, even within the larger areas, these customs, and hence the law, varied from place to place. The king had little control over the country as a whole, and there was no effective central government.

When William the Conqueror gained the English throne in 1066, he established a strong central government and began, among other things, to standardise the law. Representatives of the king were sent out to the countryside to check local administration, and were given the job of adjudicating in local disputes, according to local law.

When these 'itinerant justices' returned to Westminster, they were able to discuss the various customs of different parts of the country and, by a process of sifting, reject unreasonable ones and accept those that seemed rational, to form a consistent body of rules. During this process – which went on for around two centuries – the principle of *stare decisis* ('let the decision stand') grew up. Whenever a new problem of law came to be decided, the decision formed a rule to be followed in all similar cases, making the law more predictable.

The result of all this was that by about 1250, a 'common law' had been produced, that ruled the whole country, would be applied consistently and could be used to predict what the courts might decide in a particular case. It contained many of what are now basic points of English law – the fact that murder is a crime, for example.

The principles behind this 'common law' are still used today in creating case law (which is in fact often known as common law). From the basic idea of *stare decisis,* a hierarchy of precedent grew up, in line with the hierarchy of the modern court system, so that, in general, a judge must follow decisions made in courts which are higher up the hierarchy than his or her own (the detailed rules on precedent are discussed later in this section). This process was made easier by the establishment of a regular system of publication of reports of cases in the higher courts. The body of decisions made by the higher courts, which the lower ones must respect, is known as case law.

The English common law system was exported around the world wherever British influence dominated during the colonial period. These countries, including the US and many Commonwealth countries, are described as having common law systems. They are often contrasted with civil law systems, which can be found in Continental Europe and countries over which European countries have had influence. The best-known civil law system is the French legal system, whose civil code has been highly influential.

The Supreme Court

Rather unexpectedly, the Labour Government announced in June 2003 that it was going to abolish the House of Lords (which had existed since 1876) and replace it with a Supreme Court. It subsequently issued a consultation paper, *Constitutional Reform: A Supreme Court for the United Kingdom,* which considered the shape that this reform should take. The Constitutional Reform Act 2005 was passed, which contained provisions for the creation of the new court. The Supreme Court (Photo 1.1) was established in 2009 and replaced the House of Lords. The term 'House of Lords' is slightly confusing because this name was

Photo 1.1 The Supreme Court in Parliament Square
Source: © Justin Kase Zelevenz/Alamy

used to describe both the highest court, which sat in the Palace of Westminster, and the upper chamber of Parliament. The upper chamber still remains; it is the Committee of the House of Lords sitting as a court that has been abolished. The last case to be heard by the House of Lords was the high-profile case of Debbie Purdy, who suffered from multiple sclerosis and who was seeking clarification on the criminalisation of individuals who assist the terminally ill to commit suicide.

The Labour Government was anxious to point out that the reform did not imply any dissatisfaction with the performance of the House of Lords as the country's highest court of law:

> On the contrary its judges have conducted themselves with the utmost integrity and independence. They are widely and rightly admired, nationally and internationally. The Government believes, however, that the time has come to establish a new court regulated by statute as a body separate from Parliament.

Six of the Law Lords opposed the reform, considering the change to be unnecessary and harmful.

Separation from Parliament

The consultation paper stated that this reform was necessary to enhance the independence of the judiciary from both the legislature and the executive. It pointed to the growth of judicial review cases and the passing of the Human Rights Act 1998 as two key reasons why this reform was becoming urgent. Article 6 of the European Convention on Human Rights requires not only that the judges should be independent but also that they should be seen to be independent. The fact that the Law Lords sat as a Committee of the House of Lords in Parliament raised issues about whether it appeared to be dependent on the legislature rather than independent.

The new Supreme Court is completely separate from Parliament. Its judges have no rights to sit and vote in the upper chamber. Only the Law Lords who sat in the House of Lords before it was abolished have the right to sit and vote in the House of Lords in its legislative capacity after their retirement from the judiciary.

One advantage of this change is that the court no longer sits in the Palace of Westminster, where there is a shortage of space. The Supreme Court is based in a refurbished Neo-Gothic building opposite Parliament in Parliament Square. A disadvantage is proving to be the financial arrangements for the court. In the past, the House of Lords' running expenses fell within Parliament's budget and did not attract much attention. Now its budget falls within the accounts of the Ministry of Justice and is exposed to the general cuts being made by politicians to reduce the nation's debt.

Jurisdiction

The Supreme Court can hear appeals from the whole of the United Kingdom. It can hear both civil and criminal appeals from England and Wales and Northern Ireland, and civil appeals from Scotland. It is the ultimate arbiter on questions of domestic law. Cases from the Supreme Court raising human rights issues can be heard by the European Court of Human Rights, and cases raising European law issues can be heard by the Court of Justice of the European Union. A case can only be heard by the Supreme Court if the lower court or, more normally, the Supreme Court itself, gives permission to appeal. In 2017, 31 per cent of applications for permission to appeal were successful.

The Supreme Court does not have the power to overturn legislation, a power enjoyed by the Supreme Court in America. It is not a purely constitutional court (like the *Conseil constitutionnel* in France), partly because we do not have a written constitution so it would be difficult to determine the jurisdiction of a constitutional court for the United Kingdom. The new court does not have the power to give preliminary rulings on difficult points of law because English courts do not traditionally consider issues in the abstract, so giving such a power to the Supreme Court would sit uneasily with our judicial traditions.

Membership

The full-time Law Lords from the former House of Lords are the first judges of the Supreme Court. It has a maximum of 12 full-time judges, but can call on the help of other judges on a part-time basis. Members of the Supreme Court are called 'Justices of the Supreme Court'. The Lord Chancellor was a member of the Appellate Committee of the House of Lords, but does not have a right to sit in the Supreme Court. The judges no longer automatically become Lords, instead the new male appointments take the title of 'Sir' and the female appointments 'Dame'.

Qualifications for membership have remained the same as for the House of Lords. The Government rejected the idea that changes should be made to make it easier for distinguished academics to be appointed in order to enhance the diversity of the court. This is disappointing, as the Government itself acknowledges that the current pool of candidates for the court is very narrow, and the Government's statistics show that the current senior judiciary are not representative of society. Candidates are not subjected to confirmation hearings before Parliament as these would risk politicising the appointment process.

In the Supreme Court five judges normally hear each case but in important cases seven or nine judges sit together. The rules for permission to appeal have remained largely unchanged, so the range and number of cases heard is similar to those of the House of Lords – about 70 cases each year.

The Supreme Court at work

In the past, the public was confused as to the identity of the House of Lords and its relationship with Parliament. Increasingly the public understands the role of the Supreme Court. It is open to the public and it is physically easier to visit than the old House of Lords which was hidden inside the long corridors of the Palace of Westminster.

Having moved into separate buildings from Parliament, the Supreme Court has tried to be more open, accessible and media friendly. All of its hearings are open to the public. The judge giving the lead, majority verdict will give a short oral explanation of the judgment in the morning it is released. This is televised and is occasionally shown on a news programme. There is more media interest in its work, particularly with its growing case load involving human rights law. It is gradually getting a higher profile and moving into the role of a constitutional court.

In 2017 the Supreme Court heard 91 cases and just under a third of these appeals were successful. The success rate of appeals has dropped but the number of successful appeals has remained about the same over the last few years. It is arguable that this high success rate suggests more cases should be given permission to appeal.

The physical layout of the Supreme Court building provides more opportunity for the judges to chat with each other informally when they are preparing their judgments than the offices on the long corridor in the House of Lords (Paterson (2013)). Through this process of discussion they can iron out some of their differences, so there are fewer divergent views being expressed in the individual judgments, reducing uncertainty. In 2014, only one-fifth of cases included a dissenting judgment. There is still a role for a minority dissenting judgment as this can help shape the law where the court later decides it got the law wrong.

As mentioned above, the Supreme Court sits in panels containing an odd number of judges, normally five, but sometimes they sit in panels of seven or even nine. It is worthy of particular note that in the Article 50 case of **R (on the application of Miller and Dos Santos)** *v* **The Secretary of State for Exiting the European Union (2017)**, 11 judges sat to hear the case. On one occasion in 2017, nine judges sat to hear a case and on nine other occasions seven judges decided the case.

Hearings in the Supreme Court are relatively short, lasting an average of two days. In 2016, the longest hearing was with regard to the aforementioned **Miller** case, which lasted four days. From the trial hearing, the Supreme Court takes on average three and a half months to give its decision. Its judgments are on average 30 pages long. In over half of the cases heard by the Supreme Court, one of the parties is a public authority (such as the HM Revenue & Customs, the Crown Prosecution Service and local authorities).

Judicial precedent

Case law comes from the decisions made by judges in the cases before them (the decisions of juries do not make case law). In deciding a case, there are two basic tasks: first, establishing what the facts are, meaning what actually happened; and, secondly, how the law applies to those facts. It is the second task that can make case law, and the idea is that once a decision has been made on how the law applies to a particular set of facts, similar facts in later cases should be treated in the same way, following the principle of *stare decisis* described above. This is obviously fairer than allowing each judge to interpret the law differently, and also provides predictability, which makes it easier for people to live within the law.

The judges listen to the evidence and the legal argument and then prepare a written decision as to which party wins, based on what they believe the facts were, and how the law applies to them. This decision is known as the judgment, and is usually long, containing quite a lot of comment which is not strictly relevant to the case, as well as an explanation of the legal principles on which the judge has made a decision. The explanation of the legal principles on which the decision is made is called the *ratio decidendi* – Latin for the 'reason for deciding'. It is this part of the judgment, known as binding precedent, which forms case law.

All the parts of the judgment which do not form part of the *ratio decidendi* of the case are called *obiter dicta* – which is Latin for 'things said by the way'. These are often discussions of hypothetical situations: for example, the judge might say 'Jones did this, but if she had done that, my decision would have been . . . ' None of the *obiter dicta* forms part of the case law, though judges in later cases may be influenced by it, and it is said to be a persuasive precedent.

In deciding a case, a judge must follow any decision that has been made by a higher court in a case with similar facts. The rules concerning which courts are bound by which are known as the rules of judicial precedent, or *stare decisis*. As well as being bound by the decisions of courts above them, some courts must also follow their own previous decisions; they are said to be bound by themselves.

When faced with a case on which there appears to be a relevant earlier decision, the judges can do any of the following.

Follow If the facts are sufficiently similar, the precedent set by the earlier case is followed, and the law applied in the same way to produce a decision.

Distinguish Where the facts of the case before the judge are significantly different from those of the earlier one, then the judge distinguishes the two cases and need not follow the earlier one.

Overrule Where the earlier decision was made in a lower court, the judges can overrule that earlier decision if they disagree with the lower court's statement of the law. The outcome of the earlier decision remains the same, but will not be followed. The power to overrule cases is only used sparingly because it weakens the authority and respect of the lower courts.

Reverse If the decision of a lower court is appealed to a higher one, the higher court may change it if they feel the lower court has wrongly interpreted the law. Clearly when a decision is reversed, the higher court is usually also overruling the lower court's statement of the law.

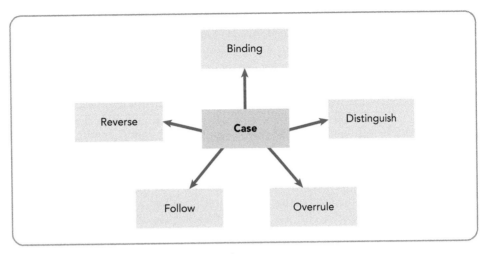

Figure 1.1 How judicial precedent works

In practice, the process is rather more complicated than this, since decisions are not always made on the basis of only one previous case; there are usually several different cases offered in support of each side's view of the question.

Numerous cases are published in law reports, legal databases and online. In **R v Erskine** (2009) the Court of Appeal said lawyers needed to select carefully the cases they referred to in court or the justice system would be 'suffocated'. Only cases which established the princi ple of law under consideration should be cited. Authorities that merely illustrated the prin ciple, or restated it, should not be cited. The court was thereby seeking to ensure that the doctrine of precedent is not overwhelmed by the sheer number of published judgments.

The hierarchy of the courts

Court of Justice of the European Union

At present, decisions of the Court of Justice of the European Union on European law are binding on all English courts (European Communities Act 1972, s. 3(1)). Although the European Court tends to follow its own previous decisions, it is not bound to do so, but we need to know what the position will be post-Brexit. Indeed, Lord Neuberger, prior to step- ping down as the President of the Supreme Court, impressed upon the Government to clarify the position. He is mindful of the separation of powers and has maintained that 'If [the Government] doesn't express clearly what the judges should do about decisions of the European Court of Justice after Brexit, or indeed any other topic after Brexit, then the judges will simply have to do their best.' This would mean that the judges need to be guided by statute otherwise they will be left with little guidance from the Government.

Supreme Court

Apart from cases concerning European law, the Supreme Court is the highest appeal court on civil and criminal matters, and all other English courts are bound by it.

The Supreme Court replaced the long-established House of Lords in 2009 and the rules of precedent are exactly the same for the Supreme Court as they were for the House of Lords before it. The House of Lords was traditionally bound by its own decisions, but in 1966 the Lord Chancellor issued a Practice Statement saying that the House of Lords was no longer bound by its previous decisions. In practice, the House of Lords only rarely overruled one of its earlier decisions, and this reluctance is illustrated by the case of **R v Kansal (No. 2)** (2001). In that case the House of Lords held that it had probably got the law wrong in its earlier decision of **R v Lambert** (2001). The latter case had ruled that the Human Rights Act 1998 would not have retrospective effect in relation to appeals heard by the House of Lords after the Act came into force, but which had been decided by the lower courts before the Act came into force. Despite the fact that the majority thought the earlier judgment of **Lambert** was wrong, the House decided in **Kansal** to follow it. This was because **Lambert** was a recent decision, it represented a possible interpretation of the statute that was not unworkable and it only concerned a temporary transitional period.

There is, however, a range of cases where the House of Lords had been prepared to apply the **1966 Practice Direction.** In **Hall v Simons** (2000), the House of Lords refused to follow the earlier case of **Rondel v Worsley** (1969), which had given barristers immunity against claims for negligence in their presentation of cases.

In **R v G and another** (2003), the House of Lords overruled an established criminal case of **R v Caldwell** (1981). Under **R v Caldwell,** the House had been prepared to convict people for criminal offences where the prosecution had not proved that the defendant personally had intended, or seen the risk of causing, the relevant harm, but had simply shown that a reasonable person would have had this state of mind on the facts. This was particularly harsh where the actual defendant was incapable of seeing the risk of harm, because, for example, they were very young or of low intelligence. **Caldwell** had been heavily criticised by academics over the years, but when the House of Lords originally reconsidered the matter, in **R v Reid** (1992), it confirmed its original decision. However, when the matter again came to the House of Lords in 2003, the House dramatically admitted that it had got the law wrong. It stated:

> The surest test of a new legal rule is not whether it satisfies a team of logicians but how it performs in the real world. With the benefit of hindsight the verdict must be that the rule laid down by the majority in Caldwell failed this test. It was severely criticised by academic lawyers of distinction. It did not command respect among practitioners and judges. Jurors found it difficult to understand; it also sometimes offended their sense of justice. Experience suggests that in Caldwell the law took a wrong turn.

In **R v Jogee** (2016), the Supreme Court was looking at the law on accomplice liability. The law on this subject had been developed by the House of Lords in **R v Powell and English** (1999). The Supreme Court decided that the House of Lords had got the law wrong on this area and that it was appropriate to change back the law to how it had been before **Powell and English.** It was justified in making this change because when the House of Lords had decided **Powell and English** not all relevant authorities were considered; the law laid down in **Powell and English** was not satisfactory and caused problems leading to a large number of appeals; and it was wrong for accomplice liability to be imposed when the accomplice had less culpability than the murderer. A change in the law did not need to be left to Parliament because accomplice liability is governed by the common law and should be corrected by the courts. This change in the law would also bring the common law into line with legislation made by Parliament (the Serious Crime Act 2007) in an overlapping area of criminal liability. The law was therefore changed even though the Supreme Court was mindful of the fact that this change was likely to lead to a number of appeals by people who had been convicted as accomplices in earlier cases under **Powell and English.**

In **Re Pinochet Ugarte** (1999), the House of Lords stated that it had the power to reopen an appeal where, through no fault of his or her own, one of the parties has been subjected to an unfair procedure. The case was part of the litigation concerning General Augusto Pinochet, the former Chilean head of state. The Lords reopened the appeal because one of the Law Lords who heard the original appeal, Lord Hoffmann, was connected with the human rights organisation Amnesty International, which had been a party to the appeal. This meant that there was a possibility of bias and so the proceedings could be viewed as unfair. The Lords stressed, however, that there was no question of them being able to reopen an appeal because the decision made originally was thought to be wrong; the Pinochet appeal was reopened because it could be said that there had not been a fair hearing, and not because the decision reached was wrong (although at the second hearing of the appeal, the Lords did in fact come to a slightly different decision).

Assange *v* **Swedish Prosecution Authority** (2012) concerned an application by the Swedish authorities for Julian Assange (involved in the Wikileaks scandal) to be extradited to Sweden to face charges concerning accusations of sexual assault. The Supreme Court allowed this application but Assange's lawyer argued that the case should be reopened because the Supreme Court had decided the case on the basis of the Vienna Convention, which had not been discussed during the hearing. This argument to reopen the case was subsequently rejected.

Privy Council

The Privy Council was established by the Judicial Committee Act 1833. It is the final appeal court for outlying British or formerly British territories, such as Jamaica, Gibraltar and the Isle of Man. The judges of the Supreme Court sit in the Privy Council. It is based in the buildings of the Supreme Court but remains a separate entity. In 2017, it heard 47 appeals.

Under the traditional rules of precedent, the decisions of the Privy Council do not bind English courts, but have strong persuasive authority because of the seniority of the judges who sit in the Privy Council (**de Lasala** *v* **de Lasala** (1980)). A national court will therefore usually follow a Privy Council decision (unless there is a decision of a superior court to the contrary), but it is not bound by precedent to do so. A judge of the Courts of England and Wales should not follow a decision of the Privy Council if it is inconsistent with the decision of a court by which the judge is otherwise bound, because the Privy Council is not part of the hierarchy of the national court structure.

Some recent cases, particularly in the context of criminal law, had thrown doubt on this limited role of the Privy Council in developing judicial precedent in England, but the traditional approach has been confirmed by the Supreme Court in **Willers** *v* **Joyce** (2016). The Supreme Court stated that a first instance judge or the Court of Appeal cannot decide to ignore this rule of precedent simply because they consider it a 'foregone conclusion' that the Privy Council view will be accepted by the Supreme Court in the future. Judges should never follow a decision of the Privy Council, if it is inconsistent with the decision of a court which is binding on them.

However, in **Willers** *v* **Joyce** the Supreme Court did state that, while a first instance judge or Court of Appeal judge cannot themselves ignore the traditional rules of precedent, the Privy Council itself can state its decision should be followed by the lower domestic courts. In an appeal to the Privy Council involving an issue of English law on which a previous decision of the House of Lords, Supreme Court or Court of Appeal is challenged, the Privy Council can expressly direct that the previous decision was wrong and that domestic courts should treat the Privy Council's decision as representing English law. The Supreme Court remarked that such an approach 'is plainly sensible in practice and justified by experience'. It takes advantage of the fact that the Privy Council judges normally consist of Justices of the Supreme Court.

In 2016 the Supreme Court and the Privy Council sat together for the first time. In **R** *v* **Jogee and Ruddock** (2016) the two courts heard two appeals jointly so that a united approach was taken to the legal issues that arose in the cases. **R** *v* **Jogee** was a domestic appeal to the Supreme Court and **R** *v* **Ruddock** was a Jamaican case on appeal to the Privy Council. The same panel of judges gave a joint judgment in the cases.

Willers *v* **Joyce** lays down as a matter of principle what effectively happened in practice in **Jersey** *v* **Holley** (2005). That case concerned the old defence of provocation in criminal law which if successful reduced a defendant's liability from murder to manslaughter.

The defence was laid down in s. 3 of the Homicide Act 1957. This section was interpreted as laying down a two-part test. The first part of the test required the defendant to have suffered from a sudden and temporary loss of self-control when he or she killed the victim. The second part of the test provided that the defence would only be available if a reasonable person would have reacted as the defendant did. This was described as an objective test, because it was judging the defendant's conduct according to objective standards, rather than their own standards. However, in practice, reasonable people almost never kill, so if this second requirement was interpreted strictly, the defence would rarely have succeeded. As a result, in **R** *v* **Smith (Morgan James)** (2000) the House of Lords held that, in determining whether a reasonable person would have reacted in this way, a court could take into account the actual characteristics of the defendant. So if the defendant had been depressed and was of low intelligence, then the test would become whether a reasonable person suffering from depression and of low intelligence would have reacted by killing the victim.

In an appeal from Jersey on the defence of provocation, **Attorney General for Jersey** *v* **Holley** (2005), the Privy Council refused to follow the case of **Smith (Morgan James)**, stating the case misinterpreted Parliament's intention when it passed the Homicide Act 1957. It considered the only characteristics that should be taken into account when considering whether the defendant had reacted reasonably were characteristics that were directly relevant to the provocation itself, but not general characteristics which simply affected a person's ability to control him- or herself.

The Court of Appeal in **James and Karimi** decided to apply the Privy Council's judgment in **Holley** rather than the House of Lords' judgment in **Smith (Morgan James)**. The Court of Appeal acknowledged this went against the established rules of judicial precedent. It gave various justifications for treating this as an exceptional case in which those established rules should not apply. It pointed out that the Privy Council had realised the importance of its judgment and had chosen to have an enlarged sitting of nine judges, all drawn from the House of Lords:

> The procedure adopted and the comments of members of the Board in **Holley** suggest that a decision must have been taken by those responsible for the constitution of the Board in **Holley** . . . to use the appeal as a vehicle for reconsidering the decision of the House of Lords in **Morgan Smith,** not just as representing the law of Jersey but as representing the law of England. A decision was taken that the Board hearing the appeal to the Privy Council should consist of nine of the twelve Lords of Appeal in Ordinary.

The judges in **Holley** were divided in their verdict six to three. The start of the first judgment of the majority stated:

> This appeal, being heard by an enlarged board of nine members, is concerned to resolve this conflict [between the House of Lords and the Privy Council] and clarify definitively the present state of English law, and hence Jersey law, on this important subject.

The dissenting judges stated:

> We must however accept that the effect of the majority decision is as stated in paragraph 1 of the majority judgment.

Thus, even the dissenting judges appear to accept that the majority decision laid down the law in England. The Court of Appeal also considered that if an appeal was taken to the House of Lords, the outcome was 'a foregone conclusion' and the House would take the same approach as **Holley**:

> Half of the Law Lords were party to the majority decision in **Holley.** Three more in that case accepted that the majority decision represented a definitive statement of English law on the issue in question. The choice of those to sit on the appeal might raise some nice questions, but we cannot conceive that, whatever the precise composition of the Committee, it would do other than rule that the majority decision in Holley represented the law of England. In effect, in the long term at least, **Holley** has overruled **Morgan Smith.**

This argument would be more convincing if the **Holley** case had been decided by a unanimous verdict. In fact, there were still potentially six House of Lords judges who preferred the **Smith (Morgan James)** approach: the three dissenting judges and the three House of Lords judges who did not hear the **Holley** case. The 'foregone conclusion' test has been rejected by the Supreme Court in **Willers** *v* **Joyce.** What matters is whether the Privy Council has expressly stated that it is laying down the law for England and Wales.

Lord Woolf recognised in **R** *v* **Simpson** (2003) that the rules of judicial precedent must provide certainty but at the same time they themselves must be able to evolve in order to do justice:

> The rules as to precedent reflect the practice of the courts and have to be applied bearing in mind that their objective is to assist in the administration of justice. They are of considerable importance because of their role in achieving the appropriate degree of certainty as to the law. This is an important requirement of any system of justice. The principles should not, however, be regarded as so rigid that they cannot develop in order to meet contemporary needs.

The Court of Appeal presumably concluded in **James and Karimi** that this was a situation where justice could only be achieved by shifting the established rules of judicial precedent. The actual outcome of the case made it more difficult for a partial defence to murder, reducing liability to manslaughter, to succeed. This may be considered to achieve justice for victims' families, but it may be an injustice to the mentally ill defendant.

Court of Appeal

This is split into Civil and Criminal Divisions; they do not bind each other. Both are bound by decisions of the old House of Lords, and the new Supreme Court.

KEY CASE

In **Young v Bristol Aeroplane Co Ltd** (1946) the Court of Appeal stated that the Civil Division is usually bound by its own previous decisions. There are four exceptions to this general rule.

1 The previous decision was made in ignorance of a relevant law (it is said to have been made *per incuriam*). This *per incuriam* rule was interpreted in **R v Cooper** (2011) as extending beyond decisions made in ignorance of legal authorities, to include decisions made in ignorance of relevant 'material and argument'. On the facts of that case, the material and arguments concerned the history of legislation banning sex offenders from working with children. Without this information the Court of Appeal had misinterpreted the legislation in an earlier case and this interpretation was corrected in the present case.
2 There are two previous conflicting decisions.
3 There is a House of Lords (or Supreme Court) decision which conflicts with the earlier Court of Appeal decision.
4 A proposition of law was assumed to exist by an earlier court and was not subject to argument or consideration by that court.

The last of these exceptions was added by **R (on the application of Kadhim) v Brent London Borough Housing Benefit Review Board** (2001).

Legal principle
The Civil Division of the Court of Appeal is usually bound by its own previous decisions.

In the Criminal Division, the results of cases heard may decide whether or not an individual goes to prison, so the Criminal Division takes a more flexible approach to its previous decisions and does not follow them where doing so could cause injustice. In **R v Simpson** (2003) the Court of Appeal stated that it had a degree of discretion to decide whether one of its earlier decisions should be treated as binding on itself when there were grounds for saying the earlier decision was wrong. This *dicta* was narrowly interpreted in **R v Magro** (2010), where the Court of Appeal held that its earlier decision in **R** *v* **Clarke** (2009) was wrong, but it was still not able to overrule it because the earlier decision had benefited from full argument of the relevant legislation and case law and the judges closely analysed the point. Thus **R** *v* **Simpson** was interpreted as simply referring to the *per incuriam* rule that an earlier case would not be binding if it was made in ignorance of a relevant law (at least when the earlier case benefits the defendant).

High Court

This court is divided between the Divisional Courts and the ordinary High Court. All are bound by the Court of Appeal, the old House of Lords and the new Supreme Court.

The Divisional Courts are the Queen's Bench Division, which deals with criminal appeals and judicial review, the Chancery Division and the Family Division, which both deal with civil appeals. The two civil Divisional Courts are bound by their previous decisions, but the Divisional Court of the Queen's Bench is more flexible about this, for the same reason as the Criminal Division of the Court of Appeal. The Divisional Courts bind the ordinary High Court.

The ordinary High Court is not bound by its own previous decisions. It can produce precedents for courts below it, but these are of a lower status than those produced by the Court of Appeal, the old House of Lords or the new Supreme Court.

Crown Court

The Crown Court is bound by all the courts above it. Its decisions do not form binding precedents, though when High Court judges sit in the Crown Court, their judgments form persuasive precedents, which must be given serious consideration in successive cases, though it is not obligatory to follow them. When a circuit or district judge is sitting, no precedents are formed. Since the Crown Court cannot form binding precedents, it is obviously not bound by its own decisions.

Magistrates' courts

The magistrates' courts hear mainly summary criminal cases. They are bound by the High Court, the Court of Appeal and the Supreme Court. Their own decisions are not reported, and cannot produce binding precedents, or even persuasive ones. Like the Crown Court, they are therefore not bound by their own decisions.

County Court

The County Court hears low-value civil cases. It is a court of record so it can set precedents for itself, but not for higher courts. It is bound by the High Court, the Court of Appeal and the Supreme Court.

European Court of Human Rights

The European Court of Human Rights (ECtHR) is an international court based in Strasbourg. It hears cases alleging that there has been a breach of the European Convention on

Human Rights. This court does not fit neatly within the hierarchy of the courts. Under s. 2 of the Human Rights Act 1998, an English court 'must take account of' the cases decided by the ECtHR. This would suggest that the decisions of the ECtHR are not completely binding on UK courts. Usually the jurisprudence of the ECtHR, having been taken into account, would be followed, but the domestic courts are not bound to do so. There is considerable debate about how s. 2 should be interpreted which is linked to a broader debate about how much influence the ECtHR should have in the United Kingdom. Under what has become known as the 'mirror principle', it has been suggested that the domestic courts should seek to mirror the interpretation of Convention rights to the interpretation given by the ECtHR. In **Manchester City Council *v* Pinnock (No. 2)** (2011) the Supreme Court stated:

> Where . . . there is a clear and constant line of decisions whose effect is not inconsistent with some fundamental substantive or procedural aspect of our law, and whose reasoning does not appear to overlook or misunderstand some argument or point of principle, we consider that it would be wrong for this court not to follow that line.

Despite this, the Supreme Court (and the House of Lords before it) has, on occasion, refused to follow an earlier decision of the ECtHR on the basis that the ECtHR has not fully understood the UK common law on this subject. In **Morris *v* UK** (2002), the ECtHR ruled that the courts martial system (which is the courts system used by the army) breached the European Convention on Human Rights as it did not guarantee a fair trial within the meaning of Art. 6 of the Convention. Subsequently, in **R *v* Boyd** (2002), three soldiers who had been convicted of assault by a court martial argued before the House of Lords that the court martial had violated their right to a fair trial under the Convention. This argument was rejected and the House of Lords refused to follow the earlier decision of the ECtHR. It stated:

> While the decision in Morris is not binding on the House, it is of course a matter which the House must take into account [s. 2(1)(a) of the Human Rights Act 1998] and which demands careful attention, not least because it is a recent expression of the European Court's view on these matters.

The House considered that the European Court was given 'rather less information than the House' about the courts martial system, and in the light of this additional information it concluded that there had been no violation of the Convention.

In **R *v* Horncastle** (2009), two appeals were heard together by the Supreme Court where defendants had been convicted using witness statements and the witness was not available to be cross-examined. In one case, the defendant was on trial for causing grievous bodily harm and the victim was a key witness but had died of natural causes before the trial. In the other case, the trial was for kidnapping and the victim had run away the day before the trial because she was too frightened to give evidence. The defendants appealed against their convictions, arguing that they had not received a fair trial in breach of Art. 6 of the European Convention. They referred, in particular, to the case of **Al-Khawaja and Tahery *v* UK** (2009) where the ECtHR had stated that convictions could not be based 'solely or to a decisive extent' on the evidence of a witness who could not be cross-examined (known as hearsay evidence). The defendants' appeals were rejected by the Supreme Court, which refused to follow the **Al-Khawaja** case. It commented that the ECtHR had developed its case law without giving full consideration to the safeguards against an unfair trial that existed under the common law. The Supreme Court stated:

> The requirement to 'take into account' the Strasbourg jurisprudence will normally result in this court applying principles that are clearly established by the Strasbourg Court. There will, however, be rare occasions where this court has concerns as to whether a decision of the Strasbourg Court sufficiently appreciates or accommodates particular aspects of our domestic process. In such circumstances it is open to this court to decline to follow the Strasbourg decision, giving reasons for adopting this course. This is likely to give the Strasbourg Court the opportunity to reconsider the particular aspect of the decision that is in issue, so that there takes place what may prove to be a valuable dialogue between this court and the Strasbourg court.

The original **Al-Khawaja and Tahery** *v* **UK** decision was given in Chamber and the UK Government requested that the case be reheard by the Grand Chamber (see p. 154). The Grand Chamber accepted in 2001 that hearsay evidence could be admissible provided there were sufficient counterbalancing safeguards. Thus, a healthy dialogue between the ECtHR and the national court resulted in modification of the European Court's position.

Where there is a conflict between a decision of the ECtHR and a national court which binds a lower court, the lower court should usually follow the decision of the binding

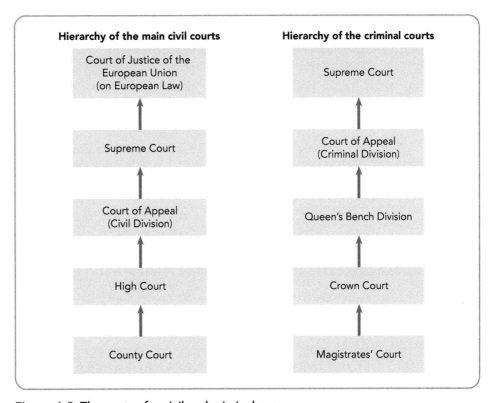

Figure 1.2 The routes for civil and criminal cases

higher national court, but give permission to appeal. Thus, in **Kay *v* Lambeth London Borough Council** (2006) the Court of Appeal had been faced with a binding precedent of the House of Lords which conflicted with a decision of the ECtHR. The Court of Appeal had applied the House of Lords' decision but gave permission to appeal. In the subsequent appeal the House had agreed that this was the appropriate course of action. We can expect to see similar tensions in the relationship between the Supreme Court and the ECtHR.

There is one exception where the usual English rules of precedent will not apply and the decision of the ECtHR will be followed rather than the decision of the House of Lords. This exception was identified in the case of **D *v* East Berkshire Community NHS Trust** (2003). In that case the Court of Appeal did not follow a decision of the House of Lords which was incompatible with the Convention because:

- the Strasbourg court had disagreed with the earlier House of Lords decision in an application made in the same case;
- the House of Lords' decision had been given before the Human Rights Act 1998;
- there had been no reference in the House of Lords' decision to the Convention;
- the policy considerations underlying the earlier House of Lords decision had been largely eroded.

How do judges really decide cases?

The independence of the judiciary was ensured by the Act of Settlement 1700, which transferred the power to sack judges from the Crown to Parliament. Consequently, judges should theoretically make their decisions based purely on the logical deductions of precedent, uninfluenced by political or career considerations.

The eighteenth-century legal commentator, William Blackstone, introduced the declaratory theory of law, stating that judges do not make law, but merely, by the rules of precedent, discover and declare the law that has always been: '[the judge] being sworn to determine, not according to his private sentiments . . . not according to his own private judgment, but according to the known laws and customs of the land: not delegated to pronounce a new law, but to maintain and expound the old one'. Blackstone does not accept that precedent ever offers a choice between two or more interpretations of the law: where a bad decision is made, he states, the new one that reverses or overrules it is not a new law, nor a statement that the old decision was bad law, but a declaration that the previous decision was 'not law', in other words that it was the wrong answer. His view presupposes that there is always one right answer, to be deduced from an objective study of precedent.

Today, however, this position is considered somewhat unrealistic. If the operation of precedent is the precise science Blackstone suggests, a large majority of cases in the higher courts would never come to court at all. The lawyers concerned could simply look up the relevant case law and predict what the decision would be, then advise whichever of the clients would be bound to lose not to bother bringing or fighting the case. In a civil case, or any appeal case, no good lawyer would advise a client to bring or defend a case that they had no chance of winning. Therefore, where such a case is contested, it can be assumed that, unless one of the lawyers has made a mistake, it could go either way, and still be in accordance with the law. Further evidence of this is provided by the fact that one can read a judgment of the Court of Appeal, argued as though it were the only possible decision in the light of the cases that had gone before, and then discover that this apparently inevitable decision has promptly been reversed by the House of Lords.

In practice, then, judges' decisions may not be as neutral as Blackstone's declaratory theory suggests: they have to make choices which are by no means spelled out by precedents. Yet, rather than openly stating that they are choosing between two or more equally relevant precedents, the courts find ways to avoid awkward ones, which give the impression that the precedents they do choose to follow are the only ones that could possibly apply. In theory, only the Supreme Court, which can overrule its own decisions as well as those of other courts, can depart from precedent: all the other courts must follow the precedent that applies in a particular case, however much they dislike it. In fact, there are a number of ways in which judges may avoid awkward precedents that at first sight might appear binding:

- By distinguishing the awkward precedent on its facts – arguing that the facts of the case under consideration are different in some important way from those of the previous case, and therefore the rule laid down does not apply to them. Since the facts are unlikely to be identical, this is the simplest way to avoid an awkward precedent, and the courts have made some extremely narrow distinctions in this way.
- By distinguishing the point of law – arguing that the legal question answered by the precedent is not the same as that asked in the present case.
- By stating that the precedent has been superseded by more recent decisions, and is therefore outdated.
- By giving the precedent a very narrow *ratio decidendi*. The only part of a decision that forms binding precedent is the *ratio*, the legal principle on which the decision is based. Since judges never state 'this is the *ratio decidendi*', it is possible to argue at some length about which bits of the judgment actually form the *ratio* and therefore bind courts in later cases. Judges wishing to avoid an awkward precedent may reason that those parts of the judgment which seem to apply to their case are not part of the *ratio*, and are only *obiter dicta*, which they are not obliged to follow.
- By arguing that the precedent has no clear *ratio decidendi*. There are usually three judges sitting in Court of Appeal cases, and five in the Supreme Court. Where each judge in the former case has given a different reason for coming to the same decision, or where, for example, two judges of the Supreme Court take one view, two more another, and the fifth agrees with none of them, it can be argued that there is no one clear *ratio decidendi* for the decision.
- By claiming that the precedent is inconsistent with a later decision of a higher court, and has been overruled by implication.
- By stating that the previous decision was made *per incuriam*, meaning that the court failed to consider some relevant statute or precedent. This method is used only rarely, since it clearly undermines the status of the court below.
- By arguing that the precedent is outdated, and no longer in step with modern thinking.

We can see that there is considerable room for manoeuvre within the doctrine of precedent, so what factors guide judicial decisions, and to what extent? The following are some of the answers that have been suggested.

Dworkin: a seamless web of principles

Ronald Dworkin argues that judges have no real discretion in making case law. He sees law as a seamless web of principles, which supply a right answer – and only one – to every possible problem. Dworkin reasons that although stated legal rules may 'run out' (in the sense of not being directly applicable to a new case) legal principles never do, and therefore judges never need to use their own discretion.

In his book *Law's Empire* (1986), Professor Dworkin claims that judges first look at previous cases, and from those deduce which principles could be said to apply to the case before them. Then they consult their own sense of justice as to which apply, and also consider what the community's view of justice dictates. Where the judge's view and that of the community coincide, there is no problem, but if they conflict, the judges then ask themselves whether or not it would be fair to impose their own sense of justice over that of the community. Dworkin calls this the interpretive approach and, although it may appear to involve a series of choices, he considers that the legal principles underlying the decisions mean that in the end only one result could possibly surface from any one case.

Dworkin's approach has been heavily criticised as being unrealistic: opponents believe that judges do not consider principles of justice but take a much more pragmatic approach, looking at the facts of the case, not the principles.

Critical theorists: precedent as legitimation

Critical legal theorists, such as David Kairys (1998), take a quite different view. They argue that judges have considerable freedom within the doctrine of precedent. Kairys suggests that there is no such thing as legal reasoning, in the sense of a logical, neutral method of determining rules and results from what has gone before. He states that judicial decisions are actually based on 'a complex mixture of social, political, institutional, experiential and personal factors', and are simply legitimated, or justified, by reference to previous cases. The law provides 'a wide and conflicting variety' of such justifications 'from which courts pick and choose'.

The process is not necessarily as cynical as it sounds. Kairys points out that he is not saying that judges actually make the decision and then consider which precedents they can pick to justify it; rather their own beliefs and prejudices naturally lead them to give more weight to precedents which support those views. Nevertheless, for critical legal theorists, all such decisions can be seen as reflecting social and political judgments, rather than objective, purely logical deductions.

Critical theory argues that the neutral appearance of so-called 'legal reasoning' disguises the true nature of legal decisions which, by the choices made, uphold existing power relations within society, tending to favour, for example, employers over employees, property owners over those without, men over women, and rich developed countries over poor undeveloped ones.

Griffith: political choices

In similar vein, Griffith (1997) argues in his book *The Politics of the Judiciary* that judges make their decisions based on what they see as the public interest, but that their view of this interest is coloured by their background and their position in society. He suggests that the narrow social background – usually public school and Oxbridge – of the highest judges (see p. 176), combined with their position as part of established authority, leads them to believe that it is in the public interest that the established order should be maintained: in other words, that those who are in charge – whether of the country or, for example, in the workplace – should stay in charge, and that traditional values should be maintained. This leads them to 'a tenderness for private property and dislike of trade unions, strong adherence to the maintenance of order, distaste for minority opinions, demonstrations and protests, the avoidance of conflict with Government policy even where it is manifestly oppressive of the most vulnerable, support of governmental secrecy, concern for the preservation of the moral and social behaviour [to which they are] accustomed'.

As Griffith points out, the judges' view of public interest assumes that the interests of all the members of society are roughly the same, ignoring the fact that within society, different groups – employers and employees, men and women, rich and poor – may have interests which are diametrically opposed. What appears to be acting in the public interest will usually mean in the interest of one group over another, and therefore cannot be seen as neutral.

Waldron: political choices, but why not?

In his book, *The Law* (1989), Waldron agrees that judges do exercise discretion, and that they are influenced in those choices by political and ideological considerations, but argues that this is not necessarily a bad thing. He contends that while it would be wrong for judges to be biased towards one side in a case, or to make decisions based on political factors in the hope of promotion, it is unrealistic to expect a judge to be 'a political neuter – emasculated of all values and principled commitments'.

Waldron points out that to be a judge at all means a commitment to the values surrounding the legal system: recognition of Parliament as supreme, the importance of precedent, fairness, certainty, the public interest. He argues that this itself is a political choice, and further choices are made when judges have to balance these values against one another where they conflict. The responsible thing to do, according to Waldron, is to think through such conflicts in advance, and to decide which might generally be expected to give way to which. These will inevitably be political and ideological decisions. Waldron argues that since such decisions have to be made 'the thing to do is not to try to hide them, but to be as explicit as possible'. Rather than hiding such judgments behind 'smokescreens of legal mystery . . . if judges have developed particular theories of morals, politics and society, they should say so up front, and incorporate them explicitly into their decision-making'.

Waldron suggests that where judges feel uncomfortable about doing this, it may be a useful indication that they should re-examine their bias, and see whether it is an appropriate consideration by which they are to be influenced. In addition, if the public know the reasoning behind judicial decisions 'we can evaluate them and see whether we want to rely on reasons like that for the future'.

Some support for Waldron's analysis can be found in Lord Hoffmann's judgment in **Arthur J.S. Hall & Co *v* Simons** (2000). In that case the House of Lords dramatically removed the established immunity of barristers from liability in negligence for court work. Lord Hoffmann stated:

> I hope that I will not be thought ungrateful if I do not encumber this speech with citations. The question of what the public interest now requires depends upon the strength of the arguments rather than the weight of authority.

Do judges make law?

Although judges have traditionally seen themselves as declaring or finding rather than creating law, and frequently state that making law is the prerogative of Parliament, there are several areas in which they clearly do make law.

In the first place, historically, a great deal of our law is and always has been case law, made by judicial decisions. Contract and tort law are still largely judge-made, and many of the most important developments – for example, the development of negligence as a tort – have had profound effects. Even though statutes have later been passed on these subjects, and occasionally Parliament has attempted to embody whole areas of common law in statutory form, these still embody the original principles created by the judges.

Secondly, the application of law, whether case law or statute, to a particular case is not usually an automatic matter. Terminology may be vague or ambiguous, new developments in social life have to be accommodated, and the procedure requires interpretation as well as application. As we have suggested, judicial precedent does not always make a particular decision obvious and obligatory – there may be conflicting precedents, their implications may be unclear, and there are ways of getting round a precedent that would otherwise produce an undesirable decision. If it is accepted that Blackstone's declaratory theory does not apply in practice, then clearly the judges do make law, rather than explaining the law that is already there. The theories advanced by Kairys, Griffith and Waldron all accept that judges do have discretion, and therefore they do to some extent make law.

Where precedents do not spell out what should be done in a case before them, judges nevertheless have to make a decision. They cannot simply say that the law is not clear and refer it back to Parliament, even though in some cases they point out that the decision before them would be more appropriately decided by those who have been elected to make decisions on changes in the law. This was the case in **Airedale NHS Trust v Bland** (1993), where the House of Lords considered the fate of Tony Bland, the football supporter left in a coma after the Hillsborough stadium disaster. The court had to decide whether it was lawful to stop supplying the drugs and artificial feeding that were keeping Mr Bland alive, even though it was known that doing so would mean his death soon afterwards. Several Law Lords made it plain that they felt that cases raising 'wholly new moral and social issues' should be decided by Parliament, the judges' role being to 'apply the principles which society, through the democratic process, adopts, not to impose their standards on society'. Nevertheless, the court had no option but to make a decision one way or the other, and the judges decided the action was lawful in the circumstances, because it was in the patient's best interests.

Thirdly, our judges have been left to define their own role, and the role of the courts generally in the political system, more or less as they please. They have, for example, given themselves the power to review decisions of any public body, even when Parliament has said those decisions are not to be reviewed. And despite their frequent pronouncements that it is not for them to interfere in Parliament's law-making role, the judges have made it plain that they will not, unless forced by very explicit wording, interpret statutes as encroaching on common law rights or judge-made law (see p. 59). They also control the operation of case law without reference to Parliament: an obvious example is that the 1966 Practice Direction announcing that the House of Lords would no longer be bound by its own decisions, which made case law more flexible and thereby gave the judges more power, was made on the court's own authority, without needing permission from Parliament.

The House of Lords has explained its approach to judicial law-making (which is the same for the Supreme Court) in the case of **C (A Minor)** *v* **DPP** (1995) which raised the issue of children's liability for crime. The common law defence of *doli incapax* provided that a defendant aged between 10 and 14 could be liable for a crime only if the prosecution could prove that the child knew that what he or she did was seriously wrong. On appeal from the magistrates' court, the Divisional Court held that the defence was outdated and should no longer exist in law. An appeal was brought before the House of Lords, arguing that the Divisional Court was bound by precedent and not able to change the law in this way. The House of Lords agreed, and went on to consider whether it should change the law itself (as the 1966 Practice Direction clearly allowed it to do), but decided that this was not an appropriate case for judicial law-making. Explaining this decision, Lord Lowry suggested five factors were important:

- Where the solution to a dilemma was doubtful, judges should be wary of imposing their own answer.
- Judges should be cautious about addressing areas where Parliament had rejected opportunities of clearing up a known difficulty, or had passed legislation without doing so.
- Areas of social policy over which there was dispute were least likely to be suitable for judicial law-making.
- Fundamental legal doctrines should not be lightly set aside.
- Judges should not change the law unless they can be sure that doing so is likely to achieve finality and certainty on the issue.

This guidance suggests that the judges should take quite a cautious approach to changing the law. In practice, however, the judges do not always seem to be following these guidelines. For example, in an important criminal case of **R** *v* **Dica** (2004) the Court of Appeal overruled an earlier case of **R** *v* **Clarence** (1888) and held that criminal liability could be imposed on a defendant for recklessly infecting another person with HIV. This change in the law was made despite the fact that the Home Office had earlier decided that legislation should not be introduced which would have imposed liability in this situation (*Violence: Reforming the Offences Against the Person Act 1861* (1998)). The Home Office had observed that 'this issue had ramifications going beyond the criminal law into wider considerations of social and public health policy'.

Some commentators feel that the judiciary's current approach is tending to go too far, and straying outside its constitutional place. Writing in the *New Law Journal* in 1999, Francis Bennion, a former parliamentary counsel, criticised what he called the 'growing appetite of some judges for changing the law themselves, rather than waiting for Parliament to do it'. Bennion cites two cases as examples of this. The first, **Kleinwort Benson Ltd** *v* **Lincoln City Council** (1998), concerns contract law, and in particular, a long-standing rule, originating from case law, that where someone made a payment as a result of a mistake about the law, they did not have the right to get the money back. The rule had existed for nearly two centuries, and been much criticised in recent years – so much so that a previous Lord Chancellor had asked the Law Commission to consider whether it should be amended by legislation, and they had concluded that it should. This would normally be taken by the courts as a signal that they should leave the issue alone and wait for Parliament to act, but in this case the Lords decided to change the rule. In doing so,

Lord Keith expressed the view that 'a robust view of judicial development of the law' was desirable. Bennion argues that, in making this decision, the Lords were usurping the authority which constitutionally belongs to Parliament. He also points out that judicial, rather than parliamentary, change of the law in this kind of area causes practical difficulties, because it has retrospective effect; a large number of transactions which were thought to be settled under the previous rule can now be reopened. This would not usually be the case if Parliament changed the law.

The second case Bennion criticises is **DPP** *v* **Jones** (1999), which concerned a demonstration on the road near Stonehenge. In that case the Lords looked at another long-held rule, that the public have a right to use the highway for 'passing and repassing' (in other words, walking along the road), and for uses which are related to that, but that there is no right to use the highway in other ways, such as demonstrating or picketing. In **Jones,** the House of Lords stated that this rule placed unrealistic and unwarranted restrictions on everyday activities, and that the highway is a public place that the public has a right to enjoy for any reasonable purpose. This decision clearly has major implications for the powers of the police to break up demonstrations and pickets.

Bennion argues that, in making decisions like these, the judiciary are taking powers to which they are not constitutionally entitled, and that they should not extend their law-making role into such controversial areas.

KEY CASE	An interesting recent example of judicial law-making is the Court of Appeal decision of **Simmons** *v* **Castle** (2012). The background to the case was that Lord Jackson (a senior judge) had produced a report recommending certain reforms should be made to the civil justice system to try to reduce the cost of litigation (see p. 616). Some of the key recommendations of this report were included by the Government in the Legal Aid, Sentencing and Punishment of Offenders Act 2012. But the legislation did not include a proposed reform to increase the award of damages by 10 per cent. The Government stated that calculation of damages was governed by the common law and it would be left to the courts to make this change. The Court of Appeal subsequently announced, in **Simmons** *v* **Castle** (2012), that this increase would take effect from 1 April 2013 at the same time as the 2012 Act would come into force. The Court of Appeal stated that when the 2012 Act was passed there was a 'clear understanding that the judges would implement the ten per cent increase'. And that it would be 'little short of a breach of faith' if the judges failed to do so. The problem with the courts changing the law in this way is that it throws into doubt how independent they are from the politicians. Also, the judges do not have the benefit of the tight parliamentary scrutiny. After the case was decided, the Association of British Insurers applied for the Court of Appeal to reopen its decision because it was unhappy that the decision would apply retrospectively to cases that had commenced before the April deadline and thereby increase the cost of these cases for the insurance companies.

Legal principle

Judges should change the law if Parliament intended them to do so and a failure to do so would be a breach of faith.

When should judges make law?

Again, this is a subject about which there are different views, not least among the judiciary, and the following are some of the approaches which have been suggested.

Adapting to social change

In 1952, Lord Denning gave a lecture called 'The Need for a New Equity', arguing that judges had become too timid about adapting the law to the changing conditions of society. They were, he felt, leaving this role too much to Parliament, which was too slow and cumbersome to do the job well (by 1984, he felt that judges had taken up the task again).

Lord Scarman, in **McLoughlin v O'Brian** (1982), stated that the courts' function is to adjudicate according to principle, and if the results are socially unacceptable Parliament can legislate to overrule them. He felt that the risk was not that case law might develop too far, but that it stood still and did not therefore adapt to the changing needs of society.

Paterson's (1982) survey of 19 Law Lords active between 1967 and 1973 found that at least 12 thought that the Law Lords had a duty to develop the common law in response to changing social conditions. A case where the judges did eventually show themselves willing to change the law in the light of social change is **Fitzpatrick v Sterling Housing Association Ltd** (2000). The case concerned a homosexual man, Mr Fitzpatrick, who had lived with his partner, Mr Thompson, for 18 years, nursing and caring for him after Mr Thompson suffered an accident which caused irreversible brain damage and severe paralysis. Mr Thompson was the tenant of the flat in which they lived and, when he died in 1994, Mr Fitzpatrick applied to take over the tenancy, which gave the tenant certain protections under the Rent Acts. The landlords refused. The Rent Act 1977 states that when a statutory tenant dies, the tenancy can be taken over by a spouse, a person living with the ex-tenant as wife or husband, or a member of the family who was living with the tenant. Mr Fitzpatrick's case sought to establish that he was a member of Mr Thompson's family, by virtue of their close and loving relationship.

The Court of Appeal agreed that 'if endurance, stability, interdependence and devotion were the sole hallmarks of family membership', there could be no doubt that the couple were a family. They also pointed out that discriminating against stable same-sex relationships was out of step with the values of modern society. However, they recognised that the law on succession to statutory tenancies was firmly rooted in the idea that families were based on marriage or kinship, and this had only ever been relaxed in terms of heterosexual couples living together, who were treated as if married. As a result, the court concluded that it would be wrong to change the law by interpreting the word family to include same-sex couples; all three judges agreed that such a change should be made, in order to reflect modern values, but it should be made by Parliament. The House of Lords, however, overturned the Court of Appeal's decision. It ruled that the appellant could not be treated as the spouse of the deceased tenant, but as a matter of law a same-sex partner could establish the necessary familial link for the purposes of the legislation.

Types of law

Lord Reid has suggested that the basic areas of common law are appropriate for judge-made law, but that the judges should respect the need for certainty in property and contract law, and that criminal law, except for the issue of *mens rea*, was best left to Parliament.

Consensus law-making

Lord Devlin (1979) has distinguished between activist law-making and dynamic law-making. He saw new ideas within society as going through a long process of acceptance. At first society will be divided about them, and there will be controversy, but eventually such ideas may come to be accepted by most members of society, or most members will at least become prepared to put up with them. At this second stage we can say there is a consensus. We can see this process in the way that views have changed over recent decades on subjects such as homosexuality and sex before marriage.

Law-making which takes one side or another while an issue is still controversial is what Devlin called dynamic law-making, and he believed judges should not take part in it because it endangered their reputation for independence and impartiality. Their role is in activist law-making, concerning areas where there is a consensus. The problem with Devlin's view is that in practice the judges sometimes have no choice but to embark on dynamic law-making. In **Gillick *v* West Norfolk and Wisbech Area Health Authority** (1985), the House of Lords was asked to consider whether a girl under the age of 16 needed her parents' consent before she could be given contraceptive services. It was an issue on which there was by no means a consensus, with one side claiming that teenage pregnancies would increase if the courts ruled that parental consent was necessary, and the other claiming that the judges would be encouraging under-age sex if they did not. The House of Lords held, by a majority of three to two, that a girl under 16 did not have to have parental consent if she was mature enough to make up her own mind. But the decision did not end the controversy, and it was widely suggested that the judges were not the right people to make the choice. However, since Parliament had given no lead, they had no option but to make a decision one way or the other, and were therefore forced to indulge in what Devlin would call dynamic law-making.

Respecting parliamentary opinion

It is often stated that judges should not make law where there is reason to believe Parliament does not support such changes. In **President of India *v* La Pintada Compañia Navigación SA** (1984), the House of Lords felt that there was a strong case for overruling a nineteenth-century decision that a party could receive no interest on a contract debt, but they noted that the Law Commission had recommended that this rule should be abolished and the legislators specifically decided not to do so. Lord Brandon said that to make new law in these circumstances would be an 'unjustifiable usurpation of the function which properly belongs to Parliament'.

Similarly, it is sometimes argued that judges should avoid making law in areas of public interest which Parliament is considering at the time. Lord Radcliffe suggested that, in such areas, judges should be cautious 'not because the principles adopted by Parliament are more satisfactory or more enlightened, but because it is unacceptable constitutionally that there should be two independent sources of law-making at work at the same time'.

Assisted voluntary euthanasia

There is an ongoing debate about whether someone should be able to lawfully assist another person to die. Under the current law such assistance could amount to murder. Campaigners in favour of voluntary euthanasia argue that the law should be changed either by Parliament or by the courts. In **R (on the application of Nicklinson)** v **Ministry of Justice** (2014) the applicant, Tony Nicklinson, had led an active life until, at the age of 51, he suffered a catastrophic stroke. This left him paralysed below the neck, unable to speak and only able to move his head and eyes. His condition is sometimes described as 'locked-in syndrome', because his active mind is locked into a virtually useless body. Tony summed up his life as 'dull, miserable, demeaning, undignified and intolerable'. He decided that he wanted to die but due to his disabilities he was not able to commit suicide without assistance unless he starved himself, which is a slow and very uncomfortable death. He sought a declaration from the courts that any doctors who assisted him in dying (known as assisted voluntary euthanasia (AVE)), would not be committing the offence of murder because they would have a defence of necessity. This declaration was refused. The court ruled that the defence of necessity was not available on these facts. To allow the defence of necessity would amount to a major change in the common law. This change could not be made by the courts, because any such change raised controversial social policy issues: parliamentary legislation would instead be required. The High Court noted that 'the subject is profoundly difficult and complex, raising a myriad of moral, medical and practical considerations'. As a result a court hearing an individual case, concentrating on the dire circumstances of the claimant, is not in a position to decide such broader questions, but its decision would create a precedent which would affect many other cases. The High Court commented:

> ... it is one thing for the courts to adopt and develop the principles of the common law incrementally in order to keep up with the requirements of justice in a changing society, but major changes involving matters of controversial social policy are for Parliament.

The High Court's decision has been confirmed by the Court of Appeal, and the Supreme Court. Parliament, unlike the courts, can control the consequences of such a move. If assisted voluntary euthanasia were legalised in this way, then the legislation would be able to put into place a surrounding framework regarding end-of-life care and procedural safeguards. The case, in effect, confirms the supremacy of Parliament. The judges did not want to be seen to be taking over the role of Parliament in making laws. The court followed the traditional role of judges as declarers of law, rather than makers of law. While the judiciary will not make law in this area, with every high-profile case the pressure for Parliament to review this area of law increases.

Protecting individual rights

In a 1992 lecture, the human rights lawyer, Anthony Lester QC, argued that while judges must have regard to precedent, they could still use their discretion within the system of precedent more effectively. He argued that, in the past, judges have abdicated responsibility for law-making by surrounding themselves with self-made rules (such as the pre-1966 rule that the House of Lords was bound by its own decisions). Since the 1960s, however, he feels that this tendency has gradually been reduced, with judges taking on more responsibility for developing the common law in accordance with contemporary values, and being more willing to arbitrate fairly between the citizen and the state. Lester praises this development, arguing that the judges can establish protection for the individual against misuse of power, where Parliament refuses to do so.

Advantages of case law

Certainty

Judicial precedent means litigants can assume that like cases will be treated alike, rather than judges making their own random decisions, which nobody could predict. This helps people to plan their affairs.

Detailed practical rules

Case law is a response to real situations, as opposed to statutes, which may be more heavily based on theory and logic. Case law shows the detailed application of the law to various circumstances, and thus gives more information than statute. The academic Roscoe Pound (1963) has written on the doctrine of precedent:

> Growth is ensured in that the limits of the principle are not fixed authoritatively once and for all but are discovered gradually by a process of inclusion and exclusion as cases arise which bring out its practical workings and prove how far it may be made to do justice in its actual operation.

Free market in legal ideas

The right-wing philosopher Hayek (1982) has argued that there should be as little legislation as possible, with case law becoming the main source of law. He sees case law as developing in line with market forces: if the *ratio* of a case is seen not to work, it will be abandoned; if it works, it will be followed. In this way the law can develop in response to demand. Hayek sees statute law as imposed by social planners, forcing their views on society whether the majority of people like it or not, and threatening the liberty of the individual.

Flexibility

Law needs to be flexible to meet the needs of a changing society, and case law can make changes far more quickly than Parliament. The most obvious signs of this are the radical changes the House of Lords made in the field of criminal law, following announcing in 1966 that its judges would no longer be bound by their own decisions.

Disadvantages of case law

Complexity and volume

There are hundreds of thousands of decided cases, comprising several thousand volumes of law reports, and more are added all the time. With the development of the internet, almost every decided case is available online or in legal databases. Judgments themselves are long, with many judges making no attempt at readability, and the *ratio decidendi* of a case may be buried in a sea of irrelevant material. This can make it very difficult to pinpoint appropriate principles.

A possible solution to these difficulties would be to follow the example of some European systems, where courts hand down a single concise judgment with no dissenting judgments. However, some of these decisions can become so concise that lawyers are required to do considerable research around the specific words used to discover the legal impact of the case, because no detailed explanation is provided by the judges.

Rigid

The rules of judicial precedent mean that judges should follow a binding precedent even where they think it is bad law, or inappropriate. This can mean that bad judicial decisions are perpetuated for a long time before they come before a court high enough to have the power to overrule them.

Illogical distinctions

The fact that binding precedents must be followed unless the facts of the case are significantly different can lead to judges making minute distinctions between the facts of a previous case and the case before them, so that they can distinguish a precedent which they consider inappropriate. This in turn leads to a mass of cases all establishing different precedents in very similar circumstances, and further complicates the law.

Unpredictable

The advantages of certainty can be lost if too many of the kind of illogical distinctions referred to above are made, and it may be impossible to work out which precedents will be applied to a new case.

Dependence on chance

Case law changes only in response to those cases brought before it, so important changes may not be made unless someone has the money and determination to push a case far enough through the appeal system to allow a new precedent to be created.

Unsystematic progression

Case law develops according to the facts of each case and so does not provide a comprehensive code. A whole series of rules can be built on one case, and if this is overruled the whole structure can collapse.

Lack of research

When making case law the judges are only presented with the facts of the case and the legal arguments, and their task is to decide on the outcome of that particular dispute. Technically, they are not concerned with the social and economic implications of their decisions, and so they cannot commission research or consult experts as to these implications, as Parliament can when changing the law. Increasingly, the senior courts have been willing to allow interveners to make representations in the public interest during court proceedings. Such an intervener might be, for example, a charitable body, such as Liberty or JUSTICE, and it will present to the court arguments about the broader impact of the case on society, provide comparisons with practice abroad and refer to socioeconomic research in the field. In the House of Lords' last year of operation, it allowed third-party interveners to make representations in almost a third of its cases.

Retrospective effect

Changes made by case law apply to events which happened before the case came to court, unlike legislation, which usually only applies to events after it comes into force. This may be considered unfair, since if a case changes the law, the parties concerned in that case could not have known what the law was before they acted. US courts sometimes get round the problems by deciding the case before them according to the old law, while declaring that in future the new law will prevail: or they may determine with what degree of retro-activity a new rule is to be enforced.

The same issue came before the courts again in **R** *v* **C** (2004). In that case the defendant was convicted in 2002 of raping his wife in 1970. On appeal, he argued that this conviction breached Art. 7 of the European Convention and tried to distinguish the earlier case of **SW** *v* **United Kingdom** (1995). He said that while in **SW** *v* **United Kingdom** the defendant could have foreseen in 1989 when he committed the offence that his conduct would be regarded as criminal, this was not the case in 1970. This argument was rejected by the Court of Appeal. It claimed, rather unconvincingly, that a husband in 1970 could have anticipated this development in the law. In fact, the leading textbooks at the time clearly stated that husbands were not liable for raping their wives.

KEY CASE

In **SW** *v* **United Kingdom** (1995), two men, who had been convicted of the rape and attempted rape of their wives, brought a case before the European Court of Human Rights, alleging that their convictions violated Art. 7 of the European Convention on Human Rights, which provides that criminal laws should not have retrospective effect. The men argued that when the incidents which gave rise to their convictions happened, it was not a crime for a man to force his wife to have sex; it only became a crime after the decision in **R** *v* **R** (1991). The court dismissed the men's argument: Art. 7 did not prevent the courts from clarifying the principles of criminal liability, providing the developments could be clearly foreseen. In this case, there had been mounting criticism of the previous law, and a series of cases which had chipped away at the marital rape exemption, before the **R** *v* **R** decision.

Legal principle

There is no breach of the European Convention when courts clarify the law, provided legal developments can be foreseen.

Recent criminal cases have shown that the retrospective effect of case law can also work to the benefit of the defendant. In **R** *v* **Powell and English** (1999) the House of Lords clarified the law that should determine the criminal liability of accomplices. An earlier controversial case that had involved the criminal liability of an accomplice was that of **R** *v* **Bentley** (1953), whose story was made into the 1992 film *Let Him Have It.* Bentley was caught and arrested after being chased across rooftops by police. Craig had a gun and Bentley is alleged to have said to Craig, 'Let him have it'. Craig then shot and killed a policeman. Craig was charged with murdering a police officer (at that time a hanging offence) and Bentley was charged as his accomplice. In court Bentley argued that when he shouted, 'Let him have it', he was telling Craig to hand over his gun rather than, as the prosecution claimed, encouraging him to shoot the police officer. Nevertheless both were convicted. Craig was under the minimum age for the death sentence, and was given life imprisonment. Bentley, who was older, was hanged. The conviction was subsequently overturned by the Court of Appeal in July 1998, following a long campaign by his family. In considering the trial judge's summing up to the jury, the Court of Appeal said that criminal liability 'must be determined according to the common law as now understood'. The common law that applied in 1998 to accomplice liability was more favourable than the common law that applied in 1952. The danger in practice is that every time the common law shifts to be more favourable to defendants, the floodgates are potentially opened for defendants to appeal against their earlier convictions. To try to avoid this problem, the Criminal Justice and Immigration Act 2008 provides that the Court of Appeal can reject as out of time references made to it by the Criminal Cases Review Commission which are based purely on a change in the common law. The court is likely to do this where a rejection of the appeal will not cause substantial injustice.

Undemocratic

Lord Scarman pointed out in **Stock** *v* **Jones** (1978) that the judge cannot match the experience and vision of the legislator; and that unlike the legislator the judge is not answerable to the people. Theories, like Griffith's, which suggest that precedent can actually give judges a good deal of discretion, and allow them to decide cases on grounds of political and social policy, raise the question of whether judges, who are unelected, should have such freedom.

Answering questions

1 **What do we mean when we say that the English Legal System is a common law system?**
University of London, International Programmes LLB

The meaning of 'common law' is discussed above (at p. 2). The term 'common law' has different meanings depending on the context in which it is being used. In the context of this question the focus is on common law being a product of England's legal history. It can be contrasted to the civil law systems which can be found in Continental Europe (for example,

France) and countries which were influenced by Continental Europe. This essay is not concerned with the distinction between equity and 'common law' (which is discussed at p. 121).

One approach to this essay would be to first provide a historical analysis of the common law (found on p. 2). Secondly, contrast the common law systems which emphasise judge-made law and the doctrine of judicial precedent, with the civil law systems which place a greater emphasis on legislative codes. Finally, provide some examples of the common law working in practice. For example, the fact that the definition of murder can be found in case law and the way that definition has been developed by the courts.

2 **Judicial reasoning in case law 'consists in the applying to new combinations of circumstances those rules of law which we derive from legal principles and judicial precedents . . . and we are not at liberty to reject them, and to abandon all analogy to them'. (Mr Justice Peak, 1833)**

Does this statement reflect the operation of precedent today? *University of London, International Programmes LLB*

Your answer could be divided into two parts. The first part could discuss how the statement of Mr Justice Peak fits within the classic declaratory theory of law provided by William Blackstone (p. 16). The basic rules that underpin judicial precedent with the hierarchy of the courts, and the ways that cases can be followed, distinguished, overruled and reversed support this view (p. 6).

The second part of your answer could point to theories and practice which undermine this view so that it may not 'reflect the operation of precedent today'. Thus, you could discuss the work of the critical theorists (p. 18), and Griffith (p. 18). The material under the heading 'Do judges make law?' (p. 20) would also be useful to answer this part of the essay.

You might conclude that while Mr Justice Peak's statement might suggest that the judges are simply applying existing legal principles and judicial precedents to a particular set of facts, there may be some flexibility in the way in which those principles and precedents can be applied, and there may be other factors that help determine the outcome of a case.

3 **Precedent must, on the one hand, provide certainty, but on the other hand, it must be flexible in adapting to social change. In view of the so-called binding nature of precedent, how are judges able to reconcile these seemingly contradictory characteristics in their use of precedent?**

You should begin by explaining what precedent is and how *stare decisis* operates, drawing on the materials in the section on 'Judicial precedent' (p. 6). Certainty and flexibility are two of the advantages of precedent. Preoccupation with certainty could lead to an overly rigid system where bad decisions have to be followed. However, there are a number of ways in which judges can exercise flexibility, and indeed, are permitted to do so. Examples that could be given include:

- use of the 1966 Practice Direction;
- the rules in **Young** v **Bristol Aeroplane Co Ltd** (1946) (relevant material can be found under the heading 'Court of Appeal' (p. 12));
- the practice of distinguishing earlier cases on their facts (see the section entitled 'How do judges really decide cases?' (p. 16)).

You could argue that this flexibility involves judges in 'making law', as opposed to applying the law, and you could express your view as to whether you think this is acceptable.

You might conclude with your view on how effectively (or not) you think judges balance certainty and flexibility, and indeed, whether you think they have to.

4 Critically evaluate the extent to which the doctrine of binding precedent inhibits judicial creativity.

The phrase 'judicial creativity' is a reference to the judges' ability to create or make law. Your essay could start by explaining the rules relating to judicial precedent including a clear explanation of the judicial hierarchy, and the exceptional rules relating to both the Court of Appeal and the Supreme Court (drawing upon material about judicial precedent and how it works under the heading 'Judicial precedent', p. 6). The relevance of the distinction between *ratio decidendi* and *obiter dicta* should be explained and the importance of decisions of the European Court of Justice and the European Court of Human Rights could also be mentioned. Explain some of the arguments in favour of precedent, such as certainty and consistency. This part of your answer would aim to show how far the rules of judicial precedent inhibit judicial freedom.

The second part of your essay could then explore how far, despite the rules of judicial precedent, 'judicial creativity' still exists. You might discuss some of the material contained under the heading 'Do judges make law?' (p. 20) in this chapter. You could discuss:

- the sheer amount of case law in our system (especially in contract and tort);
- applying the law is not usually an automatic matter in practice;
- judges have been left to define their own role in the system, in the context of the principle of the separation of powers; and
- the increased availability of reported material can afford significant judicial opportunities to distinguish cases, and thus to influence the future direction of case law.

You should finish with a conclusion, drawing on the points you have made, that states how far you think precedent does inhibit judicial creativity.

5 Evaluate the advantages of abolishing the doctrine of binding judicial precedent.

You first need to describe the doctrine of binding precedent, but do not spend too much time on this, as pure description is not what the question is asking for.

You should then consider what the law would lose if precedent were abandoned – the material on the advantages of precedent is relevant here. Then talk about the disadvantages of the system of precedent, and what might be gained by abolishing it. You could bring in the effects of the 1966 Practice Direction as an example of the relaxation of precedent, and talk about whether you feel it has benefited the law or not, mentioning appropriate cases.

You might mention innovations which would lessen the role of precedent, such as codification, and say whether you feel they would be desirable and why.

Your conclusion could state whether or not you feel precedent serves a useful role, and outline any changes which you feel should be made to its operation.

Summary of Chapter 1: Case law

Judicial precedent

In deciding a case, a judge must follow any decision that has been made by a higher court in a case with similar facts. Judges are bound only by the part of the judgment that forms the legal principle that was the basis of the earlier decision, known as the *ratio decidendi*. The rest of the judgment is known as *obiter dicta* and is not binding.

The hierarchy of the courts

The Court of Justice of the European Union is the highest authority on European law, in other matters the Supreme Court is the highest court in the UK. Under the 1966 Practice Direction, the Supreme Court is not bound by its previous decisions.

How do judges really decide cases?

According to the traditional declaratory theory laid down by William Blackstone, judges do not make law but merely discover and declare the law that has always been. Ronald Dworkin also accepts that the judges have no real discretion in making case law, but he bases this view on his concept that law is a seamless web of principles.

Very different views have been put forward by other academics. Critical theorists argue that judicial decisions are actually influenced by social, political and personal factors and that the doctrine of judicial precedent is merely used to legitimate the judges' decisions. Griffith also thinks that judges are influenced by their personal background. Waldron accepts that judges make political choices but sees no fundamental problem with this.

When should judges make law?

There is no doubt that on occasion judges make law. There is some debate as to when judges ought to make law. When judges make law they can adapt it to social change, but Francis Bennion has highlighted the danger that if the courts are too willing to make law, they undermine the position of Parliament.

Advantages of binding precedent

The doctrine of judicial precedent provides:

- certainty;
- detailed practical rules;
- a free market in legal ideas; and
- flexibility.

Disadvantages of binding precedent

Case law has been criticised because of its:

- complexity and volume;
- rigidity;
- illogical distinctions;
- unpredictability;
- dependence on chance;
- retrospective effect; and
- undemocratic character.

 ## Reading list

Bennion, F.A.R. (1999) A naked usurpation. *New Law Journal*, 149: 421.

Devlin, P. (1979) *The Judge*. Oxford: Oxford University Press.

Dworkin, R. (1986) *Law's Empire*. London: Fontana.

Griffith, J.A.G. (1997) *The Politics of the Judiciary*. London: Fontana.

Hale, Sir M. (1979) *The History of the Common Law of England.* Chicago: University of Chicago Press.

Hayek, F. (1982) *Law, Legislation and Liberty: A New Statement of the Liberal Principles of Justice and Political Economy.* London: Routledge.

Hohfeld, W.N. and Cook, W.W. (1919) *Fundamental Legal Concepts as Applied in Judicial Reasoning.* London: Greenwood Press.

Kairys, D. (1998) *The Politics of Law: A Progressive Critique.* New York: Basic Books.

Lawson, C.M. (1982) The family affinities of common law and civil law legal systems. *Hastings International Comparative Law Review,* 6: 85.

Lennan, J. (2010) A Supreme Court for the United Kingdom: a note on early days. *Civil Justice Quarterly,* 29(2): 139.

MacCormick, N. (1978) *Legal Rules and Legal Reasoning.* Oxford: Clarendon.

Paterson, A. (1982) *The Law Lords.* London: Macmillan.

(2013) *Final Judgment: The Last Law Lords and the Supreme Court.* Oxford: Hart Publishing.

Pound, R. (1963) *The Spirit of the Common Law.* Boston: Beacon Press.

Prime, T. and Scanlan, G. (2004) Stare decisis and the Court of Appeal: judicial confusion and judicial reform. *Civil Justice Quarterly,* 23: 212.

Summers, R. (1992) *Essays on the Nature of Law and Legal Reasoning.* Berlin: Duncker & Humblot.

Waldron, J. (1989) *The Law.* London: Routledge.

Weinreb, L. (2004) *Legal Reason: The Use of Analogy in Legal Argument.* Cambridge: Cambridge University Press.

On the internet

www

Decisions of the Supreme Court can be found on the website of the Supreme Court at:
https://www.supremecourt.uk/decided-cases/

The Supreme Court YouTube channel provides video-clips of the Justices of the Supreme Court handing down summaries of their judgments:
http://www.youtube.com/user/UKSupremeCourt

You can watch live broadcasts of the Supreme Court at work on the Sky News website at:
http://news.sky.com/supreme-court-live

The Supreme Court Annual Report and Accounts 2016–2017 can be found at:
https://www.supremecourt.uk/docs/annual-report-2016-17.pdf

The former House of Lords judgments are available on the House of Lords' judicial business website at:
http://www.publications.parliament.uk/pa/ld/ldjudgmt.htm

Some important judgments are published on the Court Service website at:
http://www.justice.gov.uk/about/hmcts/

You can watch an introductory film about the Supreme Court on the Supreme Court website at:
https://www.supremecourt.uk/about/introductory-film.html

2

Statute law

This chapter discusses:

- the House of Commons;
- the House of Lords;
- how an Act of Parliament is made; and
- post-legislative scrutiny.

Introduction

Statutes are made by Parliament, which consists of the House of Commons, the House of Lords and the Monarch. Another term for a statute is an Act of Parliament. In Britain, Parliament is sovereign, which has traditionally meant that the law it makes takes precedence over law originating from any other source though, as we shall see, membership of the European Union (EU) has compromised this principle. EU law aside, Parliament can make or cancel any law it chooses, and the courts must enforce it. In other countries, such as the United States of America, the courts can declare such legislation unconstitutional, but our courts are not allowed to do that.

House of Commons

The House of Commons is the democratically elected chamber of Parliament. Every four to five years Members of Parliament (MPs) are elected in a general election. There are 650 MPs who discuss the big political issues of the day and proposals for new laws.

House of Lords

The House of Lords acts as a revising chamber for legislation and its work complements the business of the Commons. Members of the House of Lords are not elected by the general public, instead the majority are appointed by the Queen on the recommendation of the House of Lords Appointments Commission. The House of Lords currently has close to 800 members, divided into four different types:

- Life peers
- Retired judges of the former House of Lords' judicial committee
- Bishops
- Elected hereditary peers.

Life peers are appointed for their lifetime only, so the right to sit in the House of Lords is not passed on to their children.

TOPICAL ISSUE

Modernising the House of Lords

The former Prime Minister, Lloyd George, described the House of Lords as 'a body of five hundred men chosen at random from amongst the unemployed'. Today's desire for reform might partly reflect public discontent at the 'cash for honours' controversy,

▶

when there were suggestions that individuals had been made Lords in return for donations to political parties. Such a reform could also provide a response to the recent scandal that some members of the Lords appear to have arranged for legislation to be amended in return for receiving large sums of money from private companies. At the moment the House of Lords is a chamber which legislates on behalf of the people but is not held to account by the people.

Traditionally, hereditary peers have sat in the House of Lords and this right was passed down from father to son. Membership of the House is currently undergoing a major reform to remove the role of the hereditary peers. Their right to sit and vote in the House of Lords was ended in 1999 by the House of Lords Act, but 92 members were elected internally to remain until the next stage of the Lords reform process.

The Royal Commission for the Reform of the House of Lords, chaired by Lord Wakeham, published its report in January 2000. It recommended that there should be a chamber of about 550 members. Only a minority would be elected, to represent the regions; the remainder would be appointed by an independent Appointments Commission. It would be responsible for selecting members who were broadly representative of British society. Approximately 20 per cent of the House of Lords' members would be politically independent and the others would reflect the political balance as expressed by the last general election. The Appointments Commission would be under a statutory duty to ensure that at least 30 per cent of new members were women and that minorities were represented in numbers at least proportionate to their representation in the total population. The powers of the new chamber would be broadly comparable with the present House of Lords.

In 2011, the coalition Government announced its proposals for House of Lords reform, with the publication of a White Paper and a House of Lords Reform Draft Bill. The key proposals were that there should be a smaller chamber of 300 members with 80 per cent elected and 20 per cent appointed. Elected members would be elected for a 15-year term on a staged basis – one third every five years. The appointed members would be chosen by an Appointments Commission, with 20 members being appointed at the same time as the elected members. The appointed members would be expected to make a 'non-party political' contribution to the work of the chamber. All members would be allowed to serve only one 15-year term.

The representatives of the Church of England would be retained but reduced in number from 26 to 12. The Prime Minister would also be able to make an unspecified number of Ministerial appointments to the House in addition to the 300 elected and appointed members. Anyone appointed in this way would only be a member of the House whilst he or she retained Ministerial office.

The existing life and hereditary peers have been removed from office. The primacy of the House of Commons over the House of Lords has been retained, as has been Parliament Acts of 1911 and 1949 (discussed on p. 40). These key recommendations, with a few minor amendments, were included in a House of Lords Bill which was presented to Parliament in 2012. However, following opposition by Conservative MPs, the Bill was abandoned after its Second Reading in the House of Commons.

Criminal Defence Service (Advice and Assistance) Act 2001

2001 CHAPTER 4

An Act to clarify the extent of the duty of the Legal Services Commission under section 13(1) of the Access to Justice Act 1999.   [10th April 2001]

B E IT ENACTED by the Queen's most Excellent Majesty, by and with the advice and consent of the Lords Spiritual and Temporal, and Commons, in this present Parliament assembled, and by the authority of the same, as follows: —

1   Extent of duty to fund advice and assistance

   (1)   Subsection (1) of section 13 of the Access to Justice Act 1999 (c. 22) (duty of Legal Services Commission to fund advice and assistance as part of Criminal Defence Service) shall be treated as having been enacted with the substitution of the following for paragraph (b) and the words after it —

   "(b)   in prescribed circumstances, for individuals who —

   (i)   are not within paragraph (a) but are involved in investigations which may lead to criminal proceedings,

   (ii)   are before a court or other body in such proceedings, or

   (iii)   have been the subject of such proceedings;

   and the assistance which the Commission may consider appropriate includes assistance in the form of advocacy."

   (2)   Regulations under subsection (1) of section 13 (as amended above) may include provision treating them as having come into force at the same time as that subsection.

2   Short title

   This Act may be cited as the Criminal Defence Service (Advice and Assistance) Act 2001.

Figure 2.1 An example of a statute: Criminal Defence (Advice and Assistance) Act 2001

Source: The Stationery Office. © Crown Copyright 2001

Making an Act of Parliament

Policy development

Before the parliamentary legislative process begins, usually a policy objective will have been identified by the Government of the day. This policy objective may have been set out in an election manifesto or included in an official consultation document, known as a Green Paper. The latter document puts forward tentative proposals, which interested parties may consider and give their views on. The Green Paper will be followed by a White Paper, which contains the specific reform plans. The Government's legislative plans for a parliamentary session are outlined in the Queen's Speech in May.

Bills

All statutes begin as a Bill, which is a proposal for a piece of legislation. There are three types of Bill:

Public Bills These are written by parliamentary counsel who specialise in drafting legislation. They are presented to Parliament by Government ministers and change the general law of the whole country.

Private Members' Bills These are prepared by an individual backbench MP (someone who is not a member of the Cabinet). MPs wanting to put forward a Bill have to enter a ballot to win the right to do so, and then persuade the Government to allow enough parliamentary time for the Bill to go through. Consequently very few such Bills become Acts, and they tend to function more as a way of drawing attention to particular issues. Some, however, have made important contributions to legislation, an example being the Abortion Act 1967 which stemmed from a Private Members' Bill put forward by David Steel.

Private Bills These are usually proposed by a local authority, public corporation or large public company, and usually only affect that sponsor. An example might be a local authority seeking the right to build a bridge or road.

The actual preparation of Bills is done by expert draftsmen known as parliamentary counsel.

Figure 2.2 Parliamentary Bills

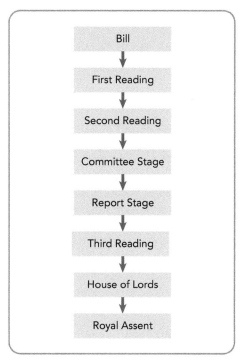

Figure 2.3 Making an Act of Parliament

First reading

The title of the prepared Bill is read to the House of Commons. This is called the first reading, and acts as a notification of the proposed measure.

Second reading

At the second reading, the proposals are debated fully, and may be amended, and members vote on whether the legislation should proceed. In practice, the whip system (party officials whose job is to make sure MPs vote with their party) means that a Government with a reasonable majority can almost always get its legislation through at this and subsequent stages.

Committee stage

The Bill is then referred to a committee of the House of Commons for detailed examination, bearing in mind the points made during the debate. At this point further amendments to the Bill may be made.

Report stage

The committee then reports back to the House, and any proposed amendments are debated and voted upon.

Third reading

The Bill is re-presented to the House. There may be a short debate, and a vote on whether to accept or reject the legislation as it stands.

House of Lords

The Bill then goes to the House of Lords, where it goes through a similar process of three readings. If the House of Lords alters anything, the Bill returns to the Commons for further consideration. The Commons then responds with agreement, reasons for disagreement, or proposals for alternative changes.

At one time legislation could not be passed without the agreement of both Houses, which meant that the unelected House of Lords could block legislation put forward by the elected House of Commons. The Parliament Acts of 1911 and 1949 lay down special procedures by which proposed legislation can go for Royal Assent without the approval of the House of Lords after specified periods of time. These procedures are only rarely used, because the House of Lords usually drops objections that are resisted by the Commons, though their use has increased in recent years. Four Acts of Parliament have been passed to date relying on the Parliament Act 1949:

- War Crimes Act 1991
- European Parliamentary Elections Act 1999
- Sexual Offences (Amendment) Act 2000
- Hunting Act 2004.

KEY CASE

It is of particular note that the procedures were used to pass the controversial Hunting Act 2004. This Act bans hunting wild animals with dogs and a form of hunting known as hare coursing. It was passed despite the House of Lords' opposition, by using the Parliament Act 1949. Members of the pressure group the Countryside Alliance brought a legal challenge to the Act in **R (on the application of Jackson and others) v Attorney General (2005)**. They argued that the Parliament Act 1949 was itself unlawful and that therefore the Hunting Act, which was passed relying on the procedures it laid down, was also unlawful. The initial Act of 1911 had required a two-year delay between the first vote in the House of Commons and reliance on the special procedures in the Act. The 1949 Act reduced this delay to one year and was itself passed using the special procedures in the 1911 Act. The Countryside Alliance claimed that the 1949 Act was unlawful because it had been passed relying on the procedures laid down in the 1911 Act, when the 1911 Act was not drafted to allow its procedures to be used to amend itself. This argument was rejected by the courts. The Law Lords stated that the 1911 and 1949 Acts could not be used to enact major constitutional reforms, such as the abolition of the House of Lords. Since the 1949 Act was simply reducing the House of Lords' delaying power from two years to one, this did not amount to a major constitutional reform and so the 1949 Act was lawful and so also, therefore, was the Hunting Act.

Legal principle
The Parliament Acts of 1911 and 1949 cannot be used to enact major constitutional reforms.

Royal Assent

In the vast majority of cases, agreement between the Lords and Commons is reached, and the Bill is then presented for Royal Assent. Technically, the Queen must give her consent to all legislation before it can become law, but in practice that consent is never refused.

The Bill is then an Act of Parliament, and becomes law, though most do not take effect from the moment the Queen gives her consent, but on a specified date in the near future or when a commencement order has been issued by a Government Minister.

Accelerated procedures

In the case of legislation about which there is no controversy, the procedure may be simplified, with the first three readings in the Lords, then three in the Commons, with the Bill passing back to the Lords only if there is disagreement. Private Bills technically go through the above procedure, and are examined to make sure that adequate warning has been given to anyone affected by the provisions, but there is little debate on

Photo 2.1 The Houses of Parliament
Source: © Maksym Gorpenyuk/Shutterstock.com

them. Consolidating Acts, which simply bring together all the existing law on one topic, also go through an accelerated procedure, with no debate, because they do not change the law; codification Bills, on the other hand, go through the normal process (see p. 134).

Post-legislative scrutiny

The Law Commission (a body responsible for looking at how the law needs to be reformed) has considered whether a formal procedure should be introduced to scrutinise legislation after it has been passed. Following a consultation process the Commission issued a report on the subject entitled *Post-Legislative Scrutiny* (2006). This report strongly supported the creation of a joint parliamentary committee on post-legislative scrutiny which would routinely check whether new legislation – both Acts of Parliament and delegated legislation (discussed in Chapter 4) – is working effectively. These recommendations were accepted by the Labour Government in its report *Post-legislative scrutiny – The Government's approach* (2008). As a result, three to five years after an Act has been passed, the relevant Government department has to produce a memorandum summarising the impact of the Act, which is given to the relevant department committee in Parliament to consider.

Devolution

Devolution is a process of decentralisation, and puts power closer to the citizen so that local factors are better recognised in decision-making. Following referendums in 1997 and 1998, a Scottish Parliament, a Welsh Assembly and a Northern Irish Assembly have been established with legislative powers. These three legislative bodies have been given some power that was previously held by the Westminster Parliament. The Westminster Parliament remains sovereign: it can change the Acts of Parliament that established these devolved legislative bodies and can legislate on anything that has been devolved. However, the Government has made it clear it will not normally do so without the consent of the devolved legislatures.

Under the Government of Wales Act 2006, the Welsh Assembly can legislate on 20 subjects listed in Schedule 7 to that Act dealing with the delivery of local services, including education, agriculture, housing and transport. This type of legislation is known as Assembly Acts. The Scotland Act 1998 specifies those matters that are reserved to the Westminster Parliament (such as defence and foreign policy) and anything else falls within the remit of the Scottish Parliament. After the Scottish Independence Referendum of September 2014, which resulted in a vote for Scotland to remain part of the UK, further powers were promised to be devolved to the Scottish Parliament, including full control over taxation. The Scottish Parliament has full legislative powers over devolved matters. Its laws are known as Acts of the Scottish Parliament. All of these devolved bodies have the power to pass primary legislation (with the authority of law in its own right) rather than just secondary legislation (discussed in Chapter 4). So Acts of these devolved bodies do not need the approval of the UK Government to take effect.

English votes for English laws

Devolution of legislative powers to Scotland, Wales and Northern Ireland raised questions about who should vote for legislation which had an impact only on England. In simple terms, why should Scottish MPs vote on legislation that only affected education in England, when English MPs no longer had the right to vote on legislation on education in Scotland? In 2015 Parliament's Standing Orders were changed to give 'English votes for English laws'. The new Standing Orders mean that prior to the Second reading the Speaker can certify a Bill, or provisions within a Bill, as 'relating exclusively to England or to England and Wales'. English only Bills are then considered by a Committee made up of only English MPs. After the Report stage, English MPs sit in a Legislative Grand Committee and are asked to consent to the Bill through a Legislative Consent Motion. Thus English MPs have effectively a veto on English Bills. Once the Legislative Consent Motion has been passed, then the Bill can proceed to its Third reading. So, apart from these Committee stages, all MPs vote as normal on the Bill.

The Housing and Planning Bill was the first Bill to be certified under the new Standing Orders and, in 2016, was the first in respect of which the new Legislative Grand Committee processes operated. The Housing Bill included an extension of the right-to-buy for housing association tenants in England and was approved by all MPs at the Third reading stage.

The new rules have been criticised as unduly complicated, and for creating two tiers of MPs: English MPs who can always vote, and other MPs who can sometimes vote. An alternative would be to have a separate English Parliament.

Reforms to legislative procedures

An experiment was carried out in 2012 looking at whether there would be benefits in introducing a new 'public reading stage' for Bills to give the public an opportunity to comment on proposed legislation online, and a dedicated 'public reading day' within a Bill's committee stage where those comments would be debated by the committee scrutinising the Bill. This procedure was piloted on three Bills, but its use has not been extended further.

More recently, in September 2016, the House of Lords Constitutional Committee launched an inquiry into the legislative process. This was in part a follow up on its previous work carried out in 2004 on the passage of legislation through Parliament. The purpose of this inquiry was to consider how outside organisations and the public are involved in the legislative process and indeed how their role could be developed. Of course Brexit was also firmly on the agenda as well. The four central questions on which evidence was sought were related to the arrangements for delivering clear draft legislation; the improvements that can be made to deliver clearer laws; the impact of Brexit; and how technology can be used to enhance the process of developing legislation.

The inquiry closed in September 2017. The final report that was published (*Preparing Legislation for Parliament* (2017)) makes the following recommendations.

- That legislation should be made more accessible and easier to understand, for practitioners and the public.
- That consolidation is urgently needed in several areas of the law (e.g. immigration law and sentencing law).
- That the Government should routinely publish the evidence base for proposals and that, if a robust evidence base is not available, the Government should explain why it is nevertheless appropriate to proceed.
- That piloting the application of policy is an important way of developing effective policies over time, and that the Government should develop guidance for departments, setting out when piloting is appropriate or desirable.
- That the Government should publish draft Bills for pre-legislative scrutiny more frequently and that it should become a regular feature of the legislative process.

The broad needs that this inquiry appears to have identified are the need for better scrutiny, a tidying up of related areas of law and ensuring that legislation is comprehensible, which in turn must contribute to facilitating access to justice.

Answering questions

1 There has been some disagreement as to the way in which the House of Lords should be reformed. What are the various options, and how do these differ from its present composition?

You could start by setting out the present composition and role of the House of Lords (as a second unelected chamber), before going on to describe the conflicting proposals (p. 35) and how these would affect the power of the House of Lords. Note that the Parliament Acts had effectively reduced the House of Lords' power, but if its members were elected it could develop the authority to exercise greater control over the House of Commons. You could give an opinion as to whether or not making the House of Lords into an elected (i.e. more democratic) chamber with greater powers would be a good or a bad thing.

2 Describe the stages of the law-making process in Parliament: to what extent is approval of the House of Lords always required?

The first part of your essay could contain a fairly full but essentially descriptive account of the legislative process, starting with the Green and White Papers and through to Royal Assent, and emphasising the principle that consent of both Houses and the Crown is usually required.

The second part of the question focuses upon the exceptional provisions of the Parliament Acts 1911 and 1949 allowing legislation to proceed to Royal Assent without the approval of the House of Lords. Mention should be made of the highly publicised case of **R (on the application of Jackson and others) v Attorney General** concerning the validity of the Hunting Act 2004. In that case the House of Lords stated that the Parliament Acts could be used for ordinary legislation but not for major constitutional reforms; and as the Hunting Act was not a major constitutional reform, the Parliament Acts had been correctly used.

Additional marks would be secured by mentioning the Law Commission Report *Post-Legislative Scrutiny*.

Summary of Chapter 2: Statute law

Introduction
Statutes are made by Parliament, which consists of the House of Commons, the House of Lords and the Monarch.

House of Commons
The House of Commons is the democratically elected chamber of Parliament.

House of Lords
Following the House of Lords Act 1999, membership of the House of Lords is currently undergoing a major reform to remove the role of the hereditary peers. The Government is considering removing the remaining 92 hereditary peers. An independent Appointments Commission selects some non-party members for the upper House and vets party appointments.

Making an Act of Parliament
All statutes begin as a Bill. There are three types of Bill:

- Public Bills
- Private Members' Bills
- Private Bills.

The legislative process usually starts in the House of Commons and proceeds as follows.

- First reading
- Second reading
- Committee stage
- Report stage
- Third reading
- House of Lords
- Royal Assent.

Role of the House of Lords
The Parliament Acts of 1911 and 1949 lay down special procedures by which proposed legislation can go for Royal Assent without the approval of the House of Lords after specified periods of time. These procedures are only rarely used, because the House of Lords usually drops objections that are resisted by the Commons, though their use has increased in recent years.

Reading list

Law Commission (2006) *Post-Legislative Scrutiny*. Cm 6945. London: HMSO.

Renton, D. (1975) *The Preparation of Legislation*. London: HMSO.

Royal Commission for the Reform of the House of Lords (2000) *A House for the Future*. Cm 4534. London: HMSO.

On the internet

Copies of Public Bills currently being considered by Parliament can be found at:
http://www.parliament.uk/business/bills-and-legislation/

Copies of recent legislation can be found at:
http://www.legislation.gov.uk/ukpga

Useful explanatory notes prepared by the Government to explain the implications of recent legislation can be found at:
http://www.legislation.gov.uk/browse

The House of Lords Constitutional Committee Report, *Preparing Legislation for Parliament* (2017), is available at:
https://www.parliament.uk/business/committees/committees-a-z/lords-select/constitution-committee/news-parliament-2017/legislative-process-part-one-report/

3

Statutory interpretation

When judges are faced with a new piece of legislation, its meaning is not always clear and they have to interpret it. Often, when interpreting the Act, the judges say that they are looking for Parliament's intention. In this chapter we will consider:

- the meaning of parliamentary intention;

- the rules of statutory interpretation;

- internal aids to statutory interpretation;

- external aids to statutory interpretation, including the Human Rights Act 1998 and the official record of what was said in Parliament (known as *Hansard*); and

- theories about how judges interpret statutes in practice.

Introduction

Although Parliament makes legislation, it is left to the courts to apply it. The general public imagines that this is simply a case of looking up the relevant law and ruling accordingly, but the reality is not so simple. Despite the fact that Acts of Parliament are carefully written by expert draftsmen, there are many occasions in which the courts find that the implications of a statute for the case before them are not at all clear.

Bennion (2005) has identified a number of factors that may cause this uncertainty:

- A word is left out because the draftsman thought it was automatically implied. For example, a draftsman writing a statute banning men with facial hair from parks might write that 'men with beards or moustaches are prohibited from parks'. Does this mean that a man who has a beard **and** a moustache would be allowed in? If the words 'and/or' were used it would be clear, but the draftsman may have thought this was automatically implied.
- A broad term was used, leaving it to the user to decide what it includes. Where a statute bans vehicles from the park, this obviously includes cars and lorries, but the courts would have to decide whether it also prohibited skateboards, bikes or roller skates, for example.
- An ambiguous word or phrase was used on purpose, perhaps because the provision is politically contentious. The European Communities Act 1972 was ambiguous about the position of UK legislation.
- The wording is inadequate because of a printing, drafting or other error.
- The events of the case before the court were not foreseen when the legislation was produced. In the example given above regarding vehicles, skateboards might not have been invented when the statute was drafted, so it would be impossible for Parliament to say whether they should be included in the term 'vehicles'.

In any of these cases, the job of the courts – in theory at least – is to discover how Parliament intended the law to apply and put that into practice. This is because, as you know, in our constitution, Parliament is the supreme source of law (excluding EU law, which will be discussed later), and therefore the judiciary's constitutional role is to put into practice what they think Parliament actually intended when it made a particular law, rather than simply what the judges themselves might think is the best interpretation in the case before them. However, as we shall see, the practice is not always as straightforward as the constitutional theory suggests.

What is parliamentary intention?

The idea of parliamentary intention is a very slippery concept in practice. The last example above is one illustration of this: how could Parliament have had any intention at all of how skateboards should be treated under the legislation, if skateboards were not invented when the legislation was passed?

More problems are revealed if we try to pin down precisely what parliamentary intention means. Is it the intention of every individual Member of Parliament at the time the law was passed? Obviously not, since not every member will have voted for the legislation or even necessarily been present when it was passed. The intention of all those who did support a particular piece of legislation is no easier to define either, since some of those are likely to be acting from loyalty to their party, and will not necessarily have detailed knowledge of the provisions, much less have thought hard about how they might apply in as yet unseen circumstances. Even among those MPs who have considered the detailed provisions, there may be many different opinions as to how they should apply in different situations. And even if one of these groups was taken to represent true parliamentary intention, how are their views to be assessed? It is hardly feasible to conduct a poll every time a legislative provision is found to be unclear.

In fact, the people who will have paid most attention to the wording of a statute are the Ministers who seek to get them through Parliament, the civil servants who advise the Ministers and the draftsmen who draw up the legislation. None of these can really be said to amount to Parliament.

Statutory interpretation and case law

Once the courts have interpreted a statute, or a section of one, that interpretation becomes part of case law in just the same way as any other judicial decision, and subject to the same rules of precedent. A higher court may decide that the interpretation is wrong, and reverse the decision if it is appealed, or overrule it in a later case but, unless and until this happens, lower courts must interpret the statute in the same way.

How are statutes interpreted?

Parliament has given the courts some sources of guidance on statutory interpretation. The Interpretation Act 1978 provides certain standard definitions of common provisions, such as the rule that the singular includes the plural and 'he' includes 'she', while interpretation sections at the end of most modern Acts define some of the words used within them – the Police and Criminal Evidence Act 1984 contains such a section. A further source of help has been provided since the beginning of 1999: all Bills passed since that date are the subject of special explanatory notes, which are made public. These detail the background to the legislation and explain the effects particular provisions are intended to have.

Apart from this assistance, it has been left to the courts to decide what method to use to interpret statutes, and four basic approaches have developed, in conjunction with certain aids to interpretation. These approaches should not be considered as rules to be followed. The Supreme Court made clear in **Cusack** *v* **London Borough of Harrow** (2013) that while these approaches have a valuable part to play in interpreting statutes, they should be treated as 'guidelines rather than railway lines'.

Rules of interpretation

The literal rule

This rule gives all the words in a statute their ordinary and natural meaning, on the principle that the best way to interpret the will of Parliament is to follow the literal meaning of the words they have used. Under this rule, the literal meaning must be followed, even if the result is silly; for example, Lord Esher stated, in **R** v **City of London Court Judge** (1892): 'If the words of an Act are clear, you must follow them, even though they lead to a manifest absurdity. The court has nothing to do with the question of whether the legislature has committed an absurdity.'

Examples of the literal rule in use are:

Whiteley v Chappell (1868) A statute aimed at preventing electoral malpractice made it an offence to impersonate 'any person entitled to vote' at an election. The accused was acquitted because he impersonated a dead person and a dead person was clearly not entitled to vote!

London and North Eastern Railway Co v Berriman (1946) A railway worker was knocked down and killed by a train, and his widow attempted to claim damages. The relevant statute provided that this was available to employees killed while engaging in 'relaying or repairing' tracks; the dead man had been doing routine maintenance and oiling, which the court held did not come within the meaning of 'relaying and repairing'.

Fisher v Bell (1961) After several violent incidents in which the weapon used was a flick-knife, Parliament decided that these knives should be banned. The Restriction of Offensive Weapons Act 1959 consequently made it an offence to 'sell or offer for sale' any flick-knife. The defendant had flick-knives in his shop window and was charged with offering these for sale. The courts held that the term 'offers for sale' must be given its ordinary meaning in law, and that in contract law this was not an offer for sale but only an invitation to people to make an offer to buy. The defendant was therefore not guilty of a crime under the Act, despite the fact that this was obviously just the sort of behaviour that Act was set up to prevent.

Advantages of the literal rule

It respects parliamentary sovereignty, giving the courts a restricted role and leaving law-making to those elected for the job.

Disadvantages of the literal rule

Where use of the literal rule does lead to an absurd or obviously unjust conclusion, it can hardly be said to be enacting the will of Parliament, since Parliament is unlikely to have intended absurdity and injustice. The case of **London and North Eastern Railway Co** v **Berriman** (above) is an example of literal interpretation creating injustice where Parliament probably never intended any – the difference in the type of work being done does not change the degree of danger to which the workers were exposed.

In addition, the literal rule is useless where the answer to a problem simply cannot be found in the words of the statute. As Hart (1994) has pointed out, some terms have a core of very clear meaning, but it may still be unclear how far that word stretches: the example above of an imaginary law banning 'vehicles' from the park clearly illustrates this. Where such a broad term is used, the answer is simply not there in the words of the statute, and the courts have to use some other method.

The Law Commission in 1969 pointed out that interpretation based only on literal meanings 'assumes unattainable perfection in draftsmanship'; even the most talented and experienced draftsmen cannot predict every situation to which legislation may have to be applied. One should not expect too much of words, which are always an imperfect means of communication. The same word may mean different things to different people, and words also shift their meanings over time.

Zander, in his book *The Law-Making Process* (2004), describes the literal approach as 'mechanical, divorced both from the realities of the use of language and from the expectations and aspirations of the human beings concerned . . . in that sense it is irresponsible'.

In **R (on the application of Haw)** *v* **Secretary of State for the Home Department** (2006), the Court of Appeal refused to apply a literal interpretation to a new piece of legislation, as it considered that this would not reflect the intention of Parliament. The case concerned Brian Haw, who had been holding a protest in Parliament Square, opposite Parliament, against the war in Iraq since June 2001. He lived on the pavement and displayed a large number of placards protesting about Government policy in Iraq. The demonstration had earlier been held to be lawful, since it neither caused an obstruction nor gave rise to any fear that a breach of the peace might arise. The Serious Organised Crime and Police Act 2005, s. 133(1) was subsequently passed, which required any person who intended to organise a demonstration in the vicinity of Parliament to apply to the police for authorisation to do so. Section 132(1) provided that a person who carried on a demonstration in the designated area was guilty of an offence if, when the demonstration started, appropriate authorisation had not been given:

(1) Any person who –

(a) organises a demonstration in a public place in the designated area, or
(b) takes part in a demonstration in a public place in the designated area, or
(c) carries on a demonstration by himself in a public place in the designated area,

is guilty of an offence if, when the demonstration **starts,** authorisation for the demonstration has not been given under section 134(2).

Haw argued that the Act did not apply to his demonstration because it had started before the Act came into force. The Court of Appeal held that the Act did in fact apply to Haw's demonstration: 'Any other conclusion would be wholly irrational and could fairly be described as manifestly absurd.' Construing the statutory language in context, Parliament's intention was clearly to regulate all demonstrations in the designated area, whenever they began. Thus, rather than following a literal interpretation of the legislation, the court looked at its context to determine the intention of Parliament. The court gave particular weight to the fact that the 2005 Act repealed a provision in the Public Order Act 1986. That provision had provided for controls to be placed on public demonstrations and would have applied to demonstrations which had been started since 1986. The Court of Appeal thought it was inconceivable that Parliament would have intended to repeal that power to control demonstrations started before 2005 and replace it with legislation which could only control demonstrations started after 2005, as this would leave a significant gap in the power of the state to control demonstrations.

Conditions were subsequently imposed on Haw's demonstration in accordance with the provisions of the 2005 Act, aimed primarily at restricting the size of the demonstration. It was accepted that Haw's demonstration in itself did not pose a security risk, but if a large number of people joined his demonstration this could be an opportunity for terrorists to join in and conceal an explosive device. A new framework for regulating protests around Parliament Square is contained in the Police Reform and Social Responsibility Act 2011, replacing the relevant provisions in the 2005 Act.

The golden rule

This provides that if the literal rule gives an absurd result, which Parliament could not have intended, then (and only then) the judge can substitute a reasonable meaning in the light of the statute as a whole. It was defined by Lord Wensleydale in **Grey v Pearson** (1857): 'The grammatical and ordinary sense of the words is to be adhered to, unless that would lead to some absurdity, or some repugnance or inconsistency with the rest of the instrument, in which case the grammatical and ordinary sense of the words may be modified so as to avoid that absurdity and inconsistency, but no further.'

Examples of the golden rule in use are:

R v Allen (1872) Section 57 of the Offences Against the Person Act 1861 stated that 'Whosoever being married shall marry any other person during the life of the former husband or wife . . . shall be guilty of bigamy.' It was pointed out that it was impossible for a person already married to 'marry' someone else – they might go through a marriage ceremony, but would not actually be married; using the literal rule would make the statute useless. The courts therefore held that 'shall marry' should be interpreted to mean 'shall go through a marriage ceremony'.

Maddox v Storer (1963) Under the Road Traffic Act 1960, it was an offence to drive at more than 30 mph in a vehicle 'adapted to carry more than seven passengers'. The vehicle in the case was a minibus made to carry 11 passengers, rather than altered to do so, and the court held that 'adapted to' could be taken to mean 'suitable for'.

Adler v George (1964) The defendant was charged under s. 3 of the Official Secrets Act 1920, with obstructing a member of the armed forces 'in the vicinity of any prohibited place'. He argued that the natural meaning of 'in the vicinity of' meant near to, whereas the obstruction had actually occurred in the prohibited place itself, an air force station. The court held that while in many circumstances 'in the vicinity' could indeed only be interpreted as meaning near to, in this context it was reasonable to construe it as including being within the prohibited place.

Advantages of the golden rule

The golden rule can prevent the absurdity and injustice caused by the literal rule, and help the courts put into practice what Parliament really means.

Disadvantages of the golden rule

The Law Commission noted in 1969 that the 'rule' provided no clear meaning of an 'absurd result'. As in practice that was judged by reference to whether a particular interpretation was irreconcilable with the general policy of the legislature, the golden rule turns out to be a less explicit form of the mischief rule (discussed below).

The mischief rule

The mischief rule was laid down in **Heydon's Case** in the sixteenth century, and provides that judges should consider three factors:

- what the law was before the statute was passed;
- what problem, or 'mischief', the statute was trying to remedy;
- what remedy Parliament was trying to provide.

The judge should then interpret the statute in such a way as to put a stop to the problem that Parliament was addressing.

Legal principle

Judges can interpret a statute so that it effectively tackles the problem that Parliament wanted to deal with: the mischief rule.

Examples of the mischief rule in use are:

Smith v Hughes (1960) The Street Offences Act 1959 made it a criminal offence for a prostitute to solicit potential customers in a street or public place. In this case, the prostitute was not actually in the street, but was sitting in a house, on the first floor, and tapping on the window to attract the attention of the men walking by. The judge decided that the aim of the Act was to enable people to walk along the street without being solicited, and since the soliciting in question was aimed at people in the street, even though the prostitute was not in the street herself, the Act should be interpreted to include this activity.

Elliott v Grey (1960) The Road Traffic Act 1930 provided that it was an offence for an uninsured car to be 'used on the road'. The car in this case was on the road, but jacked up, with its battery removed, but the court held that, as it was nevertheless a hazard of the type which the statute was designed to prevent, it was covered by the phrase 'used on the road'.

Royal College of Nursing v DHSS (1981) The Abortion Act 1967 stated that terminations of pregnancy were legal only if performed by a 'registered medical practitioner'. By 1972, surgical abortions were largely being replaced by drug-induced ones, in which the second stage of the process (attaching the patient to a drip), was carried out by nurses, under the instructions of a doctor. The House of Lords ruled that the mischief which the Act sought to remedy was the uncertain state of the previous law, which drove many women to dangerous back-street abortionists. It sought to do this by widening the grounds on which abortions could be obtained, and ensuring that they were carried out with proper skill in hygienic conditions, and the procedure in question promoted this aim, and was not unlawful. It was a controversial decision, with Lords Wilberforce and Edmund Davies claiming that the House was not interpreting legislation but rewriting it.

Advantages of the mischief rule

The mischief rule helps avoid absurdity and injustice, and promotes flexibility. It was described by the Law Commission in 1969 as a 'rather more satisfactory approach' than the two other established rules.

Disadvantages of the mischief rule

Heydon's Case was the product of a time when statutes were a minor source of law, compared to the common law. Drafting was by no means as exact a process as it is today, and the supremacy of Parliament was not really established. At that time too, what statutes there were tended to include a lengthy preamble, which more or less spelt out the 'mischief' with which the Act was intended to deal. Judges of the time were very well qualified to decide what the previous law was and what problems a statute was intended to remedy, since they had usually drafted statutes on behalf of the king, and Parliament only rubber-stamped them. Such a rule may be less appropriate now that the legislative situation is so different.

The purposive approach

Historically, the preferred approach to statutory interpretation was to look for the statute's literal meaning. However, over the last three decades, the courts have accepted that the literal approach can be unsatisfactory. Instead, the judges have been increasingly influenced by the European approach to statutory interpretation which focuses on giving effect to the purpose of the legislation. During his judicial career, Lord Denning was at the forefront of moves to establish a more purposive approach, aiming to produce decisions that put into practice the spirit of the law, even if that meant paying less than usual regard to the letter of the law – the actual words of the statute. He felt that the mischief rule could be interpreted broadly, so that it would not just allow the courts to look at the history of the case, but it would also allow them to carry out the intention of Parliament, however imperfectly this might have been expressed in the words used. In reality, the purposive approach that has developed takes a more liberal approach to statutory interpretation than is traditionally associated with the mischief rule. Denning stated his views in **Magor and St Mellons Rural District Council** *v* **Newport Corporation** (1952):

> We do not sit here to pull the language of Parliament to pieces and make nonsense of it . . . we sit here to find out the intention of Parliament and carry it out, and we do this better by filling in the gaps and making sense of the enactment than by opening it up to destructive analysis.

On appeal, the House of Lords described this approach as 'a naked usurpation of the judicial function, under the guise of interpretation . . . If a gap is disclosed, the remedy lies in an amending Act.'

In fact, over time, the House of Lords has come to accept that a purposive approach to statutory interpretation can, in certain cases, be appropriate. The move towards a purposive approach has been particularly marked in relation to the interpretation of European legislation and national legislation that is designed to implement European legislation, as the Court of Justice of the European Union (like most civil law countries) tends itself to adopt a purposive approach to statutory interpretation. Thus, in **Pickstone** *v* **Freemans** (1988) the House of Lords held that it had to read words into inadequate domestic legislation in order to give effect to European legislation which was intended to tackle the problem of women being paid less than men for the same work.

But the purposive approach has not been restricted to the context of European law, and has been applied to pure domestic legislation. In **Pepper** *v* **Hart** (1993) the House of Lords stated:

> The days have long passed when the court adopted a strict constructionist view of interpretation which required them to adopt the literal meaning of the language. The courts now adopt

a purposive approach which seeks to give effect to the true purpose of legislation and are prepared to look at much extraneous material that bears on the background against which the legislation was enacted.

KEY CASE

In **R (on the application of Quintavalle)** v **Secretary of State for Health** (2003) the House of Lords was required to interpret the Human Fertilisation and Embryology Act 1990. Section 1 of this Act defines an embryo as 'a live human embryo where fertilisation is complete' and their use was regulated by the Human Fertilisation and Embryology Authority (HFEA). After the Act had been passed, scientists developed a cloning technique whereby embryos were not created by fertilising an egg, but by replacing the nucleus of an egg with a cell from another person. The Labour Government had issued a statement saying that medical research involving cloned embryos did fall within the Act and could be regulated by HFEA. The pressure group, Pro-Life Alliance, was opposed to such research and sought a declaration of the courts that HFEA was acting outside its statutory powers. The House of Lords gave the Act a purposive interpretation to give effect to the intention of Parliament. It observed that under the influence of European legal culture 'the pendulum has swung towards purposive methods of construction':

> The basic task of the court is to ascertain and give effect to the true meaning of what Parliament has said in the enactment to be construed. But that is not to say that attention should be confined and a literal interpretation given to the particular provisions which give rise to difficulty . . . The court's task, within the permissible bounds of interpretation, is to give effect to Parliament's purpose. So the controversial provisions should be read in the context of the statute as a whole, and the statute as a whole should be read in the historical context of the situation which led to its enactment.

It concluded that Parliament could not have intended to exclude cloned embryos from being regulated by HFEA.

Legal principle
Legislation can be interpreted using a purposive approach.

Rectification

Words can be added to a statute by a judge to give effect to Parliament's intention where an obvious error has been made in drafting a statute. This was the conclusion of the House of Lords in **Inco Europe Ltd** v **First Choice Distribution** (2000) and this process of correcting mistakes is known as rectification. To be able to read words into a statute, the court must be in no doubt about what provision needs to be added. The power of rectification is restricted to plain cases of drafting mistakes. The court must not do anything that might look like judicial legislation; its role is purely interpretative. Since a statute is expressed in language that is approved and enacted by the legislature, the courts must exercise considerable caution before adding, omitting or substituting words. Therefore, before interpreting a statute in this way, the court must be sure:

- of the intended purpose of the statute;
- that the draftsman and Parliament have, by accident, failed to give effect to that purpose;

- how Parliament would have written the provision if the error had been spotted, though not necessarily the precise words Parliament would have used, had the error in the Bill been noticed.

Even where these conditions are satisfied, a court may be unable to imply a change of wording in the Act if the change in language is considered too far-reaching.

The case of **Inco Europe Ltd** was considered in **OB** *v* **Director of the Serious Fraud Office** (2012). The defendant had been sent to prison for contempt of court and sought to appeal against this decision from the Criminal Division of the Court of Appeal to the Supreme Court. The old Administration of Justice Act 1960 contained a right to appeal in such cases, but this right was not mentioned when the legislation was amended by the Armed Forces Act 2006. The defendant argued that this omission was simply a legislative error and he should still have a right of appeal. The Court of Appeal accepted that the case satisfied the requirements laid down in **Inco Europe Ltd.** In particular, when enacting the 2006 Act, Parliament had no intention of removing the right of appeal in contempt cases. In summary, the courts will correct an error in legislative drafting where common sense requires it.

TOPICAL ISSUE

The Human Rights Act 1998

The Human Rights Act 1998 incorporates into UK law the European Convention on Human Rights, which is an international treaty signed by most democratic countries, and designed to protect basic human rights. In much of Europe, the Convention has been incorporated into national law as a Bill of Rights, which means that the courts can overrule domestic legislation which is in conflict with it. This is not the case in the UK. Instead, s. 3(1) of the Human Rights Act requires that:

> So far as it is possible to do so, primary legislation and subordinate legislation must be read and given effect in a way which is compatible with the Convention rights.

Section 2 further requires that, in deciding any question which arises in connection with a right protected by the Convention, the courts 'must take into account' any relevant judgments made by the European Court of Human Rights (see p. 13). If it is impossible to find an interpretation which is compatible with the Convention, the court concerned can make a declaration of incompatibility under s. 4 of the Act. This does not affect the validity of the statute in question, but it is designed to draw attention to the conflict so that the Government can change the law to bring it in line with the Convention (although the Act does not oblige the Government to do this). Under s. 10 there is a special 'fast track' procedure by which a Minister can make the necessary changes.

When new legislation is being made, the relevant Bill must carry a statement from the relevant Minister, saying either that its provisions are compatible with the Convention, or that, even if they are not, the Government wishes to go ahead with the legislation anyway. In the latter case, the Government would be specifically saying that the legislation must override Convention rights if there is a clash, but clearly any Government intent on passing such legislation would be likely to face considerable opposition and so would have to have a very good reason, in the eyes of the public, for doing so.

If the courts consider that a literal interpretation of an Act would render the legislation in breach of the European Convention, under s. 3 the precise wording of the Act may in certain circumstances be ignored and the Act given an interpretation which conforms with the Convention. In **R v A** (2001) the House of Lords noted that:

> Under ordinary methods of interpretation a court may depart from the language of the statute to avoid absurd consequences: section 3 goes much further . . . In accordance with the will of Parliament as reflected in section 3 it will sometimes be necessary to adopt an interpretation which linguistically may appear strained.

This case was concerned with the prosecution of rape. Evidence of a complainant's past sexual experience is sometimes admissible as evidence in court in rape trials. Such evidence has in the past been used to give the jury a bad impression of the victim and make it appear that she was not a credible witness – the insinuation being that a woman who has had an active sex life with men other than a husband is immoral and cannot be trusted generally. The Labour Government was concerned that rape victims were not being adequately protected in court proceedings and legislation was passed on the matter. The Youth Justice and Criminal Evidence Act 1999, s. 41 provided that evidence of the complainant's past sexual behaviour could only be given if 'a refusal of leave might have the result of rendering unsafe a conclusion of the jury or . . . the court on any relevant issue in the case'. The clear intention of Parliament was to significantly restrict the use of past sexual history evidence in rape trials. Unfortunately, in the first case to reach the House of Lords concerning this section, the House relied on the Human Rights Act 1998 in order to ignore the clear intention of Parliament. It ruled that a defendant had to be given the opportunity to adduce evidence as to the complainant's past sexual behaviour with the defendant which had taken place over a week before the purported rape. It considered that otherwise this section would be in breach of Art. 6 of the European Convention on Human Rights guaranteeing a fair trial. The interpretation of the legislation ran contrary to Parliament's intention when it passed that Act, though it is arguable that Parliament's ultimate intention was being respected as provided for in the Human Rights Act 1998.

In **Ghaidan v Godin-Mendoza** (2004) the House of Lords encouraged the courts to use s. 3 to interpret statutes in accordance with the European Convention. Lord Steyne noted that, at the time of the judgment, ten declarations of incompatibility had been made under s. 4, of which five had been overturned on appeal, and s. 3 had only been relied on 10 times. He concluded from these statistics that s. 4 was being relied on too often, when it should only be used as a last resort, and that instead the courts should make greater use of s. 3 to interpret legislation in accordance with the Convention.

The House felt that, in the context of s. 3, the courts should be prepared to move away from the 'semantic lottery' of the words used by the draftsman and interpret the statute in the light of Convention rights:

> [O]nce it is accepted that section 3 may require legislation to bear a meaning which departs from the unambiguous meaning the legislation would otherwise bear, it becomes impossible to suppose Parliament intended that the operation of section 3 should depend critically upon the particular form of words adopted by the parliamentary draftsman in the statutory provision under consideration.

The House simply requires the courts to make sure that the meaning given to the legislation is consistent with the 'fundamental features' of the statute and the judges must avoid deciding issues calling for legislative deliberation. This potentially gives the courts considerable flexibility when relying on s. 3 to interpret a statute which risks breaching the European Convention.

The Court of Appeal went too far in **Re S (*A Minor*)** (2002). It attempted to interpret the Children Act 1989 by adding a new procedure requiring the local authority to contact the guardian of a child subjected to a care order in particular circumstances. The House of Lords allowed an appeal as it considered that the Court of Appeal had crossed the boundary between interpretation and amendment. The new procedure created by the Court of Appeal conflicted with a fundamental feature of the 1989 Act that judicial supervision of care orders was very restricted.

Thus, there are certain limits on the courts' powers of interpretation when applying s. 3 of the Human Rights Act 1998, but they still appear to have greater powers of interpretation in this context than when they are exercising their ordinary powers of statutory interpretation.

Interpreting European legislation

Section 2(4) of the European Communities Act 1972 provides that all parliamentary legislation (whether passed before or after the European Communities Act) must be construed and applied in accordance with European law. The case of **R *v* Secretary of State for Transport, *ex parte* Factortame** (1990) makes it clear that the English courts must apply European law which is directly effective even if it conflicts with English law, including statute law (these issues are discussed more fully in Chapter 5: European law).

Aids to interpretation

Whichever approach the judges take to statutory interpretation, they have at their disposal a range of material to help. Some of these aids may be found within the piece of legislation itself, or in certain rules of language commonly applied in statutory texts – these are called internal aids. Others, outside the piece of legislation, are called external aids. Since 1995, a very important new external aid has been added in the form of the Human Rights Act 1998.

Internal aids

The literal rule and the golden rule both direct the judge to internal aids, though they are taken into account whatever the approach.

The statute itself

To decide what a provision of the Act means the judge may draw a comparison with provisions elsewhere in the statute. Clues may also be provided by the long title of the Act or the subheadings within it.

Explanatory notes

Acts passed since the beginning of 1999 are provided with explanatory notes, published at the same time as the Act.

Rules of language

Developed by lawyers over time, these rules are really little more than common sense, despite their intimidating names. As with the rules of interpretation, they are not always precisely applied. Examples include:

Ejusdem generis General words which follow specific ones are taken to include only things of the same kind. For example, if an Act used the phrase 'dogs, cats and other animals' the phrase 'and other animals' would probably include other domestic animals, but not wild ones.

Expressio unius est exclusio alterius Express mention of one thing implies the exclusion of another. If an Act specifically mentioned 'Persian cats', the term would not include other breeds of cat.

Noscitur a sociis A word draws meaning from the other words around it. If a statute mentioned 'cat baskets, toy mice and food', it would be reasonable to assume that 'food' meant cat food, and dog food was not covered by the relevant provision.

Presumptions

The courts assume that certain points are implied in all legislation. These presumptions include the following.

- Statutes do not change the common law.
- The legislature does not intend to remove any matters from the jurisdiction of the courts.
- Existing rights are not to be interfered with.
- Laws which create crimes should be interpreted in favour of the citizen where there is ambiguity.

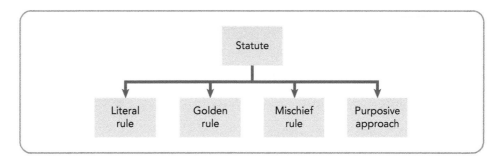

Figure 3.1 **Approaches to statutory interpretation**

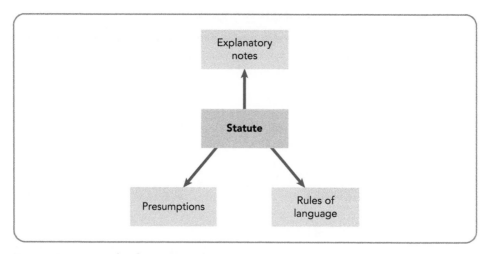

Figure 3.2 Internal aids to interpretation

- Legislation does not operate retrospectively: its provisions operate from the day it comes into force, and are not backdated.
- Statutes do not affect the Monarch.
- Statutes are 'always speaking' (see p. 65).

It is always open to Parliament to go against these presumptions if it sees fit – for example, the European Communities Act 1972 makes it clear that some of its provisions are to be applied retrospectively. But, unless the wording of a statute makes it absolutely clear that Parliament has chosen to go against one or more of the presumptions, the courts can assume that the presumptions apply.

Some indication of the weight which judges feel should be attached to presumptions can be seen in the case of **L'Office Cherifien des Phosphates Unitramp SA** *v* **Yamashita-Shinnihon Steamship Co Ltd (** *The Boucraa* **)** (1994), which concerned the presumption against retrospective effect. The House of Lords stated that the important issue was 'simple fairness': if they read the relevant statute as imposing the suggested degree of retrospective effect, would the result be so unfair that Parliament could not have intended it, even though their words might suggest retrospective effect? This could be judged by balancing a number of factors, including the nature of the rights affected, the clarity of the words used and the background to the legislation.

What remains unclear is how judges decide between different presumptions if they conflict, and why certain values are selected for protection by presumptions, and not others. For example, the presumption that existing rights are not to be interfered with serves to protect the existing property or money of individuals, but there is no presumption in favour of people claiming state benefits.

External aids

The mischief rule directs the judge to external aids, including the following:

Historical setting

A judge may consider the historical setting of the provision that is being interpreted, as well as other statutes dealing with the same subjects.

Dictionaries and textbooks

These may be consulted to find the meaning of a word, or to gather information about the views of legal academics on a point of law.

Reports

Legislation may be preceded by a report of a Royal Commission, the Law Commission or some other official advisory committee (see p. 137). The House of Lords stated in **Black Clawson International Ltd** v **Papierwerke Waldhof-Aschaffenburg AG** (1975) that official reports may be considered as evidence of the pre-existing state of the law and the mischief that the legislation was intended to deal with.

Treaties

Treaties and international conventions can be considered when following the presumption that Parliament does not legislate in such a way that the UK would be in breach of its international obligations.

Previous practice

General practice and commercial usage in the field covered by the legislation may shed light on the meaning of a statutory term.

Hansard

This is the official daily report of parliamentary debates, and therefore a record of what was said during the introduction of legislation. For over 100 years, the judiciary held that such documents could not be consulted for the purpose of statutory interpretation. During his career, Lord Denning made strenuous efforts to do away with this rule and, in **Davis** v **Johnson** (1978), justified his interpretation of the Domestic Violence and Matrimonial Proceedings Act 1976 by reference to the parliamentary debates during its introduction. The House of Lords, however, rebuked him for doing so, and maintained that the rule should stand.

KEY CASE

In 1993, the case of **Pepper** v **Hart** overturned the rule against consulting *Hansard*, and such consultation is clearly now allowed. The case was between teachers at a fee-paying school (Malvern College) and the Inland Revenue, and concerned the tax which employees should have to pay on perks (benefits related to their job). Malvern College allowed its teachers to send their sons there for one-fifth of the usual fee, if places were available. Tax law requires employees to pay tax on perks, and the amount of tax is based on the cost to the employer of providing the benefit, which is usually taken to mean any extra cost that the employer would not otherwise incur. The amount paid by Malvern teachers for their sons' places covered the extra cost to the school of having the child there (in books, food and so on), but did not cover the school's fixed costs, for paying teachers, maintaining buildings and so on, which would have been the same whether the teachers' children were there or not. Therefore the perk cost the school little or nothing, and so the teachers maintained that they should not have to pay tax on it. The Inland Revenue disagreed, arguing that the perk should be taxed on the basis of the amount it saved the teachers on the real cost of sending their children to the school.

The reason why the issue of consulting parliamentary debates arose was that, during the passing of the Finance Act 1976 which laid down the tax rules in question, the then Secretary to the Treasury, Robert Sheldon, had specifically mentioned the kind of situation that arose in **Pepper v Hart.** He had stated that where the cost to an employer of a perk was minimal, employees should not have to pay tax on the full cost of it. The question was, could the judges take into account what the Minister had said? The House of Lords convened a special court of seven judges, which decided that they could look at *Hansard* to see what the Minister had said, and that his remarks could be used to decide what Parliament had intended.

Legal principle

When interpreting a statute the courts can consult *Hansard* to see what a Minister had said about a piece of legislation in order to decide what Parliament had intended.

The decision in **Pepper v Hart** was confirmed in **Three Rivers District Council v Bank of England (No. 2)** (1996), which concerned the correct interpretation of legislation passed in order to fulfil obligations arising from an EC directive. Although the legislation was not itself ambiguous, the claimants claimed that, if interpreted in the light of the information contained in *Hansard,* the legislation imposed certain duties on the defendants, which were not obvious from the legislation itself. The defendants argued that *Hansard* could only be consulted where legislation contained ambiguity, but the court disagreed, stating that where legislation was passed in order to give effect to international obligations, it was important to make sure that it did so, and consulting legislative materials was one way of helping to ensure this. The result would appear to be that *Hansard* can be consulted not just to explain ambiguous phrases, but to throw light on the general purpose of legislation.

In **R v Secretary of State for the Environment, Transport and the Regions,** *ex parte* **Spath Holme Ltd** (2001), the House of Lords gave a restrictive interpretation of the application of **Pepper v Hart.** The applicant was a company that was the landlord of certain properties. It sought judicial review of the Rent Acts (Maximum Fair Rent) Order 1999, made by the Secretary of State under s. 31 of the Landlord and Tenant Act 1985. The applicant company contended that the 1999 Order was unlawful as the Secretary of State had made it to alleviate the impact of rent increases on certain categories of tenants, when a reading of *Hansard* showed that Parliament's intention was that such orders would only be made to reduce the impact of inflation. On the use of *Hansard* to interpret the intention of Parliament, the House of Lords pointed out that the case of **Pepper v Hart** was concerned with the meaning of an expression used in a statute ('the cost of a benefit'). The Minister had given a statement on the meaning of that expression. By contrast, the present case was concerned with a matter of policy, and in particular the meaning of a statutory power rather than a statutory expression. Only if a Minister were, improbably, to give a categorical assurance to Parliament that a power would not be used in a given situation would a parliamentary statement on the scope of a power be admissible.

KEY CASE

In **Wilson** v **Secretary of State for Trade and Industry** (2003) the House of Lords again gave a restrictive interpretation to **Pepper** v **Hart**. It held that only statements in *Hansard* made by a Minister or other promoter of legislation could be looked at by the court; other statements recorded in *Hansard* had to be ignored.

Under the British constitution, Parliament and the courts have separate roles. Parliament enacts legislation, the courts interpret and apply it. Due to the principle of the separation of powers, neither institution should stray into the other's domain. Thus, Art. 9 of the Bill of Rights 1689 provides that 'the freedom of speech and debates or proceedings in Parliament ought not to be impeached or questioned in any court or place out of Parliament'. In **Wilson**, the House of Lords emphasised the importance of the courts not straying into Parliament's constitutional role. It concluded from this that *Hansard* could only be used to interpret the meaning of words in legislation; it could not be used to discover the reasons for the legislation. The Court of Appeal in **Wilson** had used *Hansard* to look at the parliamentary debates concerning a particular Act. It was not trying to discover the meaning of words, as their meaning was not in doubt, but to discover the reason which led Parliament to think that it was necessary to pass the Act. The House of Lords held that the Court of Appeal had been wrong to do this. Referring to *Hansard* simply to check the meaning of enacted words supported the principle of parliamentary sovereignty. Referring to *Hansard* to discover the reasoning of Parliament, where there was no ambiguity as to the meaning of the words, would go against the sovereignty of Parliament.

The Human Rights Act 1998 requires the courts to exercise a new role in respect of Acts of Parliament. This new role is fundamentally different from interpreting and applying legislation. The courts are now required to determine whether the legislation violates a right laid down in the European Convention on Human Rights. If the Act does violate the Convention, the courts have to issue a declaration of incompatibility. In order to determine this question, the House of Lords stated in **Wilson** that the courts can only refer to *Hansard* for background information, such as the social policy aim of the Act. Poor reasoning in the course of parliamentary debate was not a matter which could count against the legislation when determining the question of compatibility.

Legal principle

When interpreting a statute, only statements in *Hansard* made by a Minister or other promoter of legislation can be looked at by the court.

Although it is now clear that *Hansard* can be referred to in order to find evidence of parliamentary intention, there is still much debate as to how useful it is, and whether it can provide good evidence of what Parliament intended.

Below are three key arguments in favour of using *Hansard* to assist statutory interpretation.

Usefulness

Lord Denning's argument, advanced in **Davis v Johnson,** was that to ignore it would be to 'grope in the dark for the meaning of an Act without switching on the light'. When such an obvious source of enlightenment was available, it was ridiculous to ignore it – in fact Lord Denning said after the case that he intended to continue to consult *Hansard,* but simply not say he was doing so.

Other jurisdictions

Legislative materials are used in many foreign jurisdictions, including many other European countries and the US. In such countries, these materials tend to be more accessible and concise than *Hansard* – it is difficult to judge whether they are consulted because of this quality, or whether the fact that they are consulted has encouraged those who produce them to make them more readable. It is argued that the latter might be a useful side-effect of allowing the judges to consult parliamentary materials.

Media reports

Parliamentary proceedings are reported in newspapers and on radio and television. Since judges are as exposed to these as anyone else, it seems ridiculous to blinker themselves in court, or to pretend that they are blinkered.

Below are four key arguments against the use of *Hansard*:

Lack of clarity

The House of Lords, admonishing Lord Denning for his behaviour in **Davis v Johnson,** and directing that parliamentary debates were not to be consulted, stated that the evidence provided by the parliamentary debates might not be reliable; what was said in the cut and thrust of public debate was not 'conducive to a clear and unbiased explanation of the meaning of statutory language'.

Time and expense

Their Lordships also suggested that, if debates were to be used, there was a danger that the lawyers arguing a case would devote too much time and attention to ministerial statements and so on, at the expense of considering the language used in the Act itself.

> It would add greatly to the time and expense involved in preparing cases involving the construction of a statute if counsel were expected to read all the debates in *Hansard,* and it would often be impracticable for counsel to get access to at least the older reports of debates in select committees in the House of Commons; moreover, in a very large proportion of cases such a search, even if practicable, would throw no light on the question before the court . . .

This criticism of the use of *Hansard* was highlighted by Lord Steyn, a judge in the House of Lords, in his article 'Pepper v Hart: a re-examination' (2001). He suggests that much of the work of the appellate courts is now concerned with the interpretation of documents, such as statutes, rather than the examination of precedents.

Parliamentary intention

The nature of parliamentary intention is difficult, if not impossible, to pin down. Parliamentary debates usually reveal the views of only a few members and, even then, those words may need interpretation too.

Lord Steyn (2001) criticised the way the use of *Hansard* in **Pepper v Hart** gives pre-eminence to the Government Minister's interpretation of the statute and ignores any dissenting voices by opposition MPs. The Minister only spoke in the House of Commons and the detail of what he said was unlikely to have been known by the House of Lords. He therefore queries how the Minister's statement can be said to reflect the intention of Parliament, which is made up of both Houses. He points to the nature of the parliamentary process:

> The relevant exchanges sometimes take place late at night in nearly empty chambers. Sometimes it is a party political debate with whips on. The questions are often difficult but political warfare sometimes leaves little time for reflection. These are not ideal conditions for the making of authoritative statements about the meaning of a clause in a Bill. In truth a Minister speaks for the Government and not for Parliament. The statements of a Minister are no more than indications of what the Government would like the law to be. In any event, it is not discoverable from the printed record whether individual members of the legislature, let alone a plurality in each chamber, understood and accepted a ministerial explanation of the suggested meaning of the words.

This criticism has been partly tackled by the House of Lords in **Wilson v Secretary of State for Trade and Industry** (2003). The House stated that the courts must be careful not to treat the ministerial statement as indicative of the intention of Parliament:

> Nor should the courts give a ministerial statement, whether made inside or outside Parliament, determinative weight. It should not be supposed that members necessarily agreed with the Minister's reasoning or his conclusions.

The House emphasised that the will of Parliament is expressed in the language used in its enactments.

Statutes are always speaking

The courts have developed a presumption that 'statutes are always speaking', which means they have to be interpreted in the modern day legal context, rather than being fixed with the same meaning they had when they were originally passed. For example, s. 72 of the Highways Act 1835 provides a person is committing an offence if they:

> . . . wilfully ride upon any footpath or causeway by the side of any road made or set apart for the use or accommodation of foot passengers; or shall wilfully lead or drive any horse, ass, sheep, mule, swine, or cattle or carriage of any description, or any truck or sledge, upon any such footpath or causeway; or shall tether any horse, ass, mule, swine, or cattle, on any highway, so as to suffer or permit the tethered animal to be thereon.

This piece of legislation was passed before bicycles had been invented, but in **Taylor v Goodwin** (1879) the High Court held that the statute should be interpreted as applying to bicycles because they could come within the concept of a 'carriage' and the defendant was liable for the 'furious driving of a bicycle' on a pavement.

In **Turkington v Times Newspapers** (2000), *The Times* had published an article which reported a press conference in which a law firm had been criticised. *The Times* argued that they had a defence under the Law of Libel Amendment Act 1888, which applied when newspapers published accounts of certain public meetings. The claimant argued that the defence could not apply because when the statute had been passed there was no such thing as a 'press conference'. The House of Lords held:

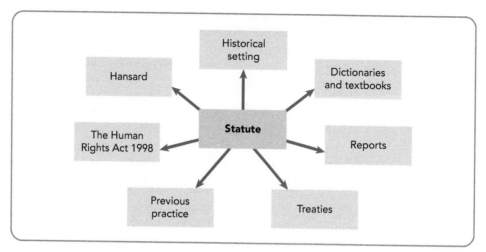

Figure 3.3 External aids to interpretation

There is a clear answer to this appeal to Victorian history. Unless they reveal a contrary intention all statutes are to be interpreted as 'always speaking statutes'.

There are two aspects of the 'always speaking' principle. The first is that courts must interpret and apply a statute to the world as it exists today. The second is that the statute must be interpreted in the light of the legal system as it exists today: a statutory provision has to be considered as a norm of the current legal system, rather than just as a product of a historically defined parliamentary assembly. The House of Lords concluded:

> . . . on ordinary principles of construction the question before the House must be considered in the light of the law of freedom of expression as it exists today. The appeal to the original meaning of the words of the statute must be rejected.

In **R** *v* **Ireland and Burstow** (1997) the House of Lords stated:

> Statutes dealing with a particular grievance or problem may sometimes require to be historically interpreted. But . . . statutes will generally be found to be of the 'always speaking' variety.

As a result, any reference to *Hansard* that determines the meaning of words at the time an Act was passed will not be conclusive about how the words will be interpreted today.

How do judges really interpret statutes?

This question has much in common with the discussion of case law and the operation of precedent (p. 6); in both cases, discussion of rules conceals a certain amount of flexibility. The so-called 'rules of interpretation' are not rules at all, but different approaches. Judges do not methodically apply these rules to every case and, in any case, the fact that they can conflict with each other and produce different results necessarily implies some choice as to which is used. There is choice too in the relative weight given to internal and external aids, and rules of language, and approaches have varied over the years.

Just as with judicial precedent, the idea that statutory interpretation is an almost scientific process that can be used to produce a single right answer is simply nonsense. There is frequently room for more than one interpretation (otherwise the question would never reach the courts) and judges must choose between them. For clear evidence of this, there is no better example than the litigation concerning Augusto Pinochet, the former head of state of Chile. He had long been accused of crimes against humanity, including torture and murder and conspiracy to torture and to murder. When he made a visit to the UK, the Spanish Government requested that he should be extradited to Spain so that they could put him on trial. This led to protracted litigation concerning whether it was legal for Britain to extradite him to Spain, and eventually the question came before the House of Lords. Pinochet's defence argued on the basis of the State Immunity Act 1978, which gives other states immunity from prosecution in English courts; the Act provides that 'states' includes heads of state. The Lords were therefore asked to decide whether this immunity extended to Pinochet's involvement in the acts he was accused of and, by a majority of three to two, they decided that it did not. Yet when the appeal was reopened (because one of the judges, Lord Hoffmann, was found to have links with Amnesty International, which was a party to the case), this time with seven Law Lords sitting, a different decision was reached. Although the Lords still stated that the General did not have complete immunity, by a majority of six to one, they restricted his liability to those acts which were committed after 1978, when torture committed outside the UK became a crime in the UK. This gave General Pinochet immunity for the vast majority of the torture allegations, and complete immunity for the allegations of murder and conspiracy to murder.

The reasoning behind both the decisions is complex and does not really need to concern us here; the important point to note is that in both hearings the Lords were interpreting the same statutory provisions, yet they came up with significantly different verdicts. Because of the way it was reopened, the case gives us a rare insight into just how imprecise and unpredictable statutory interpretation can be, and it is hard to resist the implication that if you put any other case involving statutory interpretation before two separate panels of judges, they might well come up with different judgments too.

Given then that judges do have some freedom over questions of statutory interpretation, what influences the decisions they make? As with case law, there are a number of theories.

Dworkin: fitting in with principles

Dworkin (1986) claims that, in approaching a case, the job of judges is to develop a theory about how the particular measure they are dealing with fits with the rest of the law as a whole. If there are two possible interpretations of a word or phrase, the judge should favour the one that allows the provision to sit most comfortably with the purpose of the rest of the law and with the principles and ideals of law and legality in general. This should be done, not for any mechanical reason, but because a body of law which is coherent and unified is, just for that reason, a body of law more entitled to the respect and allegiance of its citizens.

Cross: a contextual approach

Sir Rupert Cross (Bell and Engle, 1995) suggests that the courts take a 'contextual' approach in which, rather than choosing between different rules, they conduct a progressive analysis, considering first the ordinary meaning of the words in the context of the statute (taking a broad view of context), and then moving on to consider other possibilities if this provides an absurd result. Cross suggests that the courts can read in words that are necessarily implied, and have a limited power to add to, alter or ignore words that would otherwise make a provision unintelligible, absurd, totally unreasonable, unworkable or completely inconsistent with the rest of the Act.

Willis: the just result

John Willis's influential article 'Statute interpretation in a nutshell' (1938) was cynical about the use of the three 'rules'. He points out that a statute is often capable of several different interpretations, each in line with one of the rules. Despite the emphasis placed on literal interpretation, Willis suggests that the courts view all three rules as equally valid. He claims they use whichever rule will produce the result that they themselves believe to be just.

Griffith: political choices

As with case law (see p. 26), Griffith (1997) claims that, where there is ambiguity, the judiciary choose the interpretation that best suits their view of policy. An example of this was the 'Fares Fair' case, **Bromley London Borough Council** *v* **Greater London Council** (1982). The Labour-controlled GLC had enacted a policy – which was part of their election manifesto – to lower the cost of public transport in London, by subsidising it from the money paid in rates (what we now call Council Tax). This meant higher rates. Conservative-controlled Bromley Council challenged the GLC's right to do this.

The powers of local authorities (which then included the GLC) are defined entirely by statute, and there is an assumption that if a power has not been granted to a local authority by Parliament, then it is not a power the authority is entitled to exercise. The judges' job then was to discover what powers Parliament had granted the GLC, and to determine whether their action on fares and rates was within those powers.

Section 1 of the Transport (London) Act 1969 stated: 'It shall be the general duty of the Greater London Council to develop policies, and to encourage, organise and where appropriate, carry out measures which will promote the provision of integrated, efficient and economic transport facilities and services in Greater London.' The key word here was 'economic', with each side taking a different view of its meaning.

The GLC said 'economic' meant 'cost-effective', in other words, giving good value for money. They stated that good value covered any of the policy goals that transport services could promote: efficient movement of passengers, reduction of pollution and congestion, possibly even social redistribution. Bromley Council, on the other hand, said that 'economic' meant 'breaking even': covering the expenses of its operation out of the fares charged to the passengers and not requiring a subsidy.

It is not difficult to see that both sides had a point – the word 'economic' could cover either meaning, making the literal rule more or less useless. Because of this, Lord Scarman refused to consult a dictionary, stating that: 'The dictionary may tell us the several meanings the word can have but the word will always take its specific meaning (or meanings) from its surroundings.' Lord Scarman stressed that those surroundings meant not just the statute as a whole, but also the general duties of the GLC to ratepayers; that duty must coexist with the duty to the users of public transport.

Lord Scarman concluded:

> 'Economic' in s. 1 must, therefore, be construed widely enough to embrace both duties. Accordingly, I conclude that in s. 1(1) of the Act 'economic' covers not only the requirement that transport services be cost-effective but also the requirement that they be provided so as to avoid or diminish the burden on the ratepayers so far as it is practicable to do so.

Griffith has argued that the idea of a 'duty' to ratepayers as explained in the case is entirely judge-made, and that the Law Lords' ruling that the interests of transport users had been preferred over those of ratepayers is interfering with the role of elected authorities. He suggests that 'public expenditure can always be criticised on the ground that it is excessive or wrongly directed', but that it is the role of elected bodies to make such decisions, and if the public does not like them 'the remedy lies in their hands at the next election'.

It is certainly odd that when the judges make so much play of the fact that Parliament should legislate because it is elected and accountable, they do not consider themselves bound to respect decisions made in fulfilment of an elected body's manifesto. What the Lords were doing, argues Griffith, was making a choice between two interpretations, based not on any real sense of what Parliament intended, but 'primarily [on] the Law Lords' strong preference for the principles of the market economy with a dislike of heavy subsidisation for social purposes' – in other words a political choice.

The judiciary would argue against this proposition, but it is certainly difficult to see where any of the 'rules of interpretation' fitted into this case: none of the rules of interpretation or the aids to interpretation forced the judges to favour Bromley Council's interpretation of the law over that of the GLC. They could have chosen either interpretation and still been within the law, so that choice must have been based on something other than the law.

Reform of statutory interpretation

The problems with statutory interpretation have been recognised for decades but, despite several important reports, little has changed. The Law Commission examined the interpretation of statutes in 1967 and had 'little hesitation in suggesting that this is a field not suitable for codification'. Instead, it proposed certain improvements within the present system:

- More liberal use should be made of internal and external aids.
- In the event of ambiguity, the construction which best promoted the 'general legislative purpose' should be adopted. This could be seen as supporting Denning's approach.

The Renton Committee on the Preparation of Legislation produced its report in 1975, making many proposals for improving the procedure for making and drafting statutes, including the following.

- Acts could begin with a statement of purpose in the same way that older statutes used to have preambles.

- There should be a move towards including less detail in the legislation, introducing the simpler style used in countries such as France.
- More use could be made in statutes of examples showing the courts how an Act was intended to work in particular situations.
- Long, un-paragraphed sentences should be avoided.
- Statutes should be arranged to suit the convenience of the ultimate users.
- There should be more consolidation of legislation.

In 1978, Sir David Renton, in a speech entitled 'Failure to implement the Renton Report', noted that there had been a small increase in the number of draftsmen and increased momentum in the consolidation process, but that Parliament had continued to pass a huge amount of legislation, with no reduction in the amount of detail and scarcely any use of statements of purpose. Fifteen years later, in 1992, a Commission appointed by the *Hansard Society for Parliamentary Government* reported that little had changed. Having consulted widely, it concluded that there was widespread dissatisfaction with the situation, and suggested that the drafting style adopted should be appropriate for the main end users of legislation, with the emphasis on clarity, simplicity and certainty. There should be some means of informing citizens, lawyers and the courts about the general purpose behind a particular piece of legislation, and unnecessary detail should be avoided. The Commission suggested that an increase in the number of draftsmen might be necessary to achieve these aims: since its report, four more draftsmen have been recruited, but otherwise there was no immediate response to the proposals. The Labour Government, however, placed a high priority on making the workings of law and government accessible to ordinary people, and the introduction of explanatory notes to Bills passed from 1999 is an important step forward.

Answering questions

1 Using appropriate examples, explain three judicial rules of statutory interpretation.

The three traditional rules of statutory interpretation are the literal rule, the golden rule and the mischief rule. The literal rule gives the words of a piece of legislation their ordinary and natural meaning. Thus, in **Whiteley v Chappell** the accused was acquitted of impersonating a person entitled to vote as he had impersonated a person who was dead and therefore not so entitled. In **Fisher v Bell,** the offence of **offering** for sale was not committed where there had been merely an invitation to treat.

The golden rule applies where the literal rule produces an absurd result, and allows for the modification of words to avoid that absurdity but no further. Thus, in **R v Allen** the supposed offence of marrying when already married was in fact impossible, and so the courts interpreted 'shall marry' to mean 'shall go through a marriage ceremony'.

The mischief rule was established in **Heydon's Case** and provides that the judges should look at the law before the statute was passed, look at the mischief it was trying to remedy and look at the remedy Parliament provided. Thus, in **Elliott v Grey,** the offence of an uninsured car being 'used on the road' was committed even when it was jacked up as it did create a hazard.

2 The four approaches to statutory interpretation are so inconsistent with each other that a different result could be reached in the same case if the judges simply followed a different approach. Discuss.

A starting point would be to set out, briefly, the requirements/meaning of the four approaches. Then, in order to discuss the comment directly, you could take a number of case examples, such as **Royal College of Nursing** v **DHSS** (1981) (p. 61); **Smith** v **Hughes** (1960) (p. 61); and **London and North Eastern Railway Co** v **Berriman** (1946) (p. 58), and apply each of the four approaches to the disputed words in each case. This would clearly demonstrate how a different result could be reached depending on the approach taken.

You could close by expressing a preference for one of the approaches and explain why you prefer this approach – for example, if you thought the purposive approach was preferable, this might be because it does try to give effect to parliamentary intention and it responds to events not foreseen when the legislation was produced.

3 Why do judges sometimes refer to *Hansard*?

Your essay could start by observing that the application of the three traditional rules of statutory interpretation – the literal rule, the golden rule and the mischief rule – may not provide a clear answer as to the meaning of a piece of legislation. Moreover, despite the extensive use of both internal and external aids to statutory interpretation, the meaning of a term or phrase may continue to remain unclear.

In **Davis** v **Johnson,** the House of Lords rejected Lord Denning's attempts to use *Hansard* to aid statutory interpretation; but later in **Pepper** v **Hart** the House of Lords accepted that reference to *Hansard* could be made. This was later confirmed by their Lordships' opinions in **Three Rivers District Council** v **Bank of England (No. 2).** However, in **Wilson** v **SS Trade and Industry,** the Law Lords emphasised that *Hansard* could only be looked at to consider statements made by a Minister or the promoter of a Bill.

You could conclude by noting that the need to refer to *Hansard* to interpret statutes would be reduced if legislation was clearly drafted so that the aims of its promoters could be clear to the courts without the need to look at parliamentary debates.

Summary of Chapter 3: Statutory interpretation

Parliamentary intention
In interpreting statutes the courts are looking for the intention of Parliament, but this intention is frequently difficult to find.

Rules of statutory interpretation
There are four approaches to statutory interpretation:

- the literal rule;
- the golden rule;
- the mischief rule; and
- the purposive approach.

Human Rights Act 1998
Under s. 3 of the 1998 Act the courts are required to read legislation in a way that is compatible with Convention rights.

Interpreting European legislation

Under s. 2(4) of the European Communities Act 1972, all parliamentary legislation must be construed in accordance with European law.

Internal aids to statutory interpretation

Internal aids consist of the statute itself, explanatory notes (post-1999) and rules of language.

External aids to statutory interpretation

These include:

- dictionaries and textbooks;
- reports that preceded the legislation;
- treaties;
- the Human Rights Act 1998; and
- *Hansard*, following the decision of **Pepper v Hart**.

How do judges really interpret statutes?

Different academics have put forward arguments as to how judges really interpret statutes. John Willis argues that the courts use whichever rule will produce the result that they themselves believe to be just. Griffith thinks that judges interpret statutes in a way that coincides with their political preferences, referring to the case of **Bromley London Borough Council v Greater London Council** to support his arguments.

Reform of statutory interpretation

The Renton Committee on the Preparation of Legislation in 1975 recommended reforms of the procedure for making and drafting statutes, but little has changed.

Reading list

Bell, J. and Engle, G. (eds) (1995) *Cross: Statutory Interpretation* (3rd edn). London: LexisNexis/ Butterworths.

Bennion, F.A.R. (2005) *Statutory Interpretation*. London: Butterworths.

(2007) Executive estoppel: *Pepper v Hart* revisited. *Public Law*, Spring 1.

Dworkin, R. (1986) *Law's Empire*. London: Fontana.

Griffith, J.A.G. (1997) *The Politics of the Judiciary*. London: Fontana.

Hart, H.L.A. (1994) *The Concept of Law*. Oxford: Clarendon.

Manchester, C., Salter, D. and Moodie, P. (2000) *Exploring the Law: The Dynamics of Precedent and Statutory Interpretation* (2nd edn). London: Sweet & Maxwell.

Steyn, J. (2001) Pepper v Hart: a re-examination. *Oxford Journal of Legal Studies*, 59.

Willis, J. (1938) Statute interpretation in a nutshell. *Canadian Bar Review*, 16: 13.

Zander, M. (2004) *The Law-Making Process*. London: Butterworths.

On the internet

www *Hansard* is available at:

http://www.parliament.uk/business/publications/hansard/

4

Delegated legislation

This chapter discusses:

- the three forms of delegated legislation;
- why delegated legislation is necessary;
- how delegated legislation is controlled; and
- criticism made of delegated legislation.

Introduction

In many cases the statutes passed by Parliament lay down a basic framework of the law, with creation of the detailed rules delegated to others. There are three main forms of delegated legislation: statutory instruments, bye-laws and Orders in Council.

Statutory instruments

Statutory instruments were created by the Statutory Instruments Act 1946. There are four forms of statutory instrument (Pywell, 2013):

- **Regulations.** These are used to make substantive law.
- **Orders in Council.** These are made by the Privy Council and usually involve rubber-stamping the detailed rules regulating the professions.
- **Orders.** These are usually made by Government Ministers and serve a narrow purpose, such as commencement orders (stating when a statutory provision will come into force) and legislative reform orders (discussed below).
- **Rules.** These are procedural rules which lay down how things should be done, rather than what should be done, such as the Civil Procedure Rules.

Bye-laws

Bye-laws are made by local authorities, public and nationalised bodies and deal with matters within their limited jurisdiction. Bye-laws have to be approved by central Government.

Orders in Council

Orders in Council are approved by the Privy Council and signed by the Queen. They are used when an ordinary statutory instrument made by a Minister would be inappropriate, such as in times of emergency or where the order involves the transfer of ministerial power. For example, under the Civil Service (Amendment) Order in Council 1997, Tony Blair gave himself the power to appoint up to three people to the Prime Minister's Office outside the normal Civil Service recruitment procedure. He used this power to appoint his two most trusted political advisers: Alastair Campbell and Jonathan Powell. The involvement of the monarch is necessary because of the potentially far-reaching consequences of Orders in Council.

The power to make delegated legislation

Ordinary members of the public cannot decide on a whim to make delegated legislation. Instead, usually an Act of Parliament is required, known as an enabling Act, which gives this power to a branch of the state. The Act can be quite specific, giving a limited power to make legislation on a very narrow issue, or it can be quite general and allow for a wide range of delegated legislation to be made. An example of such a general provision is the European Communities Act 1972, s. 2, which allows the executive to make delegated legislation to bring into force in the UK relevant European legislation. Local authorities have been given a general power to make bye-laws under s. 235 of the Local Government Act 1972. Recent years have seen a move towards centralised government and therefore a reduced role for bye-laws. The Labour Government, however, favoured the use of local bye-laws to strengthen community involvement in regulating behaviour in their local areas. To facilitate the use of bye-laws the Local Government and Public Involvement in Health Act 2007 was passed containing provisions for a faster legislative process for some bye-laws.

TOPICAL ISSUE

Legislative reform orders

The **Legislative and Regulatory Reform Act 2006** gives the executive very wide powers to make delegated legislation. This Act was introduced following a report of the Better Regulation Task Force, *Regulation – Less is More* (2005). The official aim of the Act is to make it simpler and faster to amend existing legislation. It allows Ministers to issue statutory instruments to amend legislation to reduce a burden (such as unnecessary cost or administrative inconvenience) caused by legislation in order to promote better regulation. European Union obligations can also be implemented using this Act. Orders made under this Act are known as legislative reform orders. The first draft of the Bill was severely criticised by a panel of MPs for giving excessive powers to make delegated legislation which were disproportionate to the Bill's stated aims. In the light of this criticism some amendments were made. Thus, the effect of the order must be proportionate, it must strike a fair balance between the different interests involved and it must not be of constitutional significance. Sometimes a super-affirmative procedure (see p. 78) will have to be followed to pass a legislative reform order. Concerns remain that this is an unnecessary shift of power from a democratically elected Parliament, to the executive.

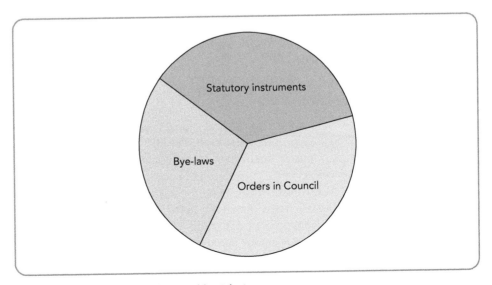

Figure 4.1 Sources of delegated legislation

Why is delegated legislation necessary?

Delegated legislation is necessary for a number of reasons:

Insufficient parliamentary time Parliament does not have the time to debate every detailed rule necessary for efficient government.

Speed It allows rules to be made more quickly than they could by Parliament. Parliament does not sit all the time, and its procedure is slow and cumbersome; delegated legislation often has to be made in response to emergencies and urgent problems.

Technicality of the subject matter Modern legislation often needs to include detailed, technical provisions – those in building regulations or safety at work rules, for example. MPs do not usually have the technical knowledge required, whereas delegated legislation can use experts who are familiar with the relevant areas.

Need for local knowledge Local bye-laws in particular can only be made effectively with awareness of the locality. Recognition of the importance of local knowledge can be found with the devolved assemblies for Scotland, Wales and Northern Ireland. These democratic bodies have important powers to make delegated legislation.

Flexibility Statutes require cumbersome procedures for enactment, and can only be revoked or amended by another statute. Delegated legislation, however, can be put into action quickly, and easily revoked if it proves problematic.

Future needs Parliament cannot hope to foresee every problem that might arise as a result of a statute, especially concerning areas such as health provision or welfare benefits. Delegated legislation can be put in place as and when such problems arise.

Control of delegated legislation

Because it is not directly made by elected representatives, delegated legislation is subject to the following range of controls, designed to ensure that the power delegated is not abused.

Consultation

Those who make delegated legislation often consult experts within the relevant field, and those bodies which are likely to be affected by it. In the case of road traffic regulations, for example, Ministers are likely to seek the advice of police, motoring organisations, vehicle manufacturers and local authorities before making the rules. Often the relevant statute makes such consultation obligatory and names the bodies which should be consulted. Under the National Insurance Act 1946, for example, draft regulations must be submitted to the National Insurance Advisory Committee. In other cases there may be a general statutory requirement for 'such consultation as the minister thinks appropriate with such organisations as appear to him to represent the interest concerned'. Statutory instruments made under the Legislative and Regulatory Reform Act 2006 (see p. 75) can only be made after interested parties have been consulted.

In **R** v **Brent London Borough Council**, *ex parte* **Gunning** (1985) it was stated that consultations had to be fair and to be fair they must:

- take place at a formative stage;
- give adequate reasons for the proposals to allow for intelligent consideration and response;
- allow adequate time for consideration and response; and
- ensure that the product of the consultation is conscientiously taken into account in finalising the proposals.

In **R (on the application of Moseley)** v **London Borough of Haringey** (2014) the Supreme Court stated that the consultation documentation needed to refer to alternative legislative options that had been rejected by the public body so that the people consulted were aware of these.

Publication

All delegated legislation is published, and therefore available for public scrutiny. Alongside the statutory instrument, the Government now publishes an explanatory memorandum detailing the statutory instrument's policy objective and legislative context. The importance of publishing legislation was emphasised in a European case in 2009. A man had been prevented from getting on a plane with a tennis racket as hand luggage. The airline had pointed to some European regulations that prohibited certain articles from being taken on board the plane for security reasons. The relevant items were listed in an appendix which had been published but when the appendix was amended the amended version was not published. The passenger claimed that the amended regulations could not be enforced against him because they had never been published. This argument was accepted by the court because governments should not be allowed to pass secret legislation; the public should be able to ascertain the scope of their rights and obligations under the law.

Supervision by Parliament

There are a number of ways in which Parliament can oversee delegated legislation.

Revocation

Parliamentary sovereignty means that Parliament can at any time revoke a piece of delegated legislation itself, or pass legislation on the same subject as the delegated legislation.

The negative resolution procedure

Much delegated legislation is put before Parliament for MPs under the negative resolution procedure. Within a specified time (usually 40 days), any member may put down a motion to annul it. An annulment motion put down by a backbencher is not guaranteed to be dealt with, but one put down by the Official Opposition (the party with the second largest number of MPs) usually will be. If, after debate, either House passes an annulment motion, the delegated legislation is cancelled.

The affirmative resolution procedure

Enabling Acts dealing with subjects of special, often constitutional, importance may require Parliament to vote its approval of the delegated legislation. This is called the affirmative resolution procedure, whereby delegated legislation is laid before one or both Houses (sometimes in draft), and becomes law only if a motion approving it is passed within a specified time (usually 28 or 40 days). Since a vote has to be taken, the procedure means that the Government must find parliamentary time for debate, and opposition parties have an opportunity to raise any objections. In practice, though, it is very rare for the Government not to achieve a majority when such votes are taken and the process amounts to little more than a rubber-stamping exercise. An instrument has not been struck down under this procedure since 1969.

The super-affirmative procedure

The super-affirmative procedure is sometimes required to check legislative reform orders (see p. 75) and is required for some orders made under the Public Bodies Act 2011 and the Localism Act 2011. Under this procedure Parliament has more power to scrutinise the proposed delegated legislation than under the ordinary affirmative resolution procedure. First, the Minister must lay before Parliament for 60 days a draft of the proposed legislative reform order. During this period two parliamentary committees will automatically review the order and produce a report. The Minister then takes into account these reports and any other representations and decides whether to proceed with the legislation and whether to make any amendments to it. If he or she decides to proceed, the draft order, with any amendments, is formally made available in each House (described as 'being laid before Parliament'). This ability to make changes to the draft order is a key feature of the procedure, which is not available to statutory instruments made under the ordinary negative or affirmative resolution procedures. The two committees then produce a report, normally within 15 days. Each House considers the relevant committee report on the draft order. An order dealt with under this procedure must be expressly approved by both Houses of Parliament before it can be made.

Committee supervision

Several parliamentary committees monitor new delegated legislation. The Joint Committee on Statutory Instruments watches over the making of delegated legislation and reports to each House on any delegated legislation which requires special consideration, including any regulations made under an Act that prohibit challenge by the courts, or which seem to make unusual or unexpected use of the powers granted by the enabling Act. However, the Committee may not consider the merits of any piece of delegated legislation. This is the responsibility of the House of Lords' Merits of Statutory Instruments Committee. In addition, the House of Lords' Select Committee on Delegated Powers and Regulatory Reform looks at the extent of legislative powers proposed to be delegated by Parliament to Government Ministers. It is required to report on whether the provision of any Bill inappropriately delegates legislative power, or subjects the exercise of legislative power to an inappropriate level of parliamentary scrutiny.

Questions from MPs

MPs can ask Ministers questions about delegated legislation at a ministerial question time, or raise them in debates.

The House of Lords

Although the House of Lords cannot veto proposed Acts following the Parliament Acts 1911 and 1949 (see p. 40), the same does not apply to delegated legislation. Instead there is a Convention that dates back to 1968 that the House of Lords should only exceptionally reject a statutory instrument. This has only happened five times since 1968. Most recently, in 2015 the House of Lords rejected the draft Tax Credits (Income Thresholds and Determination of Rates) (Amendment) Regulations 2015. As a result of this defeat, the Government commissioned the former leader of the House of Lords, Lord Strathclyde, to carry out a review looking at the relationship between the two Houses of Parliament in the context of delegated legislation, and to ensure that the elected chamber plays the decisive role in the passage of such legislation. The Strathclyde Review was published in December 2015. It outlined three options for change:

- no power of scrutiny by the House of Lords;
- the passing of a resolution by the House of Lords establishing a convention that the Lords' ability to reject secondary legislation would be left unused; or
- new legislation removing the Lords' powers to reject secondary legislation, but allowing them to ask the Commons to 'think again'.

The House of Lords has rejected all three of these recommendations and the Government has not yet acted upon them.

Control by the courts: judicial review

While the validity of a statute can never be challenged by the courts because of parliamentary sovereignty, delegated legislation can. It may be challenged on any of the following grounds under the procedure for judicial review.

Procedural *ultra vires*

Here the complainant claims that the procedures laid down in the enabling Act for producing delegated legislation have not been followed. In **Agricultural, Horticultural and Forestry Industry Training Board *v* Aylesbury Mushrooms Ltd** (1972), an order was declared invalid because the requirement to consult with interested parties before making it had not been properly complied with.

Substantive *ultra vires*

This is usually based on a claim that the measure under review goes beyond the powers Parliament granted under the enabling Act. In **Customs and Excise Commissioners *v* Cure & Deeley Ltd** (1962), the powers of the Commissioners to make delegated legislation under the Finance (No. 2) Act 1940 were challenged. The Act empowered them to produce regulations 'for any matter for which provision appears to them necessary for the purpose of giving effect to the Act'. The Commissioners held that this included allowing them to make a regulation giving them the power to determine the amount of tax due where a tax return was submitted late. The High Court invalidated the regulation on the ground that the Commissioners had given themselves powers far beyond what Parliament had intended; they were empowered only to collect such tax as was due by law, not to decide what amount they thought fit.

R *v* Secretary of State for Social Security, *ex parte* **Joint Council for the Welfare of Immigrants** (1996) concerned the Asylum and Immigration Appeals Act 1993 which provided a framework for determining applications for asylum, and for appeals after unsuccessful applications. It allowed asylum seekers to apply for social security benefits while they were waiting for their applications or appeals to be decided, at a cost of over £200 million per year to British taxpayers. This led to concern from some quarters that the provisions might attract those who were simply seeking a better lifestyle than that available in their own countries (often called economic migrants), as opposed to those fleeing persecution, whom the provisions were actually designed to help.

In order to discourage economic migrants, the then Secretary of State for Social Security exercised his powers to make delegated legislation under the Social Security (Contributions and Benefits) Act 1992, and produced regulations which stated that social security benefits would no longer be available to those who sought asylum after they had entered the UK, rather than immediately on entry, or those who had been refused leave to stay here and were awaiting the outcome of appeals against the decision.

The Joint Council for the Welfare of Immigrants challenged the regulations, claiming that they fell outside the powers granted by the 1992 Act. The Court of Appeal upheld their claim, stating that the 1993 Act was clearly intended to give asylum seekers rights which they did not have previously. The effect of the regulations was effectively to take those rights away again since, without access to social security benefits, most asylum seekers would either have to return to the countries from which they had fled, or live on nothing while their claims were processed. The court ruled that Parliament could not have intended to give the Secretary of State powers to take away the rights it had given in the 1993 Act: this could only be done by a new statute, and therefore the regulations were *ultra vires*.

The decision was a controversial one, because the regulations had themselves been approved by Parliament, and overturning them could be seen as a challenge to the power of the legislature, despite the decision being explained by the court as upholding that power.

Unreasonableness

If rules are manifestly unjust, have been made in bad faith (for example, by someone with a financial interest in their operation) or are otherwise so perverse that no reasonable official could have made them, the courts can declare them invalid.

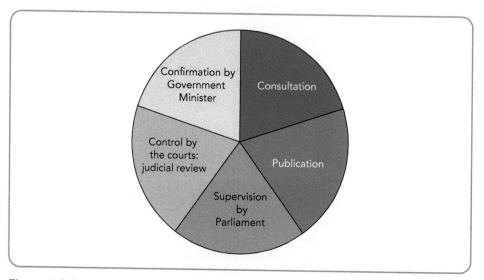

Figure 4.2 Control of delegated legislation

Confirmation by Government Minister

Under s. 235(2) of the Local Government Act 1972, bye-laws passed by local authorities often need to be confirmed by the relevant Government Minister. This confirmation process checks that:

- the local authority had the power to make the legislation;
- the consultation process was undertaken;
- there is no duplication or conflict with existing legislation;
- the bye-law deals with a genuine and specific local problem (rather than a national issue); and
- there is no conflict with Government policy.

Following the passing of the Local Government and Public Involvement in Health Act 2007, regulations can be passed allowing bye-laws dealing with specified issues to be made under an accelerated procedure which does not require confirmation by a Government Minister. This power has been extended to where councils want to repeal outdated bye-laws under the Localism Act 2011.

Criticism of delegated legislation

Lack of democratic involvement

This argument is put forward because delegated legislation is usually made by civil servants, rather than elected politicians. This is not seen as a particular problem where the delegated legislation takes the form of detailed administrative rules, since these would clearly take up impossible amounts of parliamentary time otherwise. However, in the latter years of the John Major-led Conservative Government (1990–97) there was increasing concern that delegated legislation was being used to implement important policies.

The power to overturn an Act of Parliament by ministerial order is known as a Henry VIII power because Henry VIII legislated to give his declarations the same legal status as Acts of Parliament. Henry VIII clauses in legislation amount to an attack on parliamentary supremacy. While ordinary delegated powers create a mechanism for the executive to supplement parliamentary statutes, Henry VIII clauses allow the executive to amend or repeal such statutes. The executive should not be able to overrule primary legislation because this undermines Parliament's power. The Public Bodies Act 2011 contains a list of public bodies (called quangos) which the Government is entitled to abolish by delegated legislation – the media has called this the 'bonfire of the quangos'. This power amounts to a Henry VIII power because it allows Ministers by order to amend or abolish bodies that were established by primary legislation.

The role of the Privy Council in passing delegated legislation is particularly sensitive because it is not a democratic body. The civil rights group, JUSTICE, published a report in 2009 pointing out that Orders in Council made by the Privy Council had been used to abolish the right of trade union membership for some civil servants and to force residents of the Chagos Islands to leave their homes and prevent them from returning.

Overuse

Critics argue that there is too much delegated legislation; this is linked to the point above, as there would be little problem with increasing amounts of delegated legislation if its purpose was merely to flesh out technical detail.

Sub-delegation

Delegated legislation is sometimes made by people other than those who were given the original power to do so.

Lack of control

Despite the above list of controls over delegated legislation, the reality is that effective supervision is difficult. First, publication has only limited benefits, given that the general public are frequently unaware of the existence of delegated legislation, let alone on what grounds it can be challenged and how to go about doing so. This in turn has an effect on the ability of the courts to control delegated legislation, since judicial review relies on individual challenges being brought before the courts. This may not happen until years after a provision is enacted, when it finally affects someone who is prepared and able to challenge it. The obvious result is that legislation which largely affects a class of individuals who are not given to questioning official rules, are unaware of their rights, or who lack the financial resources to go to court, will rarely be challenged.

A further problem is that some enabling Acts confer extremely wide discretionary powers on Ministers; a phrase such as 'the Minister may make such regulations as he sees fit for the purpose of bringing the Act into operation' would not be unusual. This means that there is very little room for anything to be considered *ultra vires,* so judicial review is effectively frustrated.

The main method of control over delegated legislation is therefore parliamentary, but this too has its drawbacks. Although the affirmative resolution procedure usually ensures that parliamentary attention is drawn to important delegated legislation, it is rarely possible to prevent such legislation being passed. The Select Committee on the Scrutiny of Delegated Powers makes an important contribution, and has been able to secure changes to a number of important pieces of legislation. However, it too lacks real power, as it is unable to consider the merits of delegated legislation (as opposed to whether the delegated powers have been correctly used) and its reports have no binding effect.

Answering questions

1 To what extent is there any parliamentary or judicial control over delegated legislation?

Your introduction could explain that delegated legislation normally takes the form of statutory instruments, bye-laws and Orders in Council. The authority to make such legislation usually derives from an enabling Act, in other words, an Act which enables an individual or organisation to make legislation on a specific issue.

Your essay could then be divided into two parts: parliamentary controls and judicial controls. Considering first parliamentary controls, Parliament exercises control over delegated legislation through requiring a consultation process, the publication of all draft legislation, parliamentary supervision through the affirmative, super-affirmative and negative resolution process, and the scrutiny by relevant parliamentary committees.

Looking secondly at the judicial controls, the courts exercise scrutiny through the process of judicial review, which will check whether the delegated legislation has met the procedural and substantive requirements. In respect of procedural *ultra vires*, the courts ensure that the correct procedure has been followed: see for example, **Agricultural, Horticultural and Forestry Industry Training Board** v **Aylesbury Mushrooms Ltd.** They check that the delegated legislation does not go beyond the provisions of the enabling Act – see **CEC** v **Cure & Deeley Ltd** (p. 79), where the court held that the Commissioners could not give themselves powers that went significantly beyond those intended by Parliament.

2 The effect that delegated legislation has on daily life is significantly greater than that of primary legislation (Acts of Parliament). What are the benefits of delegated legislation? In your view, do its benefits outweigh its weaknesses?

You need to begin by setting out what the benefits and criticisms of delegated legislation are (which are discussed on pp. 76 and 81 respectively). In order to answer the question properly though, you must then express your view as to whether or not the former outweigh the latter, and explain your reasoning. You could certainly use the democracy argument (raised in the 'Topical issue' section on p. 74).

3 Read the source material below and answer parts (a), (b) and (c) which follow.

Exercise on Delegated Legislation

Source A

Police and Criminal Evidence Act 1984

(1984 c.60)
Section 60

Tape-recording of Interviews

(1) It shall be the duty of the Secretary of State –

. . .

(b) to make an order requiring the tape-recording of interviews of persons suspected of the commission of criminal offences, or of such descriptions of criminal offences as may be specified in the order . . .

(2) An order under subsection (1) above shall be made by statutory instrument and shall be subject to annulment in pursuance of a resolution of either House of Parliament.

Source B

Statutory Instrument
1991 No. 2687
The Police and Criminal Evidence Act 1984

(Tape-recording of Interviews) (No. 1) Order 1991

Made	29th November 1991
Laid before Parliament	6th December 1991
Coming into force	1st January 1992

Now, therefore, in pursuance of the said section 60(1)(b), the Secretary of State hereby orders as follows:

. . .

2. This Order shall apply to interviews of persons suspected of the commission of indictable offences which are held by police officers at police stations in the police areas specified in the schedule to this Order and which commence after midnight on 31st December 1991.

3. (1) Subject to paragraph (2) below, interviews to which this Order applies shall be tape-recorded in accordance with the requirements of the code of practice on tape-recording which came into operation on 29th July 1988 . . .

(2) The duty to tape-record interviews under paragraph (1) above shall not apply to interviews –

(a) where the offence of which a person is suspected is one in respect of which he has been arrested or detained under section 14(1)(a) of the Prevention of Terrorism (Temporary Provisions) Act 1989; . . .

(a) Using Sources A and B to illustrate your answer, compare the legislative process in relation to an Act of Parliament on the one hand and delegated legislation on the other.

(b) What are the advantages and disadvantages of delegated legislation?

(c) Each of the following interviews was conducted by police officers and took place at a police station covered by SI 1991/2687, but none of the interviews was tape-recorded.

(i) On 30th November 1991 Alice was charged with an indictable offence and interviewed;

(ii) Bertie, who was suspected of an indictable offence, was interviewed on 1st April 1998;

(iii) Cedric, detained under s. 14(1)(a) of the Prevention of Terrorism (Temporary Provisions) Act 1989 was interviewed in April 1998.

Discuss interviews (i), (ii) and (iii) with reference to Source B.

(a) For material on the legislative process in relation to an Act of Parliament see Chapter 2 and for delegated legislation pp. 74–81. You could point out that the Police and Criminal Evidence Act 1984 (PACE) was an enabling Act which allowed the Secretary of State to make the Statutory Instrument 1991/2687. You could mention that statutory instruments are made by Government departments and contrast this with bye-laws and Orders in Council (p. 74). When explaining the negative resolution procedure (p. 76) you could refer to the fact that the statutory instrument on tape-recording interviews was laid before Parliament on 6 December 1991 and that s. 60(2) of PACE refers to this process.

(b) Material on the advantages of delegated legislation can be found on p. 75 under the heading 'Why is delegated legislation necessary?' Criticisms can be found on p. 81.

(c) (i) As Statutory Instrument 1991/2687 provides that its provisions only apply to interviews that take place after midnight on 31 December 1991, the police were under no obligation to tape-record Alice's interview.

(ii) Bertie's interview should have been tape-recorded as he was suspected of committing an indictable offence and the interview took place after the provisions of the statutory instrument came into force. You could look at possible remedies, particularly the exclusion of the evidence obtained.

(iii) There was no obligation to tape-record Cedric's interview as he had been detained under the Prevention of Terrorism (Temporary Provisions) Act 1989.

Summary of Chapter 4: Delegated legislation

There are three main forms of delegated legislation:

● Statutory instruments
● Bye-laws
● Orders in Council.

The power to make delegated legislation
Usually an Act of Parliament is required giving the power to make delegated legislation to a branch of the state.

Why is delegated legislation necessary?
Delegated legislation is necessary because it saves parliamentary time, constitutes a quick form of legislation, and is suited to technical subject areas or where local knowledge is needed.

Control of delegated legislation
Delegated legislation is controlled through:

● the consultation of experts;
● publication of the legislation;
● supervision by Parliament;
● the courts with the judicial review procedure; and
● confirmation by a Government Minister.

Criticism of delegated legislation
Delegated legislation has been criticised due to:

● lack of democratic involvement;
● overuse;
● sub-delegation; and
● lack of controls.

Reading list

Better Regulation Task Force (2005) *Regulation – Less is More: Reducing Burdens, Improving Outcomes.* London: Cabinet Office.

Burns, S. (2006) Tipping the balance. *New Law Journal,* 156: 787.

McHarg, A. (2006) What is delegated legislation? *Public Law,* Autumn: 539.

Pywell, S. (2013) Untangling the law. *New Law Journal,* 163: 321.

On the internet

www Statutory instruments are published on the legislation.gov.uk website at:
www.legislation.gov.uk/uksi

5

European law

This chapter discusses:

- the six key institutions of the European Union: the Council of Ministers, the European Council, the Commission, the European Parliament, the Court of Justice of the European Union and the European Central Bank;

- how European law is made;

- the four main sources of European law: treaties, regulations, directives and decisions; and

- the impact of European Union law on the UK.

Introduction

The European Union (EU) currently comprises 28 European countries. The original members – France, West Germany, Belgium, Luxembourg, Italy and the Netherlands – laid the foundations in 1951, when they created the European Coal and Steel Community (ECSC). Six years later, they signed the Treaty of Rome, creating the European Economic Community (EEC) and the European Atomic Energy Community (Euratom). The original six were joined by the UK, Ireland and Denmark in 1973, Greece in 1981 and Spain and Portugal in 1986 and, in the same year, the member countries signed the Single European Act, which developed free movement of goods and people within the Community (the single market), and greater political unity. Finland, Austria and Sweden joined in 1995. Following the Nice summit in 2004, the EU increased its membership from 15 to 27, with most of the new members coming from eastern Europe. The last country to join was Croatia in 2013. Five countries are currently in formal negotiations to join the EU: Iceland, Macedonia, Montenegro, Serbia and Turkey. Due to its financial difficulties there is a possibility that Greece may leave the EU.

In 1993 the Maastricht Treaty renamed the European Economic Community the European Community and also created the European Union (EU). Following the Lisbon Treaty in 2009 the European Community has now been totally replaced by the European Union.

TOPICAL ISSUE

BREXIT

In June 2016 a referendum was held to decide whether the United Kingdom should remain a member of the European Union or withdraw. The citizens of the United Kingdom voted by a small majority in favour of leaving the European Union (sometimes described in the media as Brexit). The political and legal implications of this withdrawal are very significant, though the precise impact of this planned withdrawal is still unclear. A formal procedure has to be followed under Article 50 of the Treaty on European Union before the withdrawal takes effect. The terms of Article 50 are as follows:

1 Any Member State may decide to withdraw from the Union in accordance with its own constitutional requirements.
2 A Member State which decides to withdraw shall notify the European Council of its intention. In the light of the guidelines provided by the European Council, the Union shall negotiate and conclude an agreement with that State, setting out the arrangements for its withdrawal, taking account of the framework for its future relationship with the Union. That agreement shall be negotiated in accordance with Article 218(3) of the Treaty on the Functioning of the European Union. It shall be concluded on behalf of the Union by the Council, acting by a qualified majority, after obtaining the consent of the European Parliament.
3 The Treaties shall cease to apply to the State in question from the date of entry into force of the withdrawal agreement or, failing that, two years after the notification

▶

referred to in paragraph 2, unless the European Council, in agreement with the Member State concerned, unanimously decides to extend this period.

4 For the purposes of paragraphs 2 and 3, the member of the European Council or of the Council representing the withdrawing Member State shall not participate in the discussions of the European Council or Council or in decisions concerning it. A qualified majority shall be defined in accordance with Article 238(3)(b) of the Treaty on the Functioning of the European Union.

5 If a State which has withdrawn from the Union asks to rejoin, its request shall be subject to the procedure referred to in Article 49.

The Article 50 procedure commences with the UK contacting the European Council by letter informing them of their intention to withdraw. Following the decision of the Supreme Court in **R (on the application of Miller and Dos Santos)** v **The Secretary of State for Exiting the European Union** (2017) Parliament has to pass an Act of Parliament to authorise Government Ministers to initiate the withdrawal process. Once the withdrawal process has begun by this notification, two years are allowed to complete the withdrawal process. In March 2017 the European Union (Notification of Withdrawal) Act 2017 was passed with two seemingly simple lines:

The Prime Minister wrote to the President of the European Council, Donald Tusk on 29 March 2017 to begin the process of withdrawal under Article 50. The withdrawal process is scheduled to be completed by 29 March 2019. The terms of the withdrawal have to be negotiated and agreed with the Council acting by qualified majority vote with the consent of the European Parliament. If the two-year period ends without agreement, the withdrawing country is no longer a member. Article 50 does not provide for a cancellation of the notification. Following the March 2017 notification, negotiations of the withdrawal have taken place through monthly meetings each extending over four days. The fifth round of negotiations in October closed with progress being cited as being made on the rights of British citizens residing in the EU and vice versa once withdrawal takes place. However, it was also widely reported that negotiations thus far remained deadlocked on the vital issue of the financial settlement which needs to be reached for withdrawal to take place. This has been a thorny issue and the cause of much political and financial uncertainty. Essentially it has been debated and some might say disputed, what level of financial contribution the UK is expected to make after leaving the EU. The debates about financial contributions have been so fragile that the Government has remarked several times during the process that 'no deal is better than a bad deal'.

At a national level, the UK Parliament will repeal the European Communities Act 1972 (discussed on p. 99), removing the automatic incorporation of European law into UK law. The European Parliament and European Court of Justice will stop having any direct power over the courts and Parliament in the United Kingdom. In terms of what will become of current EU legislation that is embedded in the UK, in the second reading of The European Union (Withdrawal) Bill, one of the aims set out was to end the supremacy of European Union (EU) law in UK law and convert EU law as it stands at the moment of exit into domestic law. Further secondary legislation will be created where necessary to enable corrections to be made to the laws that would otherwise no longer operate appropriately once the UK has left the EU, so that the domestic legal system continues to function correctly outside the EU.

ELIZABETH II   c. **9**

European Union (Notification of Withdrawal) Act 2017

2017 CHAPTER 9

An Act to confer power on the Prime Minister to notify, under Article 50(2) of the Treaty on European Union, the United Kingdom's intention to withdraw from the EU.   [16th March 2017]

B E IT ENACTED by the Queen's most Excellent Majesty, by and with the advice and consent of the Lords Spiritual and Temporal, and Commons, in this present Parliament assembled, and by the authority of the same, as follows:—

1   Power to notify withdrawal from the EU

(1)   The Prime Minister may notify, under Article 50(2) of the Treaty on European Union, the United Kingdom's intention to withdraw from the EU.

(2)   This section has effect despite any provision made by or under the European Communities Act 1972 or any other enactment.

2   Short title

This Act may be cited as the European Union (Notification of Withdrawal) Act 2017.

Figure 5.1 European Union (Notification of Withdrawal) Act 2017

The aims of the European Union

The original aim of the first treaty signed, the Treaty of Paris (1951), was to create political unity within Europe and prevent another world war. The ECSC placed the production of steel and coal in all the member states under the authority of a single community organisation, with the object of indirectly controlling the manufacture of arms and therefore helping to prevent war between member states. The ECSC ceased to exist in 2002. Euratom was designed to produce cooperative nuclear research, and the EEC to improve Europe's economic strength.

It is the EEC (now known as the EU) that has had the most significance, particularly for law. Its object now is to weld Europe into a single prosperous area by abolishing all restrictions affecting the movement of people, goods and money between member states, producing a single market of over 500 million people, available to all producers in the member states. This, it is hoped, will help Europe to compete economically with countries such as

Table 5.1 Membership of the European Union

Year	Country
1951	Belgium
	France
	Italy
	Luxembourg
	Netherlands
	West Germany
1973	Denmark
	Ireland
	United Kingdom
1981	Greece
1986	Portugal
	Spain
1995	Austria
	Finland
	Sweden
2004	Cyprus
	Czech Republic
	Estonia
	Hungary
	Latvia
	Lithuania
	Malta
	Poland
	Slovakia
	Slovenia
2007	Bulgaria
	Romania
2013	Croatia

the US, Japan, China and India, the member states being stronger as a block than they could possibly be alone. The Single European Act 1986 was a major step towards this goal, setting a target of 1992 for the abolition of trade barriers between member states. The practical effect is that, for example, a company manufacturing rivets in Leeds, with an order from a company in Barcelona, can send the rivets all the way there by lorry without the driver having to fill in customs forms as he or she crosses every border. The rivets will be made to a common EU standard, so the Spanish firm will know exactly what they are going to receive, while any trademarks or other rights over the design of the rivets will be protected throughout the member states. Just as goods can now move freely throughout the EU, so can workers: for example, a designer from Paris can go and work in London, or Milan, or Dublin, with no need for a work permit and no problem with immigration controls.

Along with these closer economic ties, it is intended that there should be increasing political unity, though there is some disagreement – particularly, though not exclusively, in Britain – as to how far this should go. Nevertheless, progress is being made: the Treaty on European Union (TEU, also known as the Maastricht Treaty), signed in 1992, was the first major move in this direction, establishing the aims of a single currency (the euro), joint defence and foreign policies, and inter-governmental cooperation on justice and home affairs. The introduction of the euro began in 1999 (though not in the UK, which had negotiated the right to opt out of the programme), and the Amsterdam Treaty, signed in 1997, gave more precise definition to the common foreign and security policy and cooperation in justice and home affairs. These matters now fall within the scope of the EU.

Photo 5.1 **The European flag**
Source: © Jules Selmes/Pearson Education Ltd. 2008

Modernising the European Union

The European institutions and decision-making structures were originally designed 50 years ago for a small community of six countries. These structures became out of date and inadequate to cope with the expanded membership of Europe. A new European Constitution was drawn up with a view to modernising the European institutions, making them more democratic and efficient. However, referendums in the Netherlands and France rejected this Constitution. After a two-year period of reflection, the Lisbon Treaty was agreed in 2007 adopting the most important of the planned reforms of the failed Constitution in a pragmatic and minimalist format, rather than the more grandiose presentation of the Constitution (which would have got rid of all the previous EU treaties and replaced them with a single Constitution). The Lisbon Treaty leaves all the existing European treaties in place and simply makes key amendments. It was ratified by all the member states and came into force in December 2009.

The institutions of the European Union

There are six key European institutions: the Commission, the Council of Ministers, the European Council, the European Parliament of the European Union, the Court of Justice of the European Union and the European Central Bank. Each of these institutions will be considered in turn.

The Commission

The Commission is composed of 28 members, called Commissioners, who are each appointed by the member states, subject to approval by the European Parliament, for five years. During the preparation of the Lisbon Treaty, efforts were made to include provisions to reduce the number of Commissioners to make the organisation more streamlined and potentially more efficient, but these efforts proved unsuccessful. They must be nationals of a member state, and in practice there tend to be two each from the largest states – France, Germany, Italy, Spain and the UK – and one each from the rest. However, the Commissioners do not represent their own countries: they are independent, and their role is to represent the interests of the EU overall. The idea is that the Commission's commitment to furthering EU interests balances the role of the European Council, whose members represent national interests.

In addition to its part in making EU legislation (see p. 99), the Commission is responsible for ensuring that member states uphold EU law, and has powers to investigate breaches by member states and, where necessary, bring them before the Court of Justice. It also plays an important role in the relationship of the EU with the rest of the world, negotiating trade agreements and the accession of new members, and draws up the annual draft budget for the EU. It is assisted in all these functions by an administrative staff, which has a similar role to that of the civil service in the UK.

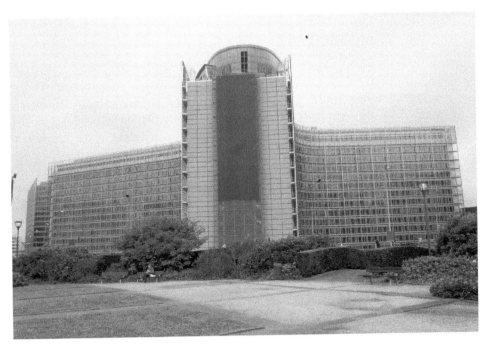

Photo 5.2 The European Commission
Source: © iStockphoto/Luke Daniek

The reputation of the Commission was seriously damaged in 1999 when an independent report found evidence of fraud, mismanagement and nepotism, forcing all the Commissioners to resign.

European Council

The members of the European Council are the president of the European Commission and the 28 heads of state of the member countries (for example, the Prime Minister of the United Kingdom, the President of France and the Chancellor of Germany). The European Council meets twice a year and has the same powers as the Council of Ministers, though the two are technically separate institutions. Many of the key decisions affecting the future direction of Europe are taken at these meetings. The Presidency of the Council is held by each member state, in rotation, for a period of six months.

Following the Lisbon Treaty, the President of the European Council will be elected by a qualified majority for a term of two-and-a-half years (renewable once), replacing the six-monthly rotating presidency. The newly defined role of the President includes ensuring the 'external representation of the Union on issues concerning its common foreign and security policy', which has led those opposed to a stronger Europe to be concerned that the President could effectively become a head of state for Europe – a move towards a president of the United States of Europe. In fact, the office enjoys only limited powers which cannot be compared with the extensive executive powers of an American president. The former British Prime Minister, Tony Blair, was considered for this position, but was found to be too controversial a figure due to his involvement in instigating the Iraq War.

Instead, a former Prime Minister of Belgium was selected to be the first person to hold this prestigious position.

The Council of Ministers

The Council of Ministers represents the interests of individual member states. It is a very powerful body in Europe and plays an important role in the passing of legislation. It does not have a permanent membership – in each meeting the members, one from each country, are national government ministers chosen according to the subject under discussion (so, for example, a discussion of matters relating to farming would usually be attended by the Ministers for Agriculture of each country). The Council meets most weeks to agree legislation and policy.

The Council may be questioned by the European Parliament, but the chief control is exercised by the national governments controlling their ministers who attend the Council.

The European Parliament

The Parliament is composed of 751 members (MEPs), including one President, who are directly elected in their own countries. In Britain they are elected to represent a geographical area which is much larger than for MPs, since there are only 73 MEPs for the whole country. Elections are held every five years.

The individual member countries are each allocated a number of seats, roughly according to population, although on this basis the smaller countries are over-represented. Members sit in political groupings rather than with others from their own country.

The Treaty of Lisbon has increased the powers of the European Parliament, to try and strengthen the democratic process within Europe. As well as taking part in the legislative process (discussed below), the Parliament has a variety of roles to play in connection with the other institutions. Over the Commission, it exercises a supervisory power. It has a right of veto over the appointment of the Commission as a whole, and can also sack the whole Commission by a vote of censure. In 1999, the entire Commission resigned during a crisis over fraud and mismanagement within the Commission, to avoid a vote of censure. The Commission must make an annual report to Parliament, and Parliament can also require Commissioners to answer written or oral questions. The Commission has to submit each proposed budget of the European Union to the European Parliament for its approval.

The Council is not accountable to Parliament in the same way, but the Parliament reports on it three times a year, and the President of the Council is obliged to address the Parliament once a year, followed by a debate. The Parliament can also bring actions against other EU institutions for failure to implement EU law.

The Parliament appoints an Ombudsman, who investigates complaints of maladministration by EU institutions from individuals and MEPs. It can also be petitioned by any natural or legal person living or having an office within a member state, on any issue within the EU field which affects that person directly.

Court of Justice of the European Union

The whole court system of the European Union is known as the Court of Justice of the European Union. This, in fact, consists of three courts: the main Court of Justice of the European Union, the General Court, and the Civil Service Tribunal.

Following the Lisbon Treaty of 2009, the official court name is the 'Court of Justice of the European Union (CJEU)' but it is still often referred to as the 'European Court of Justice' (ECJ). The CJEU has the task of supervising the uniform application of EU law throughout the member states, and in so doing it can create case law. It is important not to confuse it with the European Court of Human Rights, which deals with alleged breaches of human rights by countries that are signatories to the European Convention on Human Rights. That court is completely separate, and not an institution of the EU.

The CJEU, which sits in Luxembourg, has 28 judges, appointed for a period of six years (which may be renewed). The judges are assisted by nine Advocates General, who produce opinions on the cases assigned to them, indicating the issues raised and suggesting conclusions. These are not binding, but are nevertheless usually followed by the court. Both judges and Advocates General are chosen from those who are eligible for the highest judicial posts in their own countries.

Most cases are heard in plenary session, that is, with all the judges sitting together. Only one judgment will be delivered, giving no indication of the extent of agreement between the judges, and these often consist of fairly brief propositions, from which it can be difficult to discern any *ratio decidendi.* Consequently, lawyers seeking precedents often turn to the opinions written by the Advocates General. Since September 1989 the full CJEU has been assisted by a new Court of First Instance (now known as the General Court) to deal with specialist economic law cases. Parties in such cases may appeal to the full CJEU on a point of law.

The majority of cases heard by the CJEU are brought by member states and institutions of the Community, or are referred to it by national courts. It has only limited power to deal with cases brought by individual citizens, and such cases are rarely heard.

The CJEU has two separate functions: a judicial role, deciding cases of dispute; and a supervisory role.

The judicial role of the CJEU

The CJEU hears cases of dispute between parties, which fall into two categories: proceedings against member states, and proceedings against European institutions.

Proceedings against member states may be brought by the Commission, or by other member states, and involve alleged breaches of European law by the country in question. For example, in **Re Tachographs: EC Commission** *v* **UK** (1979), the CJEU upheld a complaint against the UK for failing to implement a European regulation making it compulsory for lorries used to carry dangerous goods to be fitted with tachographs (devices used to record the speed and distance travelled, with the aim of preventing lorry drivers from speeding, or from driving for longer than the permitted number of hours). The Commission usually gives the member state the opportunity to put things right before bringing the case to the CJEU.

Proceedings against EU institutions may be brought by member states, other EU institutions and, in limited circumstances, by individual citizens or organisations. The procedure can be used to review the legality of EU regulations, directives or decisions, on the grounds that proper procedures have not been followed, the provisions infringe a European Treaty or any rule relating to its application, or powers have been misused. In **United Kingdom** *v* **Council of the European Union** (1996) the UK sought to have the Directive on the 48-hour working week annulled on the basis that it had been unlawfully adopted by the Council. The application was unsuccessful.

In the past, there was no machinery for enforcing judgments against states. Following the Maastricht Treaty, there is now provision for member states to be fined.

Decisions made in these kinds of cases cannot be questioned in UK courts.

The supervisory role of the CJEU

Article 267 of the Treaty on the Functioning of the European Union provides that any court or tribunal in a member state may refer a question on EU law to the CJEU if it considers that 'a decision on that question is necessary to enable it to give judgment'. The object of this referral system is to make sure that the law is interpreted in the same way throughout Europe.

Article 267 states that a reference must be made if the national court is one from which there is no further appeal – so in Britain, the Supreme Court must refer such questions, while the lower courts usually have some discretion about whether or not to do so. The European Court has clarified in **Cilfit v Ministry of Health** (1983) when a court is required to refer a point of law for its consideration. It stated that a reference should be made by the final appellate court where a question of European law is raised unless:

1 The question raised is irrelevant.
2 The provision of European law has already been interpreted by the European Court.
3 The correct application of European law is so obvious as to leave no scope for any reasonable doubt (known as *acte claire*). This must be assessed in the light of the specific characteristics of European law, the particular difficulties to which its interpretation gives rise and the risk of divergence in judicial decisions between European member states.

About 20 references a year are made from UK courts. The Art. 267 procedure is expensive and time-consuming, often delaying a decision on the case for a long time (about nine months), and so lower courts have been discouraged from using it. Consequently, attempts have been made to set down guidelines by which a lower court could determine when a referral to the CJEU would or would not be necessary.

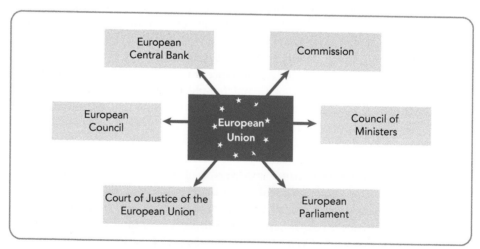

Figure 5.2 Institutions of the European Union

KEY CASE

In **Bulmer** v **Bollinger** (1974), the Court of Appeal was asked to review a judge's exercise of discretion to refer a question under what is now Art. 267. They pointed out that the European Court could not interfere with the exercise of a judge's discretion to refer, and Lord Denning set down guidelines on the points which should be taken into account in considering whether a reference was necessary. He emphasised the cost and delay that a reference could cause, and stated that no reference should be made:

- where it would not be conclusive of the case, and other matters would remain to be decided;
- where there had been a previous ruling on the same point;
- where the court considers that point to be reasonably clear and free from doubt; and
- where the facts of the case had not yet been decided.

Unless the point to be decided could be considered 'really difficult and important', said Lord Denning, the court should save the expense and delay of a reference and decide the issue itself.

Denning's view has since been criticised by academics, who point out that it can be cheaper and quicker to refer a point at an early stage, than to drag the case up through the English courts first. In addition, the clear and consistent interpretation of EU law can come to depend on whether individual litigants have the resources to take their cases all the way up to the Supreme Court. Critics also note that the apparent importance of the case should not be decisive, as many important decisions of the CJEU have arisen from cases where the parties actually had little at stake.

Legal principle
Lord Denning laid down guidance on when courts should make references to the Court of Justice of the European Union under Art. 267.

Although the judiciary still use Denning's **Bulmer** guidelines, in the 1980s and 1990s there appeared to be a greater willingness to refer cases under the Art. 267 procedure. In **Customs and Excise Commissioners** v **APS Samex** (1983), Bingham J pointed out that, in interpreting European law, the Court of Justice has certain advantages over national courts: it can take a panoramic view of the whole of European law, compare the legislation as it is written in different member states' languages, and it is experienced in the purposive approach to interpretation for which European legislation was designed. In addition, it has the facility to allow member states to make their views on an issue known. As a result, it is better placed than a national court to decide issues of interpretation. In **R** v **International Stock Exchange**, *ex parte* **Else** (1993), the same judge (by then Master of the Rolls), said that if, once the facts have been found, it is clear that an issue of European law is vital to a court's final decision, that court should normally make an Art. 267 referral: English courts should only decide such issues without referral if they have real confidence that they can do so correctly, without the help of the CJEU.

More recently, as euro-scepticism has increased, the Supreme Court has again become reluctant to refer cases to the CJEU, relying on the fact that the interpretation of the EU legislation is obvious: an *acte claire*. For example, in **X** v **Mid-Sussex Citizens Advice**

Table 5.2 Membership of the European institutions

Commission	28 Commissioners
European Council	The president of the European Commission and 28 heads of state
Council of Ministers	It does not have a permanent membership. For each meeting one minister is chosen from each country according to the subject of the meeting
European Parliament	A maximum of 751 Members of the European Parliament (MEPs)
Court of Justice of the European Union	28 judges
European Central Bank	It manages the Euro and EU economic and monetary policy

Bureau (2012), the Supreme Court stated that the word 'occupation' in a European Directive obviously did not extend to volunteers.

Where a case is submitted, proceedings will be suspended in the national court until the CJEU has given its verdict. This verdict does not tell the national court how to decide the case, but simply explains what EU law on the matter is. The national court then has the duty of making its decision in the light of this.

Regardless of which national court submitted the point for consideration, a ruling from the CJEU should be followed by all other courts in the EU – so, theoretically, a point raised by a County Court in England may result in a ruling that the highest courts in all the member states have to follow. Where a ruling reveals that national legislation conflicts with EU law, the national Government usually enacts new legislation to put the matter right.

The court's decisions can be changed only by its own subsequent decision or by an amendment of the Treaty, which would require the unanimous approval of member states through their own Parliaments. Decisions of the European Court cannot be questioned in English courts. This principle has limited the jurisdiction of the Supreme Court as a final appellate court.

An illustration of the use of Art. 267 is the case of **Marshall v Southampton and South West Hampshire Area Health Authority** (1986). Miss Marshall, a dietician, was compulsorily retired by the Authority from her job when she was 62, although she wished to continue to 65. It was the Authority's policy that the normal retiring age for its employees was the age at which state retirement pensions became payable: for women this was 60, though the Authority had waived the rule for two years in Miss Marshall's case. She claimed that the Authority was discriminating against women by adopting a policy that employees should retire at state pension age, hence requiring women to retire before men. This policy appeared to be legal under the relevant English legislation but was argued to be contrary to a Council directive providing for equal treatment of men and women. The national court made a reference to the CJEU asking for directions on the meaning of the directive. The CJEU found that there was a conflict with UK law, and the UK later changed its legislation to conform.

It is important to note that the CJEU is not an appeal court from decisions made in the member states. It does not substitute its own decisions for those of a lower court (except those of its own Court of First Instance, discussed below). It will assist a national court at any level in reaching a decision, but the actual decision remains the responsibility of the national court. When parties in an English case talk of taking the case to Europe, the only way they can do this is to get an English court to make a referral for an Art. 267 ruling, and they may have to take their case all the way to the Supreme Court to ensure this.

General Court

This court was originally known as the European Court of First Instance and was established in 1988 to reduce the workload of the then European Court of Justice. It was renamed by the Lisbon Treaty in 2009, becoming the General Court. It primarily hears direct actions against EU institutions. Appeals on points of law are heard by the Court of Justice of the European Union.

Civil Service Tribunal

The Civil Service Tribunal hears disputes between the European Union and its civil servants.

European Central Bank

The European Central Bank (ECB) gained the official status of being an institution of the European Union under the Lisbon Treaty in 2009. The ECB was established in 1998 and has its headquarters in Frankfurt in Germany. It is responsible for the economic and monetary policy of the 18 member states that have adopted the euro as their national currency, known together as the eurozone. The primary objective of the ECB is to maintain price stability within the eurozone, in other words to keep inflation below 2 per cent. It has responsibility for fixing the interest rate within the eurozone. It takes its decisions independently of governments and the other European institutions.

Making European legislation

The Council of Ministers (often called simply 'the Council'), the Commission and the European Parliament all play a role in making EU legislation. A complicated range of different procedures has been developed to make these laws. All legislation starts with a proposal from the Commission, and the Council enjoys the most power in the legislative process.

Parliament's legislative role was historically purely advisory, with the Commission and the Council having a much more powerful role in the legislative process. This led to concern over the lack of democracy within Europe, for while Parliament is directly elected by the citizens of Europe, the Commission and Council members are not. The role of the European Parliament in the passing of European legislation has gradually been increased by the Single European Act, the Maastricht Treaty, the Amsterdam Treaty and the Lisbon Treaty. Increasingly, the passing of EU legislation requires the approval of the European Parliament as well as the Council, through the co-decision process.

The Council continues to play an important role in the passing of European legislation. There are three systems of voting in the Council:

- **unanimity,** where proposals are only passed if all members vote for them;
- **simple majority,** where proposals only require more votes for than against; and

- **qualified majority,** which allows each state a specified number of votes (the larger the state, the more votes it has), and provides that a proposal can only be agreed if there are a specified number of votes in its favour.

These voting procedures have been controversial, because where unanimity is not required a member state can be forced to abide by legislation for which it has not voted, and which it believes is against its interests. This is seen as compromising national sovereignty. However, requiring unanimity makes it difficult to get things done quickly (or sometimes at all) and, as a result, initial progress towards the single market was very slow. The need to speed up progress led to both the Single European Act and the Maastricht Treaty requiring only qualified majority voting more often. The Amsterdam Treaty and the Lisbon Treaty extended its use a little more, and it is now the norm for many areas.

Types of European legislation

There is a range of different forms of European legislation: treaties, regulations, directives and decisions. In considering the impact of this legislation on UK law a distinction has to be drawn between direct applicability and direct effect. Direct applicability refers to the fact that treaty articles, regulations and some decisions immediately become part of the law of each member state. Directives are not directly applicable.

Where European legislation has direct effect, it creates individual rights which national courts must protect without any need for implementing legislation in that member state. In the UK the national courts were given this power under s. 2(1) of the European Communities Act 1972.

There are two types of direct effect: vertical direct effect gives individuals rights against Governments; and horizontal direct effect gives rights against other people and organisations.

Provisions of treaties, regulations and directives only have direct effect if they are clear, unconditional and their implementation requires no further legislation in member states. These conditions were first laid down in the context of treaties in **Van Gend en Loos** *v* **Nederlandse Tariefcommissie** (1963).

The ability of individuals to rely on European law before their national courts greatly enhances its effectiveness. National courts can quickly apply directly effective legislation and can draw on a wide range of remedies. Where legislation does not have direct effect, the only method of enforcement available in the past was an action brought by the Commission or a member state against a member state before the CJEU. This process can be slow and provides no direct remedy for the individual.

However, in the 1990s the European Court recognised the right of individuals to be awarded damages by their national courts for breach of European legislation by a member state, even where the legislation did not have direct effect. Originally, in **Francovich** *v* **Italy** (1991), this right was applied where directives had not been implemented but it has been developed to extend to any violation of European law. In **Francovich,** an Italian company went into liquidation, leaving its employees, including Francovich, unpaid arrears of salary. Italy had not set up a compensation scheme for employees in such circumstances as was required by a European directive. Francovich sued in the Italian courts.

The court held that although the directive was not sufficiently precise to have direct effect it gave a right to damages.

Liability will be imposed on a member state if:

- the legislation was intended to confer rights on individuals;
- the content of those rights is clear from the provisions of the legislation; and
- there is a direct causal link between the breach of the member state's obligation and the damage sustained by the individual.

In addition, a fourth condition was added by **Brasserie du Pêcheur SA** *v* **Germany** (1996) and **R** *v* **Secretary of State for Transport,** *ex parte* **Factortame** (1990):

- there was a serious breach of European law.

Article 288 of the Treaty on the Functioning of the European Union states:

> To exercise the Union's competences, the institutions shall adopt regulations, directives, decisions, recommendations and opinions.
> A regulation shall have general application. It shall be binding in its entirety and directly applicable in all Member States.
> A directive shall be binding, as to the result to be achieved, upon each Member State to which it is addressed, but shall leave to the national authorities the choice of form and methods.
> A decision shall be binding in its entirety. A decision which specifies those to whom it is addressed shall be binding only on them.
> Recommendations and opinions shall have no binding force.

The four different types of European law will now be examined in turn.

Treaties

The Treaties of the European Union are international treaties agreed between all the member states. They effectively constitute the European Constitution, establishing the six key European institutions and the aims of the European Union. There are now two main treaties of equal importance: the Treaty on European Union (also known as the Maastricht Treaty) and the Treaty on the Functioning of the European Union (historically known as the Rome Treaty). These treaties have been amended over the years and their article numbers changed as the European Union has evolved. Treaty provisions can create rights and obligations.

An example of a directly effective treaty provision is Art. 157 of the Treaty on the Functioning of the European Union. This provides 'equal pay for male and female workers for equal work of equal value'. In **Macarthys Ltd** *v* **Smith** (1979), Art. 157 was held to give a woman in the UK the right to claim the same wages as were paid to the male predecessor in her job, even though she had no such right under the UK equal pay legislation passed in 1970, before the UK joined the EEC.

Treaty provisions which are merely statements of intent or policy, rather than establishing clear rights or duties, require detailed legislation to be made before they can be enforced in the member states.

Parliament has passed the European Union Act 2011 which requires a national referendum before the EU treaties can be amended or a new treaty signed involving a transfer of power or competence from the UK to the EU.

Regulations

A regulation is the nearest European law comes to an English Act of Parliament. Regulations apply throughout the EU, usually to people in general, and they become part of the law of each member nation as soon as they come into force, without the need for each country to make its own legislation.

> **KEY CASE**
>
> The case of **Van Gend en Loos** (1963) decided that a treaty provision has direct effect if it is unconditional, clear and precise as to the rights or obligations it creates, and leaves member states no discretion on implementing it. Treaty provisions which are unconditional, clear and precise, and allow no discretion on implementation, have both horizontal and vertical direct effect.
>
> > *Legal principle*
> > Treaty provisions have direct effect if they are unconditional, clear and precise and impose an obligation on member states to implement them.

Regulations must be applied even if the member state has already passed legislation which conflicts with them. In **Leonesio** *v* **Italian Ministry for Agriculture and Forestry** (1972), a regulation to encourage reduced dairy production stated that a cash premium should be payable to farmers who slaughtered cows and agreed not to produce milk for five years. Leonesio had fulfilled this requirement, but was refused payment because the Italian constitution required legislation to authorise government expenditure. The CJEU said that once Leonesio had satisfied the conditions, he was entitled to the payment; the Italian Government could not use its own laws to block that right.

Directives

Directives are less precisely worded than regulations, because they aim to set out broad policy objectives, leaving the member states to create their own detailed legislation in order to put those objectives into practice (within specified time limits). As a result, it was originally assumed by most member states that directives could not have direct effect, and would not create individual rights until they had been translated into domestic legislation. However, the CJEU has consistently refused to accept this view, arguing that direct effect is an essential weapon if the EU is to ensure that member states implement directives.

The reasoning behind the approach taken in **Van Duyn** was explained in **Pubblico Ministero** *v* **Ratti** (1979), where the European Court pointed out that member states could not be allowed to rely on their own wrongful failure to implement directives as a means of denying individual rights.

Directives have vertical direct effect but not horizontal direct effect. This means that they impose obligations on the state and not individuals. Thus, they have direct effect in proceedings against a member state (vertical) but not in proceedings between individuals (horizontal). A directive with direct effect can be utilised by an individual against the state when the state has failed to implement the directive properly or on time.

KEY CASE

The case which initially established direct effect for directives was **Van Duyn v Home Office** (1974). The Home Office had refused Van Duyn permission to enter the UK because she was a member of a religious group, the Scientologists, which the Government wanted to exclude from the country at the time. Van Duyn argued that her exclusion was contrary to provisions in the Treaty of Rome on freedom of movement. The Government responded by pointing out that the Treaty allowed exceptions on public policy grounds, but Van Duyn then relied on a later directive which said that public policy could only be invoked on the basis of personal conduct, and Van Duyn herself had done nothing to justify exclusion. The case was referred to the CJEU, which found that the obligation conferred on the Government was clear and unconditional, and so created enforceable rights.

Legal principle
Directives have direct effect where they impose clear and unconditional obligations on a government.

The issue of direct effect was important in the high-profile case of **R (on the application of Westminster City Council)** *v* **Mayor of London** (2002). Westminster Council had applied for judicial review of the decision to introduce a congestion charge to enter central London. The decision had been taken by the Mayor of London, Ken Livingstone. The High Court rejected the application. Westminster Council had sought to rely on a provision of a directive. The High Court stated that the Council could not do this, as when directives had direct effect they only gave rights to individuals and not to Government institutions.

The CJEU has found a number of ways to widen access where the principle of vertical direct effect applies. First, it has defined 'the state' very broadly to include all public bodies

Table 5.3 Impact of European legislation

Impact	Meaning of term
Direct applicability	Legislative provisions immediately become part of the law of each member state.
Direct effect	Legislation creates individual rights which national courts must protect without any need for implementing legislation in the member state.
Horizontal direct effect	Legislation gives rights against governments, individuals and private organisations.
Vertical direct effect	Legislation gives rights against governments.
Indirect effect	National courts should interpret national law in accordance with relevant European legislation.

and 'emanations of the state', including local authorities and nationalised industries. In **Foster *v* British Gas plc** (1990) the CJEU stated that:

> [A] body, whatever its legal form, which has been made responsible, pursuant to a measure adopted by the State, for providing a public service under the control of the State and has for that purpose special powers beyond those which result from the normal rules applicable in relations between individuals, is included in any event among the bodies against which the provisions of a directive capable of having direct effect may be relied upon. (para 20)

This meant, for example, that in **Marshall *v* Southampton and South West Hampshire Area Health Authority** (discussed at p. 98), Miss Marshall was able to take advantage of the relevant directive even though she was not suing the Government itself, because her employer was a health authority and therefore considered to be a public body.

Secondly, in **Von Colson *v* Land Nordrhein-Westfalen** (1984), the court introduced the principle of indirect effect, stating that national courts should interpret national law in accordance with relevant directives, whether the national law was designed to implement a directive or not. The principle was confirmed in **Marleasing SA *v* La Comercial Internacional de Alimentación SA** (1990). Here, Marleasing alleged that La Comercial, a Spanish company, had been formed with the express purpose of defrauding creditors (of which they were one) and sought to have its articles of association (the document under which a company is formed) declared void. Spanish contract law allowed this, but the EU had passed a directive which did not. Which should the member state court follow? The European Court held that where a provision of domestic law was 'to any extent open to interpretation', national courts had to interpret that law 'as far as possible' in line with the wording and purpose of any relevant directive. This would apply whether the domestic law was passed before or after the directive, except that domestic law passed before a directive would only be affected once the time limit for implementation of the directive had expired.

Marleasing has been much discussed by academics, but it is still unclear quite how far national courts are expected to go in implementing directives having indirect effect. EU law experts Craig and de Búrca (2007) suggest, however, that the principle of indirect effect probably only applies where national law is sufficiently ambiguous to allow it to be interpreted in line with directives; where there is a conflict, but the national law is clear, member state courts are unlikely to be required to override that law.

Thirdly, some recent cases have allowed an unimplemented directive to act as a shield, though not as a sword, to the benefit of private individuals. In other words, the directive could be relied upon to provide a defence but not to provide a right of action. For example, **CIA Security International SA *v* Signalson** (1996) concerned the failure by the Belgian Government to notify the Commission of its law on security systems in accordance with a European directive on the subject (Notification Directive 98/34). Litigation arose between two private companies, CIA Security and Signalson. Signalson tried to prevent CIA from marketing an alarm system which had not been approved under Belgian law. CIA successfully argued that the Belgian law did not apply because the Commission had not been notified about it in accordance with the European directive. Thus, CIA was able to rely on the directive to provide a defence in the litigation between two private individuals. On the surface it looked as if the directive was being given horizontal direct effect in breach of established principles of European law, but in fact the case has been interpreted as merely allowing a directive to give private individuals a defence. Another interpretation of the case was that Signalson was effectively acting as an agent of the state, bringing proceedings for the withdrawal of a product which potentially did not conform with Belgian law.

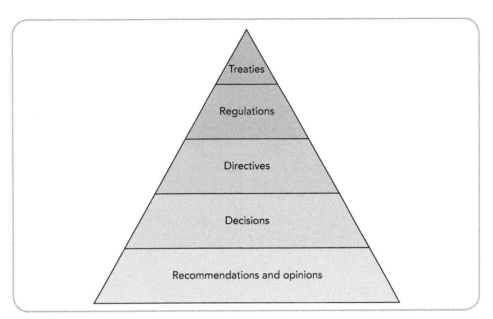

Figure 5.3 European legislation

In **R (on the application of Wells) *v* Secretary of State for Transport, Local Government and the Regions** (2005), there was a plan by a private company to reopen a quarry in an environmentally sensitive area. No environmental impact assessment had been carried out by the state in accordance with the Environmental Impact Assessment Directive (Directive 85/337). A local resident asked the Secretary of State to remove or modify the planning permission pending the carrying out of the assessment, but he refused. In the subsequent litigation, the court had to consider whether the local resident could rely on the directive. The court acknowledged that a directive cannot be used as a sword to impose obligations on a private individual. But a directive could be used as a shield, even if in doing so there would be a negative impact on a private individual: in this case the quarry owners would have to stop work on the quarry until the completion of the environmental impact assessment. As the quarry owners were not required to carry out an obligation, this did not amount to the imposition of direct horizontal effect.

Finally, the European Court has suggested in **Kucukdeveci *v* Swedex GmbH** (2009) that where a general principle of European law is being applied by a directive, the provisions of the directive can be applied by a private individual against another private individual. Thus, the national court can refuse to apply a national law in breach of a directive in litigation between private parties. On the facts of the case, the general principle identified was the principle of equal treatment and the directive was concerned with age discrimination. German national legislation would have allowed a person to be discriminated against on the basis of his or her age, and the European Court said the national court would be entitled not to apply the national law. It is understandable that the European Court wanted to give the employee a remedy, but the private employer had acted in accordance with clear provisions of German employment law, and found themselves penalised for the German Government's mistake. This is a new development in European law, but its impact remains uncertain, as it is difficult to predict what will be treated as a general principle of European law. In **Mangold *v* Helm** (2006), which also involved age discrimination, the

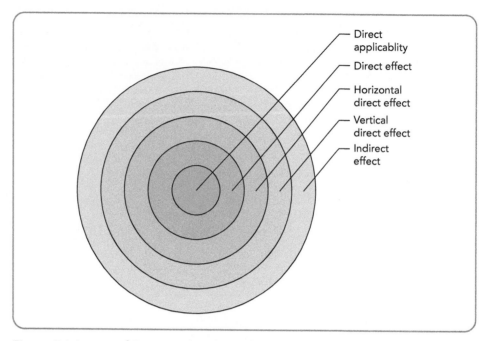

Figure 5.4 Impact of European legislation

European Court stated that the general principle of equality was found 'in various international instruments and in the constitutional traditions common in the member states'.

Decisions

A decision may be addressed to a state, a person or a company and is binding only on the recipient. Examples include granting, or refusing, export licences to companies from outside the EU.

Recommendations and opinions

The Council and the Commission may issue recommendations and opinions which, although not to be disregarded, are not binding law.

How does EU law affect the UK?

Membership of the EU has had a number of effects on UK law and our legal system.

New sources of law

Joining the original EEC created new and very important sources of law for the UK. Section 2(4) of the European Communities Act 1972 provides that English law should be interpreted and have effect subject to the principle that European law is supreme; this means that European law now takes precedence over all domestic sources of law. As a result, it has had a profound effect on the rights of citizens in this country and, in particular, on the rights of employees, especially female workers. For example, in **R** *v* **Secretary of State for Employment,** *ex parte* **Equal Opportunities Commission** (1994), the House of Lords found that parts of the Employment Protection (Consolidation) Act 1978 were incompatible with European law on equal treatment for male and female employees, because the Act gave part-time workers fewer rights than full-timers. Since most part-time workers were women, this was held to discriminate on the basis of sex, and the UK Government was forced to change the law, and greatly improve the rights of part-time workers.

The role of the courts

Because EU law takes precedence over domestic legislation, the role of the courts has changed as a result of membership. Before the UK joined the EEC, statutes were the highest form of law, and judges had no power to refuse to apply them. Now, however, they can – in fact they should – refuse to apply statutes which are in conflict with directly effective EU law.

KEY CASE

The leading case in this area is **R** *v* **Secretary of State for Transport, ex parte Factortame** (1990). It arose from the fishing policy decided by member states in 1983, which allowed member states to limit fishing within 12 miles of their own shores to boats from their own country, and left the remainder of the seas around the European Community open to fishing boats from any member state. In addition, to preserve stocks of fish, each state was allocated a quota of fish, and required not to exceed it. Soon after the new rules were in place, the UK Government became concerned that Spanish fishing boats were registering as British vessels, so that their catches counted against the British quota rather than the Spanish, and genuine British fishermen were as a result getting a smaller share. The Government therefore passed the Merchant Shipping Act 1988, which contained provisions to prevent the Spanish trawlers taking advantage of the British quota.

Spanish boat owners challenged the Act, claiming it was in conflict with EU law on the freedom to set up business anywhere in Europe, and the House of Lords agreed. They stated that s. 2(4) of the European Communities Act 'has precisely the same effect as if a section were incorporated in . . . [the 1988 Act, saying] that the provisions with respect to registration of British fishing vessels were to be without prejudice to the directly enforceable Community rights of nationals of any member state . . . '

The decision was criticised as compromising the rights of the UK Parliament to make law for this country, as the House of Lords rendered effectively unenforceable the Merchant Shipping Act. But the House of Lords was firm in dismissing such complaints, pointing out that it was very clear before the UK joined the EEC that doing so would mean giving up some degree of sovereignty over domestic law, and that this was accepted voluntarily when the UK joined the Community. 'Under . . . the Act of 1972, it has always been clear that it was the duty of a United Kingdom court, when delivering final judgment, to override any rule of national law found to be in conflict with any directly enforceable rule of Community law . . . '

Legal principle
Judges should refuse to apply statutes which are in conflict with directly effective EU law.

Lord Justice Laws stated in **Thoburn *v* Sunderland City Council** (2002) that the European Communities Act 1972 was a constitutional Act which could only be repealed by express provisions of an Act of Parliament (and not by implication). The case concerned a group of market stallholders who became known in the tabloid press as the 'metric martyrs'. They had refused to sell their fruits and vegetables in kilos and grammes, preferring to stick to the old weighing system of pounds and ounces. They argued they had not breached the law because part of the 1972 Act had been impliedly repealed by a later Act of Parliament: the Weights and Measures Act 1985, which allowed for the use of the old imperial measures. In essence, they were arguing that it was not a criminal offence to sell a pound of bananas.

In his judgment, Lord Justice Laws stated that Acts of Parliament should be divided between 'ordinary' statutes and 'constitutional' statutes. The European Communities Act was a constitutional Act and could only be repealed if Parliament used express words to show its intention to do so.

In **R (on the application of HS2 Action Alliance Ltd) *v* Secretary of State for Transport** (2014), the Supreme Court considered that Art. 9 of the Bill of Rights of 1689 was unquestionably part of whatever constitution the UK has. Article 9 prevents courts from considering proceedings in Parliament, and the Supreme Court would take a lot of persuasion that EU legislation could change that position. The case was concerned with the development of a high-speed rail link between London and Birmingham known as HS2. EU directives laid down procedures that had to be followed before giving permission for this type of project, to ensure the environmental impact of the project would be carefully considered. The government proposed agreeing to the construction of the HS2 using an Act of Parliament. The claimants argued that the parliamentary procedures followed to pass the Act of Parliament approving the HS2 project would not satisfy these EU directives, partly because they would not allow effective public participation in the consultation process. The appeal was rejected by the Supreme Court, as the Court was not prepared to question the parliamentary procedures involved in passing an Act of Parliament because Art. 9 of the Bill of Rights 1689 bans it from doing so in order to respect Parliamentary sovereignty in a democratic system.

The Supreme Court noted that if there is a conflict between a constitutional principle, such as that embodied in Art. 9 of the Bill of Rights 1689, and EU law, that conflict has to be resolved by our courts as an issue arising under the constitutional law of the United Kingdom. The impact of **Factortame** and the principle of the Supremacy of Europe was restricted by pointing out that **Factortame** was not concerned with a principle of constitutional law. While **Thoburn *v* Sunderland City Council** drew a simple binary distinction between constitutional and ordinary legislation, the Supreme Court in the HS2 case seems to suggest a distinction should also be drawn between fundamental constitutional principles in legislation and common law and less important constitutional principles. The United Kingdom does not have a written constitution, but it has a number of constitutional instruments, such as the Magna Carta, the Bill of Rights, the European Communities Act 1972 and the Human Rights Act 1998. The Supreme Court observed: 'Article 9 of the Bill of Rights, one of the pillars of the constitutional settlement which established the rule of law in England in the seventeenth century, precludes the impeaching or questioning in any court of debates or proceedings in Parliament.' Article 9 was described by Lord Browne-Wilkinson in the House of Lords in **Pepper *v* Hart** as 'a provision of the highest constitutional importance' which 'should not be narrowly construed'.

An EU directive could not succeed in setting aside such a fundamental constitutional principle. The interpretation in **Factortame** of the European Communities Act 1972 does not require national courts to accord primacy to EU law over *all* domestic law. **Thoburn** treats the European Communities Act as a constitutional statute which was therefore immune from implied repeal, so later legislation that was inconsistent (but not *explicitly* inconsistent) with EU law would cede priority to the 1972 Act and hence to the EU law to which that Act gives effect. But the **HS2** case goes further by introducing the notion that not all constitutional measures are equal; some constitutional measures are more fundamental than others. Parliament in a given constitutional measure, such as the 1972 Act, may not have intended the repeal of a more fundamental, but conflicting, constitutional measure. Whilst ordinary legislation will always (unless explicitly inconsistent) yield in the face of conflicting European law, a fundamental constitutional measure will not.

So there are two fundamental limitations on the principle of the Supremacy of European Union law:

1 Parliament cannot bind itself so it can expressly repeal the European Communities Act 1972.
2 Parliament can impliedly repeal European Community law which conflicts with a fundamental constitutional principle in the UK constitution.

The role of the courts is also affected by the principle stated in **Marleasing** (see p. 104), which effectively means that the courts now have a new external aid to consider when interpreting statutes, and should take notice of it wherever they can do so without straining the words of the statute.

The UK courts are subjected to the supervisory jurisdiction of the CJEU (as explained on p. 94), and this gives a further source of law, since the courts of all member states are bound by CJEU decisions on the interpretation and application of EU law.

The future

One view of the influence of UK membership of Europe on our national law was given by Lord Denning, in poetic mood, in **Bulmer** *v* **Bollinger**: 'The Treaty is like an incoming tide. It flows into the estuaries and up the rivers. It cannot be held back.' Lord Scarman, obviously in an equally lyrical frame of mind, commented:

> For the moment, to adopt Lord Denning's imagery, the incoming tide has not yet mingled with the home waters of the common law: but it is inconceivable that, like the Rhone and the Arve where those two streams meet at Geneva, they should move on, side by side, one grey with the melted snows and ice of the distant mountains of our legal history, the other clear blue and clean, reflecting modern opinion. If we stay in the Common Market, I would expect to see its principles of legislation and statutory interpretation, and its conception of an activist court whose role is to strengthen and fulfil the purpose of statute law, replace the traditional attitudes of English judges and lawyers to statute law and the current complex style of statutory drafting.

What Lord Scarman was referring to was the difference in approach between the English legal system and those in mainland Europe. When drafting statutes, for example, English law has tended towards tightly written, very precise rules, whereas the continental style is looser, setting out broad principles to be followed. As a result, the continental style of statutory interpretation takes a very purposive approach, paying most attention to putting into practice the spirit of the legislation, and filling in any gaps in the wording if necessary, as opposed to the more literal style traditionally associated with English judges. The CJEU tends to take the continental approach, and it has been suggested that, as time goes on, this will influence our own judges more and more, leading to more creative judicial decision-making, with corresponding changes in the drafting of statutes.

Following the **Factortame** litigation there was concern that Europe was threatening the sovereignty of the UK Parliament, as the European Court ruling had caused an Act of Parliament to be set aside. Lord Denning revised his description of European law as like an 'incoming tide' and stated:

> No longer is European law an incoming tide flowing up the estuaries of England. It is now like a tidal wave bringing down our sea walls and flowing inland over our fields and houses – to the dismay of all. (*The Independent,* 16 July 1996)

The academic Seamus Burns (2008) has suggested that, in the light of subsequent legal developments, Lord Denning 'might have to revise his image of EU law being like an incoming tide permeating our existing legal order, and more realistically compare it to a tsunami, enveloping everything in its path with irresistible force'.

In **R v Secretary of State for Foreign and Commonwealth Affairs,** *ex parte* **Lord Rees-Mogg** (1994) an unsuccessful attempt was made to demonstrate that the UK could not legally ratify the Maastricht Treaty. In rejecting this claim, the court pointed out that the Treaty did not involve the abandoning or transferring of powers, so that a Government could choose later to denounce the Treaty, or fail to honour its obligations under it.

Parliament has passed the European Union Act 2011 which includes a provision to protect the sovereignty of Parliament. Section 18 of the Act states that the status of EU law is dependent on the continuing statutory authority of the European Communities Act 1972. So if this statute is repealed by Parliament then EU law would cease to have effect in the United Kingdom. Section 18 states:

Section 18. Status of EU law dependent on continuing statutory basis

Directly applicable or directly effective EU law (that is, the rights, powers, liabilities, obligations, restrictions, remedies and procedures referred to in section 2(1) of the European Communities Act 1972) falls to be recognised and available in law in the United Kingdom only by virtue of that Act or where it is required to be recognised and available in law by virtue of any other Act.

In 2016, the UK voted in a referendum to leave the EU. Brexit will constitute a major change in the UK's relationship with the EU. The extent of this change will depend on the exit negotiations. **In R (Miller and Dos Santos) v Secretary of State for Exiting the European Union** the Supreme Court confirmed the fundamental principle of the Supremacy of Parliament and that the United Kingdom could only withdraw from the European Union if Parliament had voted an Act authorising it to do so which it now has (see p. 87).

Answering questions

1 What have been the major consequences of the United Kingdom's membership of the European Union for the character of the English legal system? *University of London, International Programmes LLB*

Some of the relevant material that you need to answer this question can be found under the subheading 'How does EU law affect the UK?' (p. 106). A possible answer to this question could be broken up into four parts which would look at:

- parliamentary sovereignty;
- the influence of civil legal systems;
- practical impact of membership; and
- future impact.

You could use these subheadings in your essay, to show clearly to the reader your essay structure.

Parliamentary sovereignty
The greatest impact of membership of the European Union has been on the principle of the sovereignty of Parliament with the courts having the power to refuse to apply statutes which are in conflict with directly effective EU law (see p. 97).

The influence of civil legal systems
Most of the other members of the European Union have a civil legal system, as opposed to a common law system (see p. 2). Because the UK was not a member of the European Union at the time of its creation (when it was known as the European Economic Community), it was the institutions from the civil legal systems that had the greatest impact on the institutions of the European Union. The European Union is therefore a means by which the English legal system has been influenced by the civil legal systems. It provides an opportunity for the English legal practitioners to see alternative ways of functioning and to consider whether they wish changes to be made to the English legal system in the light of these alternatives. The Government considered adopting some of the procedures used in the Court of Justice of the European Union (CJEU) for its new Supreme Court, but has rejected them (see p. 3). For example, abstract questions of law can be referred to the CJEU under Art. 267. The British Government has decided that this sits uncomfortably with the English legal tradition of deciding issues of law in the context of specific factual cases and has not given the new Supreme Court the power to hear such cases. Also all the judges sit in the CJEU to hear each case. While there were 12 full-time House of Lords judges, these usually divided up, and sat as panels of five. The Supreme Court is continuing this practice rather than following the CJEU model.

Practical impact of membership
Through its legislation, the European Union has a direct impact on the content and form of English law. The courts have also been forced to take a different approach to the interpretation of European legislation, which has influenced generally the courts' approach to statutory interpretation (see p. 58).

Future impact

You could conclude your essay with a discussion of the likely impact of the UK's exit from the EU following the 2016 referendum. (Material for this section can be found at p. 87.)

2 European law provisions have had a profound impact on UK law. In particular, explain how it has affected the use of precedent by judges in UK courts.

You should begin by explaining what precedent is and what it means (refer back to Chapter 1). Then, you could divide your answer into five main parts:

- A discussion of s. 2(4) of the European Communities Act 1972, which is considered under the heading 'New sources of law' (p. 106). The impact of this provision can be illustrated by the case of **Factortame** (see p. 107) as judges should refuse to apply domestic legislation which conflicts with directly effective EU law.
- The effect of **Marleasing** (p. 104) in providing a new external aid to statutory interpretation.
- In cases against other member states, decisions cannot be questioned by UK courts (see p. 94).
- UK courts are subject to the supervisory jurisdiction of the CJEU since the courts of all member states are bound by CJEU decisions on the interpretation and application of EU law. See in particular the sub-section entitled 'The supervisory role of the CJEU' (p. 96).
- You could argue that in reality EU provisions have only a limited effect, because they apply only to the interpretation of EU law.

There may be evidence to suggest that UK courts are adopting a more purposive continental approach to statutory interpretation (see Chapter 3).

3 To what extent has the English legal system irrevocably accommodated European Union law?

An introduction to this essay could observe that the principle of parliamentary sovereignty gives Parliament an unfettered discretion to enact laws, and foreign treaties do not automatically become part of domestic law. When the United Kingdom became a member of what is now the European Union, the European Communities Act 1972 provided authority for the application of EU law over UK domestic law. This has led to the courts refusing to apply domestic legislation inconsistent with EU law as occurred in **R v Secretary of State for Transport, ex parte Factortame.** Your essay could point to the different sources of European law and give specific examples of European law which now form an integral part of UK law.

As the application of EU law derives from the 1972 Act, Parliament could, in theory, revoke it and so the principle of parliamentary sovereignty remains intact. This was confirmed by the Supreme Court in **R (Miller and Dos Santos) v Secretary of State for Exiting the European Union.** In **Thoburn v Sunderland City Council,** Lord Justice Laws emphasised that revocation would have to be explicit and not by implication.

4 Explain the role of the Court of Justice of the European Union.

Although the responsibility of applying EU law falls upon the domestic courts of the respective EU member states, the CJEU is responsible for the uniform application of EU law throughout Europe. In fulfilling this duty, the CJEU has both a judicial and a supervisory role.

In its judicial role it hears disputes between parties – against either member states (for example, **Re Tachographs: EC Commission v UK**) or European institutions (for example,

UK v **Council of the European Union**). Following the Maastricht Treaty, members can be fined for failing to enforce judgments.

In its supervisory role, under Art. 267 the CJEU receives cases from domestic courts where a piece of European legislation needs to be interpreted to enable the domestic court to give judgment (for example, **Bulmer** v **Bollinger**). In **Customs and Excise Commissioners** v **APS Samex,** Bingham J emphasised that the European Court can take a panoramic view of EU law and apply a purposive approach.

A ruling from the CJEU has application throughout the EU, and so its decisions promote cohesion and certainty whilst leaving individual domestic courts to apply its principles in their decisions.

Summary of Chapter 5: European law

Introduction
The European Union currently has 28 members. It was established to create political unity within Europe and to prevent another world war. In 2016 the UK voted in a referendum to leave the EU, and the withdrawal process is scheduled to be completed by 29 March 2019.

The institutions of the European Union
There are six key institutions of the European Union: the Commission, the Council of Ministers, the European Council, the European Parliament, Court of Justice of the European Union and the European Central Bank. The Court of Justice of the European Union has two separate functions: a judicial role where it decides cases of dispute and a supervisory role under Art. 267 of the Treaty on the Functioning of the European Union.

Making European legislation
The Council of Ministers, the Commission and the European Parliament all play a role in making European legislation. All legislation starts with a proposal from the Commission, though the Council enjoys the most power in the legislative process. Increasingly, the qualified majority system of voting is being used by the Council in agreeing new legislation.

Types of European legislation
The different forms of European legislation are:

- treaties;
- regulations;
- directives; and
- decisions.

How does EU law affect the UK?
Membership of the EU has had a number of effects on UK law and on our legal system. Joining the original EEC created new and very important sources of law for the UK. Because EU law takes precedence over domestic legislation, the role of the courts has changed as a result of membership of the Union. Now judges should refuse to apply statutes which are in conflict with directly effective European law. Post Brexit, however, the judiciary needs guidance from the Government on how to manage the juxtaposition of English law and EU law.

Reading list

Booth, A. (2002) Direct effect. *Solicitors Journal*, 924.

Burns, S. (2008) An incoming tide. *New Law Journal*, 158: 44.

Craig, P. and de Búrca, G. (2007) *EU Law: Text, Cases and Materials*. Oxford: Oxford University Press.

Levitsky, J. (1994) The Europeanization of the British legal style. *American Journal of Comparative Law*, 42: 347.

On the internet

www Access to the homepages of the European institutions can be obtained from the following website:
http://europa.eu/about-eu/institutions-bodies/index_en.htm

European legislation is available at:
http://eur-lex.europa.eu/en/index.htm

A European Commission Fact Sheet on Brexit is at:
http://europa.eu/rapid/press-release_MEMO-17-648_en.htm

Parliament's perspective on how Brexit will work in the UK is at:
http://www.parliament.uk/business/publications/research/eu-referendum/how-will-brexit-work/

6

Custom

This chapter discusses:

- the history of custom as a source of law; and
- when custom can be a source of law today.

Introduction

As we have seen, the basis of the common law was custom. The itinerant justices sent out by William the Conqueror (see p. 2) examined the different local practices of dealing with disputes and crime, filtered out the less practical and reasonable ones, and ended up with a set of laws that were to be applied uniformly throughout the country. As Sir Henry Maine, a nineteenth-century scholar who studied the evolution of legal systems, has pointed out, this did not mean that custom itself was ever law – the law was created by the decisions of judges in recognising some customs and not others.

Custom still plays a part in modern law, but a very small one. Its main use is in cases where a traditional local practice – such as fishermen being allowed to dry their nets on a particular piece of land, or villagers holding a fair in a certain place – is being challenged. Custom was defined in the **Tanistry Case** (1608) as 'such usage as has obtained the force of law' and, in these cases, those whose practices are being challenged assert that the custom has existed for so long that it should be given the force of law, even though it may conflict with the general common law.

When can custom be a source of law?

To be regarded as conferring legally enforceable rights, a custom must fulfil several criteria.

'Time immemorial'

It must have existed since 'time immemorial'. This was fixed by a statute in 1275 as meaning 'since at least 1189'. In practice today claimants usually seek to prove the custom has existed as far back as living memory can go, often by calling the oldest local inhabitant as a witness. However, this may not always be sufficient. In a dispute over a right to use local land in some way, for example, if the other side could prove that the land in question was under water until the seventeenth or eighteenth century, the right could therefore not have existed since 1189. In **Simpson v Wells** (1872), a charge of obstructing the public footway by setting up a refreshment stall was challenged by a claim that there was a customary right to do so derived from 'statute sessions', ancient fairs held for the purpose of hiring servants. It was then proved that statute sessions were first authorised by the Statute of Labourers in the fourteenth century, so the right could not have existed since 1189.

Reasonableness

A legally enforceable custom cannot conflict with fundamental principles of right and wrong, so a customary right to commit a crime, for example, could never be accepted. In **Wolstanton Ltd v Newcastle-under-Lyme Corporation** (1940) the lord of a manor claimed a customary right to take minerals from under a tenant's land, without paying compensation for any damage caused to buildings on the land. It was held that this was unreasonable.

Certainty and clarity

It must be certain and clear. The locality in which the custom operates must be defined, along with the people to whom rights are granted (local fishermen, for example, or tenants of a particular estate) and the extent of those rights. In **Wilson** *v* **Willes** (1806) the tenants of a manor claimed the customary right to take as much turf as they needed for their lawns from the manorial commons. This was held to be too vague, since there appeared to be no limit to the amount of turf which could be taken.

Locality

It must be specific to a particular geographic area. Where a custom is recognised as granting a right, it grants that right only to those specified – a custom giving fishermen in Lowestoft the right to dry their nets on someone else's land would not give the same right to fishermen in Grimsby. Custom is only ever a source of local law.

Continuity

It must have existed continuously. The rights granted by custom do not have to have been exercised continuously since 1189, but it must have been possible to exercise them at all times since then. In **Wyld** *v* **Silver** (1963), a landowner, wishing to build on land where the local inhabitants claimed a customary right to hold an annual fair, argued that the right had not been exercised within living memory. The court nevertheless granted an injunction preventing the building.

Exercised as of right

It must have been exercised peaceably, openly and as of right. Customs cannot create legal rights if they are exercised only by permission of someone else. In **Mills** *v* **Colchester Corporation** (1867) it was held that a customary right to fish had no legal force where the right had always depended on the granting of a licence, even though such licences had traditionally been granted to local people on request.

Consistency

It must be consistent with other local customs. For example, if a custom is alleged to give the inhabitants of one farm the right to fish in a lake, it cannot also give the inhabitants of another the right to drain the lake. The usual course where a conflict arises is to deny that the opposing custom has any force, though this is not possible if it has already been recognised by a court.

Obligatory

Where a custom imposes a specific duty, that duty must be obligatory – a custom cannot provide that the lord of a manor grants villagers a right of way over his land only if he likes them, or happens not to mind people on his land that day.

Custom in international law

Custom is particularly important in the context of international law where fixed legal rules (for example in treaties and the Geneva Conventions) are less developed. In 2005, the International Committee of the Red Cross published a study aimed at promoting customary international humanitarian law. It identified 161 rules of customary international humanitarian law, which provide legal protection for people affected by armed conflict. These customs derive from the practice of states as expressed, for example, in military manuals, national legislation and diplomatic statements. They are considered to be binding custom in international law if they reflect the widespread, representative and uniform practice of states and are accepted as law.

These customs are particularly important during civil wars as treaty law is primarily concerned with international conflicts. The study showed that customary international humanitarian law applicable in non-international armed conflict goes beyond the rules of treaty law. While treaty law covering internal armed conflict does not expressly prohibit attacks on civilians, international customs do. Customs are particularly important in this context because, while only states are bound by international treaties, all those involved in internal fighting, including rebel groups, are bound by international customs.

Conformity with statute

A custom which is in conflict with a statute will not be held to give rise to law.

Answering questions

1 Custom is one of the sources of UK law. In reality, how useful is it as such a source?

Start by listing the sources of law, which include custom (as covered in Part 1 of the text). Arguments that could be put forward on the limited usefulness of custom include that:

- custom plays only a small part;
- custom is not, of itself, 'law' (p. 116) and;
- the criteria applied – including proof of its existence since time immemorial – is very restrictive.

However, custom may be important in international law.

Summary of Chapter 6: Custom

Introduction
The basis of the common law was custom. Custom still plays a part in modern law, but a very small one. Its main use is in cases where a traditional local practice is being challenged.

When can custom be a source of law?
To be regarded as conferring legally enforceable rights, a custom must fulfil several criteria:

'Time immemorial'
It must have existed since 'time immemorial'. This was fixed by a statute in 1275 as meaning 'since at least 1189'.

Reasonableness
A legally enforceable custom cannot conflict with fundamental principles of right and wrong.

Certainty and clarity
It must be certain and clear.

Locality
It must be specific to a particular geographic area.

Continuity
It must have existed continuously.

Exercised as of right
It must have been exercised peaceably, openly and as of right.

Consistency
It must be consistent with other local customs.

Obligatory
Where a custom imposes a specific duty, that duty must be obligatory.

Conformity with statute
A custom which is in conflict with a statute will not be held to give rise to law.

 ### Reading list

Maine, Sir H. (2001) *Ancient Law*. London: Dent.

7

Equity

This chapter looks at:

- how equity became a source of law;
- the difference between common law and equity;
- reforms introduced by the Judicature Acts 1873–75;
- equity today; and
- the future of equity as a source of law.

Introduction

In ordinary language, equity simply means fairness, but in law it applies to a specific set of legal principles, which add to those provided in the common law. It was originally inspired by ideas of fairness and natural justice, but is now no more than a particular branch of English law. Lawyers often contrast 'law' and equity, but it is important to know that when they do this they are using 'law' to mean common law. Equity and common law may be different, but both are laws. Equity is an area of law which can only be understood in the light of its historical development.

How equity began

As we have seen, the common law was developed after the Norman Conquest through the 'itinerant justices' travelling around the country and sorting out disputes. By about the twelfth century, common law courts had developed which applied this common law. Civil actions in these courts had to be started by a writ, which set out the cause of the action or the grounds for the claim made, and there grew up different types of writ. Early on, new writs were created to suit new circumstances, but in the thirteenth century this was stopped. Litigants had to fit their circumstances to one of the available types of writ: if the case did not fall within one of those types, there was no way of bringing the case to the common law court. At the same time, the common law was itself becoming increasingly rigid, and offered only one remedy, damages, which was not always an adequate solution to every problem – if a litigant had been promised the chance to buy a particular piece of land, for example, and the seller then went back on the agreement, damages might not be an adequate remedy since the buyer really wanted the land, and may have made arrangements on the basis that it would be acquired.

Consequently, many people were unable to seek redress for wrongs through the common law courts. Many of these dissatisfied parties petitioned the king, who was thought of as the 'fountain of justice'. These petitions were commonly passed to the Chancellor, the king's chief minister, as the king did not want to spend time considering them. The Chancellor was usually a member of the clergy, and was thought of as 'keeper of the king's conscience'. Soon litigants began to petition the Chancellor himself and, by 1474, the Chancellor had begun to make decisions on the cases on his own authority, rather than as a substitute for the king. This was the beginning of the Court of Chancery.

Litigants appeared before the Chancellor, who would question them, and then deliver a verdict based on his own moral view of the question. The court could insist that relevant documents be disclosed, as well as questioning the parties in person, unlike the common law courts which did not admit oral evidence until the sixteenth century, and had no way of extracting the truth from litigants. Because the court followed no binding rules, relying entirely on the Chancellor's view of right and wrong, it could enforce rights not recognised by the common law, which, restricted by precedent, was failing to adapt to new circumstances. The Court of Chancery could provide whatever remedy best suited the case – the decree of specific performance, for example, would have meant that the seller of land referred to above could be forced to honour the promise. This type of justice came to be known as equity.

Common law and equity

Not surprisingly, the Court of Chancery became popular, and caused some resentment among common lawyers, who argued that the quality of decisions varied with the length of the Chancellor's foot – in other words, that it depended on the qualities of the individual Chancellor. Because precedents were not followed and each case was considered purely on its merits, justice could appear arbitrary, and nobody could predict what a decision might be.

On the other hand, this very flexibility was seen as the great advantage of equity – where any rules are laid down, there will always be situations in which those rules produce injustice. The more general the rule, the more likely this is, yet it is impossible to foresee and lay down all the specific exceptions in which it should not apply. Equity dealt with these situations by applying notions of good sense and fairness, but in doing so laid itself open to the charge that fairness is a subjective quality.

The common lawyers particularly resented the way in which equity could be used to restrict their own jurisdiction. Where the common law gave a litigant a right which, in the circumstances, it would be unjust to exercise, the Court of Chancery could issue a common injunction, preventing the exercise of the common law right. An example might be where a litigant had made a mistake in drawing up a document. Under common law the other party could enforce the document anyway, even if they were aware of the mistake but failed to draw attention to it. This was considered inequitable, and a common injunction would prevent the document being enforced.

Nevertheless, the rivalry continued for some time, but gradually abated as equity too began to be ruled by precedent and standard principles, a development related to the fact that it was becoming established practice to appoint lawyers rather than clergy to the office of Lord Chancellor. By the nineteenth century, equity had a developed case law and recognisable principles, and was no less rigid than the common law.

KEY CASE

Tensions between equity and the common law came to a head in 1615 in **The Earl of Oxford's Case**, where conflicting judgments of the common law courts and the Court of Chancery were referred to the king for a decision; he advised that where there was conflict, equity should prevail. Had this decision not been made, equity would have been worthless – it could not fulfil its role of filling in the gaps of the common law unless it was dominant.

Legal principle

Where there is a conflict between equity and the common law, then equity should prevail.

The Judicature Acts

Once equity became a body of law, rather than an arbitrary exercise of conscience, there was no reason why it needed its own courts. Consequently, the Judicature Acts of 1873–75, which established the basis of the court structure we have today, provided that equity and common law could both be administered by all courts, and that there would no longer be different procedures for seeking equitable and common law remedies. Although the Court of Chancery remained as a division of the High Court, like all other courts it can now apply both common law and equity.

Equity today

It is important to note that the Judicature Acts did not fuse common law and equity, only their administration. There is still a body of rules of equity which is distinct from common law rules, and acts as an addition to it. Although they are implemented by the same courts, the two branches of the law are separate. Where there is conflict, equity still prevails.

Equitable maxims

Although both the common law and equity lay down rules developed from precedents, equity also created maxims which had to be satisfied before equitable rules could be applied. These maxims were designed to ensure that decisions were morally fair. The following are some of them.

'He who comes to equity must come with clean hands'

This means that claimants who have themselves been in the wrong in some way will not be granted an equitable remedy. In **D&C Builders *v* Rees** (1966) a small building firm did some work on the house of a couple named Rees. The bill came to £732, of which the Reeses had already paid £250. When the builders asked for the balance of £482, the Reeses announced that the work was defective, and they were only prepared to pay £300. As the builders were in serious financial difficulties (as the Reeses knew), they reluctantly accepted the £300 'in completion of the account'. The decision to accept the money would not normally be binding in contract law, and afterwards the builders sued the Reeses for the outstanding amount. The Reeses claimed that the court should apply the doctrine of equitable estoppel, which can make promises binding when they would normally not be. However, Lord Denning refused to apply the doctrine, on the grounds that the Reeses had taken unfair advantage of the builders' financial difficulties, and therefore had not come 'with clean hands'.

'He who seeks equity must do equity'

Anyone who seeks equitable relief must be prepared to act fairly towards their opponent. In **Chappell *v* Times Newspapers Ltd** (1975), newspaper employees who had been threatened that they would be sacked unless they stopped their strike action applied for an injunction to prevent their employers from carrying out the threat. The court held that, in order to be awarded the remedy, the strikers should undertake that they would withdraw their strike action if the injunction was granted. Since they refused to do this, the injunction was refused.

'Delay defeats equity'

Where a claimant takes an unreasonably long time to bring an action, equitable remedies will not be available. The unreasonableness of any delay will be a matter of fact to be assessed in view of the circumstances in each case. In **Leaf *v* International Galleries** (1950) the claimant bought a painting of Salisbury Cathedral described (innocently) by the seller as a genuine Constable. Five years later, the buyer discovered that it was nothing of the sort, and claimed the equitable remedy of rescission, but the court held that the delay had been too long.

These maxims (there are several others) mean that where a claimant's case relies on a rule of equity, rather than a rule of common law, that rule can only be applied if the maxims are satisfied – unlike common law rules which have no such limitations.

Equitable remedies

Equity substantially increased the number of remedies available to a wronged party. The following are the most important:

Injunction This orders the defendants to do or not to do something.

Specific performance This compels a party to fulfil a previous agreement.

Rectification This order alters the words of a document which does not express the true intentions of the parties to it.

Rescission This restores parties to a contract to the position they were in before the contract was signed.

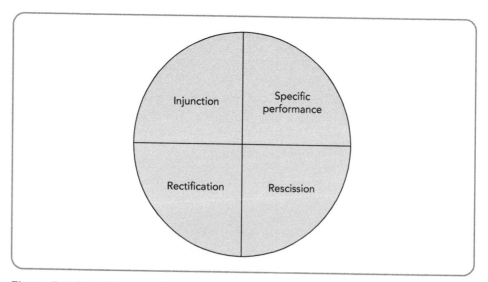

Figure 7.1 Equitable remedies

Equitable remedies are discretionary. A claimant who wins the case is awarded the common law remedy of damages as of right, but the courts may choose whether or not to award equitable remedies. They are very much an addition to common law remedies, and usually only available if common law remedies are plainly inadequate.

Equitable principles have had their greatest impact in the development of the law of property and contract, and remain important in these areas today. The two best-known contributions come from property law, and are the developments of the law of trusts, and the basis of the rules which today govern mortgages. The creation of alternative remedies has also been extremely important.

TOPICAL ISSUE

Equity's future?

Equity has shown itself capable of adapting and expanding to meet new needs, and so creating law reform. During the 1950s and 1960s, it responded to increasing marital breakdown by stating that a deserted wife could acquire an equitable interest in the family home, providing an interim solution to a growing problem until legislation could be passed in the form of the Matrimonial Homes Act 1967. And in the 1970s, two important new remedies were created by extending the scope of injunctions: the Anton Piller order, by which the court can order defendants to allow their premises to be searched and relevant documents to be removed, and the Mareva injunction, a court order to a third party, such as a bank, to freeze the assets of a party to a dispute where there is a danger that they may be removed from the court's jurisdiction (by being taken out of the country, for example, and therefore made unavailable if damages were ordered by the court).

However, further attempts to extend equitable jurisdiction, notably in **Scandinavian Trading Tanker Co AB v Flota Petrolera Ecuatoriana** (1983) and **Sport International Bussum BV v Inter-Footwear Ltd** (1984), have been firmly resisted by the House of Lords.

The availability of discretionary remedies means that equity still fulfils the traditional function of supplementing the common law, providing just and practical remedies where the common law alone is not enough, but restricting itself to cases where those remedies are felt to be genuinely and justly deserved.

Answering questions

1 Critically analyse the role of equity – both historical and modern – in the English and Welsh legal system today.

The historical background of equity and how it came about as a separate source of law is discussed on p. 121. Today, equity and the common law remain separate bodies of law, albeit they are dealt with by the same courts. Although equity supports the common law, in the event of a conflict, equity prevails. Your answer should set out some of the maxims and explain that equity implies notions of fairness and good sense. You should note the wide range of remedies available under equity and equity's ability to adapt to changing needs ('Topical issue', p. 125). However, you should also acknowledge that equitable remedies are only discretionary and that they are mostly useful in a limited number of fields, such as in contract and property law.

2 To what extent does equity remain a separate source of law?

Historically equity developed separately from the common law to remedy the shortcomings of the common law and was dispensed from separate courts (the Court of Chancery). The **Earl of Oxford's Case** in 1615 established that where common law and equity judgments conflicted, equity prevailed. Equity continued to evolve into a set of principles. The Judicature Acts 1873–75 abolished different procedures and provided that equity and common law be administered by all courts; but these measures did not fuse common law and equity.

Equity remains distinct from the common law and is epitomised in the equitable maxims such as 'delay defeats equity' – as illustrated by **Leaf v International Galleries.** Equity also provides remedies not available at common law (for example, injunctions and specific performance) but these are in addition to remedies available at common law.

Thus today equity can be accessed through the normal courts but remains a separate, supplementary strand of law, although in cases such as **Sport International Bussum BV v Inter-Footwear Ltd,** the House of Lords has firmly resisted extension of equitable principles.

Summary of Chapter 7: Equity

Introduction
In law the term 'equity' refers to a specific set of legal principles, which add to those provided in the common law.

How equity began
By the thirteenth century the common law had become inflexible and, in order to obtain justice in specific cases, individuals petitioned the king who passed the cases to the Lord Chancellor to consider. By 1474, the Chancellor had begun to make decisions on the cases on his own authority, rather than as a substitute for the king. This was the beginning of the Court of Chancery.

Common law and equity
Tensions developed between the common law and the Court of Chancery. Matters came to a head in 1615 in **The Earl of Oxford's Case,** where conflicting judgments of the common law courts and the Court of Chancery were referred to the king for a decision; he advised that where there was conflict, equity should prevail. By the nineteenth century, equity had a developed case law and recognisable principles, and was no less rigid than the common law.

The Judicature Acts
The Judicature Acts of 1873–75 provided that there would no longer be separate courts administering equity and common law.

Equity today

Although equity and the common law are implemented by the same courts, the two branches of the law are separate. Where there is conflict, equity still prevails.

Equitable maxims

Equity developed maxims to ensure that decisions are morally fair. The following are some of them.

- 'He who comes to equity must come with clean hands.'
- 'He who seeks equity must do equity.'
- 'Delay defeats equity.'

Equitable remedies

The following are the most important equitable remedies, all of which are available at the discretion of the court.

- injunction;
- specific performance;
- rectification;
- rescission.

Reading list

Burrows, A. (2002) We do this at common law but that in equity. *Oxford Journal of Legal Studies,* 22: 1.

Millett, L. (2000) Modern equity: a means of escape. *Judicial Studies Board Journal,* 21.

Salter, M. and Doupe, M. (2006) Concealing the past? Questioning textbook interpretations of the history of equity and trusts. *Liverpool Law Review,* 22: 253.

8

Treaties

This chapter discusses:

- treaties as an important source of international and national law; and

- the implementation of treaties.

Introduction

When the UK enters into treaties with other countries, it undertakes to implement domestic laws that are in accordance with the provisions of those treaties. For the purposes of the legal system, probably the most important treaties signed by the UK Government are those setting up and developing the European Union, and the European Convention on Human Rights (discussed on p. 153).

Implementation of treaties

In many countries, treaties automatically become part of domestic law when the country signs them. However, in the UK, the position is that signing treaties usually does not instantly make them law, so citizens cannot rely on them in proceedings brought in UK courts. Only when Parliament produces legislation to enact its treaty commitments do those commitments become law – the Taking of Hostages Act 1982 is an example of legislation incorporating the provisions of international treaties. Until such legislation is produced, individuals cannot usually take advantage of the protections envisaged by treaties.

However, there are some treaties which do not precisely follow this rule. Parts of the treaties setting up the European Communities are directly applicable in British courts, and can be relied on to create rights and duties just like an English statute (this subject is discussed in Chapter 5: European law).

TOPICAL ISSUE

Treaties under a modern constitution

In 2008, the Minister of Justice published a White Paper looking at ways to improve the current constitution: *The Governance of Britain: Constitutional Renewal* (2008). The Constitutional Reform and Governance Act 2010 puts on a statutory footing the procedures followed for the ratification of a treaty. In essence, it provides for treaties to be ratified by following a negative resolution procedure (see p. 77). The relevant Government Minister has to lay a copy of the treaty before Parliament and 21 days have to pass without either of the parliamentary Houses resolving that the treaty should not be ratified. If either House resolves that the treaty should not be ratified, a further condition is triggered requiring the Secretary of State to lay a statement before Parliament explaining why he or she is of the opinion that the treaty should nevertheless be ratified. Should it be the House of Commons that has resolved that the treaty should not be ratified, the Minister has to wait a further 21 days after the above statement has been laid, and the treaty cannot be ratified if the Commons again resolves to oppose it within that period. In exceptional circumstances, these procedures do not have to be followed.

Answering questions

1 In what way can treaties be said to be a source of law?

In order to answer this question you should read this chapter in conjunction with Chapter 5 'European law'. Start by explaining what treaties are and give some important examples, such as the Treaty of Rome and the Maastricht Treaty. You need to explain that some provisions in treaties can be directly applicable and that they can have direct effect. Use of cases such as **Van Gend en Loos** (1963) will illustrate this and will also help to show in what way treaties form a source of law (see p. 100 onwards).

Remember that in the UK, to maintain the sovereignty of Parliament, treaties must be implemented into UK law by the passing of an Act of Parliament. This applied even to the Treaty of Rome and the European Convention on Human Rights (see Chapter 10).

On the internet

www

The European Convention on Human Rights is available on the website of the European Court of Human Rights at:

http://www.echr.coe.int/Documents/Convention_ENG.pdf

9

Law reform

This chapter discusses:

- judicial and parliamentary law reform in practice;

- the impetus for law reform from pressure groups, political parties, the civil service, treaty obligations, public opinion and media pressure;

- the different agencies that have been set up to consider the need for reform in areas referred to them by the Government, including the Law Commission, Royal Commissions and public inquiries; and

- the success of these agencies of law reform.

Introduction

An effective legal system cannot stand still. Both legal procedures and the law itself must adapt to social change if they are to retain the respect of at least most of society, without which they cannot survive. Many laws which were made even as short a time ago as the nineteenth century simply do not fit the way we see society today – until the early part of the twentieth century, for example, married women were legally considered the property of their husbands, while, not much earlier, employees could be imprisoned for breaking their employment contracts.

Most legislation in this country stands until it is repealed – the fact that it may be completely out of date does not mean it technically ceases to apply. The offences of challenging to fight, eavesdropping and being a common scold for example, which long ago dropped out of use, nevertheless remained on the statute book until they were abolished by the Criminal Law Act 1967. In practice, of course, many such provisions simply cease to be used, but where it becomes clear that the law may be out of step with social conditions, or simply ineffective, change can be brought about in a range of ways.

Judicial change

Case law can bring about some reform – a notable example was the decision in **R** *v* **R** (1991), in which the House of Lords declared that a husband who has sexual intercourse with his wife without her consent may be guilty of rape. Before this decision, the law on rape within marriage was based on an assertion by the eighteenth-century jurist Sir Matthew Hale, that 'by marrying a man, a woman consents to sexual intercourse with him, and may not retract that consent'. This position had been found offensive for many years before **R** *v* **R.** In 1976, Parliament considered it during a debate on the Sexual Offences Act, but decided not to make changes at that time, and it was not until 1991 that the Court of Appeal and then the House of Lords held that rape within marriage should be considered an offence.

Lord Keith stated that Hale's assertion reflected the status of women within marriage in his time, but since then both the status of women and the marriage relationship had completely changed. The modern view of husband and wife as equal partners meant that a wife could no longer be considered to have given irrevocable consent to sex with her husband; the common law was capable of evolving to reflect such changes in society, and it was the duty of the court to help it do so.

Sometimes individuals try to force a change in the law by bringing a case to court. Debbie Purdy suffered from multiple sclerosis. When her condition deteriorated, she wanted her husband to be able to assist her to commit suicide without facing the risk of prosecution for the offence of assisting suicide. She successfully brought legal proceedings to force the Director of Public Prosecutions to publish guidelines on when he would prosecute for this offence – **R (on the application of Purdy)** *v* **Director of Public Prosecutions** (2009).

In practice, however, major reforms like this are rarely produced by the courts, and would not be adequate as the sole agency of reform. Norman Marsh's article 'Law reform in the United Kingdom' (1971) puts forward a number of reasons for this.

1 First, as we saw in the chapter on case law, there is no systematic, state-funded process for bringing points of law in need of reform to the higher courts. The courts can only deal with such points as they arise in the cases before them, and this depends on the parties involved having sufficient finance, determination and interest to take their case up through the courts. Consequently, judge-made reform proceeds not on the basis of which areas of law need changes most, but on a haphazard presentation of cases.

2 Secondly, judges have to decide cases on the basis of the way the issues are presented to them by the parties concerned. They cannot commission research, or consult with interested bodies to find out the possible effects of a decision on individuals and organisations other than those in the case before them – yet their decision will apply to future cases.

3 Thirdly, judges have to recognise the doctrine of precedent, and for much of the time this prohibits any really radical reforms.

4 Marsh's fourth point is that reforming decisions by judges have the potential to be unjust to the losing party. Law reforms made by Parliament are prospective – they come into force on a specified date, and we are not usually expected to abide by them until after that date. Judicial decisions, on the other hand, are retrospective, affecting something that happened before the judges decided what the law was. The more reformatory such a decision is, the less the likelihood that the losing party could have abided by the law, even if they wanted to.

5 Finally, Marsh argues, judges are not elected, and therefore feel they should not make decisions which change the law in areas of great social or moral controversy. They themselves impose limits on their ability to make major changes and will often point out to Parliament the need for it to make reforms, as happened in the **Bland** case concerning the Hillsborough stadium disaster victim (see p. 28).

Reform by Parliament

The majority of law reform is therefore carried out by Parliament. It is done in four ways:

- **Repeal** of old and/or obsolete laws.
- **Creation** of completely new law, or adaptation of existing provisions, to meet new needs. The creation of the offence of insider dealing (where company officials make money by using information gained by virtue of a privileged position) in the Companies Act 1980 was a response to public concern about 'sharp practice' in the City.
- **Consolidation.** When a new statute is created, problems with it may become apparent over time, in which case further legislation may be enacted to amend it. Consolidation brings together successive statutes on a particular subject and puts them into one statute. For example, the legislation in relation to companies was consolidated in 1985.

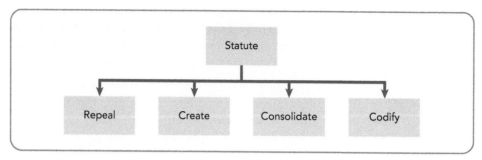

Figure 9.1 Reforming legislation

- **Codification.** Where a particular area of the law has developed over time to produce a large body of both case law and statute, a new statute may be created to bring together all the rules on that subject (case law and statute) in one place. That statute then becomes the starting point for cases concerning that area of the law, and case law, in time, builds up around it. The Criminal Attempts Act 1981 and the Police and Criminal Evidence Act 1984 are examples of codifying statutes. Codification is thought to be most suitable for areas of law where the principles are well worked out; areas that are still developing, such as tort, are less suitable for codifying.

These types of reform often happen together – the Public Order Act 1986, for example, created new public order offences designed to deal with specific problems of the time, such as football hooliganism and, at the same time, repealed out-of-date public order offences.

Some significant law reforms have come about as a result of Private Members' Bills (see p. 46) – an example is the Abortion Act 1967 which resulted from a Private Members' Bill put forward by David Steel.

Pressures for reform

The inspiration for reform may come from a variety of sources, alone or in combination. As well as encouraging Parliament to consider particular issues in the first place, they may have an influence during the consultation stage of legislation.

Pressure groups

Groups concerned with particular subjects may press for law reform in those areas – examples include charities such as Shelter, Age UK and the Child Poverty Action Group; professional organisations such as the Law Society and the British Medical Association; and business representatives such as the Confederation of British Industry. JUSTICE is a pressure group specifically concerned with promoting law reform in general.

Pressure groups use a variety of tactics, including lobbying MPs, gaining as much publicity as possible for their cause, organising petitions, and encouraging people to write to their own MP and/or relevant Ministers. Some groups are more effective than others: size obviously helps, but sheer persistence and a knack for grabbing headlines can be just as productive – the anti-porn campaigner Mary Whitehouse almost single-handedly pressurised the Government to create the Protection of Children Act 1978, which sought to prevent child pornography. The amount of power wielded by the members of a pressure group is also extremely important – organisations involved with big business tend to be particularly effective in influencing legislation, and there is a growing industry set up purely to help them lobby effectively, for a price. On the other hand, pressure groups made up of ordinary individuals can be very successful, particularly if the issue on which they are campaigning is one which stirs up strong emotion in the general public. An example was the Snowdrop Petition, organised after the shooting of 16 young children and their teacher in Dunblane, Scotland. Despite enormous opposition from shooting clubs, it managed to persuade the then Government to ban most types of handguns.

Political parties

Some of the most high-profile legislation is that passed in order to implement the Government party's election manifesto, or its general ideology – examples include the privatisations of gas and water and the creation of the Poll Tax by the Conservative Government, which began in 1989.

The civil service

Although technically neutral, the civil service nevertheless has a great effect on legislation in general. It may not have party political goals, but various departments will have their own views as to what type of legislation enables them to achieve departmental goals most efficiently – which strategies might help the Home Office control the prison population, for example, or the Department of Health make the NHS more efficient. Ministers rely heavily on senior civil servants for advice and information on the issues of the day, and few would consistently turn down their suggestions.

Treaty obligations

The UK's obligations under the treaties establishing the EU and the European Convention on Human Rights both influence changes in British law.

Public opinion and media pressure

As well as taking part in campaigns organised by pressure groups, members of the public make their feelings known by writing to their MPs, to Ministers and to newspapers. This is most likely to lead to reform where the ruling party has a small majority. The media can also be a very powerful force for law reform, by highlighting issues of concern. In 1997, media pressure helped secure a judicial inquiry into the racially motivated killing of South London teenager Stephen Lawrence. The inquiry was authorised to look not only at the Lawrence case itself, but also at the general issue of how racially motivated killings are investigated.

Public opinion and media pressure interact; the media often claims to reflect public opinion, but can also whip it up. What appears to be a major epidemic of a particular crime may in fact be no more than a reflection of the fact that once one interesting example of it hits the news, newspapers and broadcasting organisations are more likely to report others.

Photo 9.1 Brixton riots
Source: © David Hoffman Photo Library/Alamy

An example of this is the rash of stories during 1993 about parents going on holiday and leaving their children alone, which caught the headlines largely because of a popular film about just such a situation, *Home Alone*. Leaving children alone like this may have been common practice for years, or it may be something done by a tiny minority of parents, but the media's selection of stories gave the impression of a sudden epidemic of parental negligence. In 2000, there was a high-profile campaign by the *News of the World* to 'name and shame' paedophiles. The Government subsequently introduced a limited reform of the law.

TOPICAL ISSUE

Reforming the law on abortion

A recent example of pressure for law reform is the current wave for change on abortion law in the UK. It is currently a criminal offence punishable by life imprisonment for a woman to terminate her pregnancy. The Offences Against the Person Act 1861, ss.58 and 59 make it illegal to carry out an abortion. It is only legal to carry out an abortion pursuant to the Abortion Act 1967 with the involvement of doctors up until 24 weeks into the pregnancy. This is to say that should a woman attempt to undertake an abortion using pills in the privacy of her own home, at whatever stage of her pregnancy, she could be punished by life imprisonment. In 2017 the MP Diana Johnson successfully introduced a Bill called the Abortion (Foetus Protection) Bill. The first reading took place on 5 July 2017, which marked the start of its journey through the House of Lords. If the Bill becomes an Act, it will see the decriminalisation of (non-doctor assisted) termination

▶

of unwanted pregnancies up until 12 weeks. This Bill has thus far courted a lot of public interest especially because many feel that women should have autonomy in making decisions about their lives and that the old law reflects a time when abortions were being carried out using unsafe practices by sometimes unqualified individuals. These were commonly referred to as backstreet abortions. This no longer reflects the state of affairs today. Even the British Medical Association has sought to influence the laws on abortion, arguing that its doctors should not face criminal sanctions for assisting in a termination of an unwanted pregnancy. Heightened public and media interest, as well as interest from the parties involved such as the British Medical Association, will no doubt maintain the momentum for reform in this area.

Agencies of law reform

Much law reform happens as a direct response to pressure from one or more of the above sources, but there are also a number of agencies set up to consider the need for reform in areas referred to them by the Government. Often problems are referred to them as a result of the kind of pressures listed above – the Royal Commission on Criminal Justice 1993 was set up as a result of public concern and media pressure about high-profile miscarriages of justice, such as the Birmingham Six and the Guildford Four.

The Law Commission

Established in 1965 (along with another for Scotland), the Law Commission is a permanent body, comprising five people drawn from the judiciary, the legal profession and legal academics. In practice, the chairman tends to be a High Court judge, and the other four members to include a QC experienced in criminal law, a solicitor with experience of land law and equity, and two legal academics. They are assisted by legally qualified civil servants.

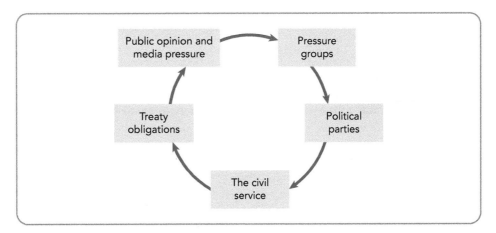

Figure 9.2 Pressures for reform

Under the Law Commissions Act 1965, the Law Commission's task is to:

- codify the law;
- remove anomalies in the law;
- repeal obsolete and unnecessary legislation;
- consolidate the law; and
- simplify and modernise the law.

The Commission works on reform projects referred to it by the Lord Chancellor or a Government department, or on projects which the Commission itself has decided would be suitable for its consideration. At any one time the Commission will be engaged on between 20 and 30 projects of law reform.

A typical project will begin with a study of the area of law in question, and an attempt to identify its defects. Foreign legal systems will be examined to see how they deal with similar problems. The Commission normally publishes a consultation paper inviting comments on the subject. The consultation paper describes the present law and its shortcomings and sets out possible options for reform. The Commission's final recommendations are set out in a report which contains a draft Bill where legislation is proposed. It is then essentially for the Government to decide whether it accepts the recommendations and to introduce any necessary Bill in Parliament.

Royal Commissions

These are set up to study particular areas of law reform, usually as a result of criticism and concern about the relevant area. They are made up of a wide cross-section of people: most have some expertise in the area concerned, but usually only a minority are legally qualified. The Commissions are supposed to be independent and non-political.

A Royal Commission can commission research, and also take submissions from interested parties. It produces a final report detailing its recommendations, which the Government can then choose to act upon or not. Usually a majority of proposals are acted upon, sometimes in amended form.

Important recent Royal Commissions include the 1981 Royal Commission on Criminal Procedure, the Royal Commission on Criminal Justice, which reported in 1993, and the Royal Commission on Reform of the House of Lords, which reported in 2000.

Public inquiries

Where a particular problem or incident is causing social concern, the Government may set up a one-off, temporary committee to examine possible options for dealing with it. Major disasters, such as the Hillsborough football stadium disaster, the sinking of the ferry *Herald of Free Enterprise* and railway accidents; events such as the Brixton riots during the 1980s; and advances in technology, especially medical technology (such as the ability to fertilise human eggs outside the body and produce 'test tube babies') may all be investigated by bodies set up especially for the job. In recent years inquiries have been set up following the BSE crisis, the murder of Victoria Climbié (a young girl living away from her parents), and the conviction of the serial killer Harold Shipman. These inquiries usually comprise individuals who are independent of Government, often with expertise in the particular area. Academics are frequent choices, as are judges – Lord

Photo 9.2 *News of the World*: its campaign to name and shame paedophiles

Source: News Syndication (front cover), © John Conner Press Associates Ltd (photograph of Sarah Payne)

Scarman headed the inquiry into the Brixton riots and Lord Hutton (2004) headed the inquiry into the suicide of Dr David Kelly following the war in Iraq. The Leveson Inquiry was set up following the News International phone hacking scandal, where private phone calls of celebrities had been listened to by journalists employed by the *News of the World*.

Public inquiries consult interested groups, and attempt to discover the truth, conducting their investigation as far as possible in a non-political way. Unlike a court, an inquiry is not required to reach a decision in favour of one party or the other. Instead, a report is produced which states the facts as the inquiry finds them to be and puts forward recommendations as to how problems could be avoided in the future.

Photo 9.3 Victoria Climbié

Source: Rex Features

The independent inquiry into child sexual abuse

In 2014, the Home Secretary announced that an independent inquiry into child sexual abuse would be established because of the growing evidence of organised child sexual abuse, conducted over many years, and institutional failures to protect children from this abuse. The inquiry is intended to be an overarching investigation into how state and non-state institutions handled their duty of care to protect children from sexual abuse; it will consider the extent to which any failings have since been addressed; and identify further action needed to address these failings. The institutions to be scrutinised include the police, the courts, the education system, the BBC and the NHS.

Initially the inquiry was going to be relatively informal with only limited powers, but following complaints by sex abuse victims and campaigners this is now a statutory inquiry established under the Inquiries Act 2005 with the power to compel witnesses to attend to give evidence in person and to order individuals and institutions to produce evidence. The inquiry will therefore have the powers it needs to penetrate deeply into the institutions that have failed children in the past, and to identify those institutions that are reportedly continuing to fail children today.

The first person to be appointed as the chair of the inquiry was Baroness Butler-Sloss who was a retired judge. Her selection was criticised as she was part of the 'establishment' as a member of the House of Lords and her brother, Lord Havers, was the Attorney General of England and Wales during the 1980s, so his conduct in the handling of sex abuse files could have fallen within the inquiry. She was therefore viewed by some victims of sex abuse as being part of the 'establishment' that the inquiry was being set up to look at. In 2011, she had carried out a review of sex abuse in the Church of England and had been criticised as being biased in favour of the Church. She therefore stood down. The corporate lawyer and Lord Mayor of London, Fiona Woolf, was appointed. But she lived in the same street and was an acquaintance of Lord Brittan, a former Home Secretary whose handling of sex abuse accusations would fall within the inquiry. As a result, she was not seen as sufficiently independent and she stood down. A High Court judge from New Zealand, Justice Dame Lowell Goddard was then appointed as the chair, but she resigned after a year in office. She had been criticised in the media for the number of days she had spent abroad, and she blamed a 'legacy of failure'. The current chair is Professor Alexis Jay, who has 30 years' experience in child protection and led the inquiry into child sexual exploitation and abuse in the town of Rotherham. The inquiry is expected to take three years to complete.

Other temporary inquiries

From time to time, various Government departments set up temporary projects to investigate specific areas of law. One of the most important examples is the inquiry by Lord Woolf into the Civil Justice System.

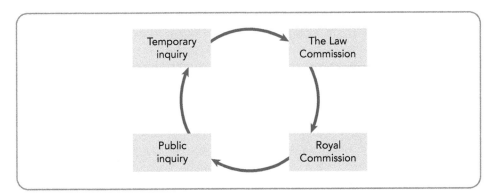

Figure 9.3 Agencies of law reform

Performance of the law reform bodies

The Law Commission

One of the principal tasks of the Commission at its inception was codification, and this programme has not on the whole been a success. The Commission's programme was ambitious: in 1965 it announced that it would begin codifying family law, contract, landlord and tenant, and evidence. Attempts in the first three were abandoned – family in 1970, contract in 1973 and landlord and tenant in 1978. Evidence was never begun.

Zander (1988) suggests the reasons for the failure are 'a mixture of conservatism and a realisation on the part of draftsmen, legislators and even judges that [codification] simply did not fit the English style of lawmaking'. The draftsmen were not keen on the idea that codes would have to be drawn up in a broader manner than was normal for traditional statutes. Legislators were doubtful of the concept of a huge Bill which would attempt to state the law in a vast area such as landlord and tenant. The judges objected to the vision promoted by Lord Scarman, the Commission's first chairman, of the code coming down like an iron curtain making all pre-code law irrelevant. As Zander explains, this appeared to the judges like 'throwing the baby out with the bathwater – losing the priceless heritage of the past and wasting the fruits of legislation and litigation on numerous points which would still be relevant to interpret the new code'.

The Law Commission is particularly concerned with the Government's failure to codify the criminal law. Between 1968 and 1974 the Commission produced a series of working papers, but in 1980 announced that its shortage of resources would not allow it to continue, and appealed for help with the task. The Society of Public Teachers of Law responded, and set up a four-person committee, which by 1985 had produced a draft code. But this has never been legislated as law. In most countries criminal law is contained in a single code so that it is accessible to the people against whom it will be applied. The Commission has now embarked upon a programme to produce a series of draft Bills, based on the code but incorporating appropriate law reform proposals, which will in themselves make substantial improvements in the law. If enacted, these Bills will form a criminal code. But at the moment there is no tangible sign of progress in implementation of any of their major reports dating back to 1993. Decisions of the courts continue to draw attention to defects in the substantive law in areas on which they have already reported. One ray of hope has been the passing of legislation consolidating the sentencing regime, and further impetus for codification has been given by the review of criminal procedure under Lord Justice Auld (2001). In the Home Office White Paper, *Criminal Justice: the Way Ahead* (2001) it stated that it did intend to codify the criminal law as part of its modernisation process.

However, opinions are mixed on whether codification would prove to be of very great value even if it ever becomes possible. Supporters say it would provide accessibility, comprehensibility, consistency and certainty. A code allows people to see their rights and liabilities more clearly than a mixture of case law and separate statutes could, and should encourage judges and others who use it to look for and expect to find answers within it. Lord Hailsham has said that a good codification would save a great deal of judicial time and so reduce costs, and the academic Glanville Williams (1983) makes the point that criminal law is not like the law of procedure, meant for lawyers only, but is addressed to all classes of society, and so the greater accessibility and clarity of a code should be particularly welcomed in this area.

Critics say a very detailed codification could make the law too rigid, losing the flexibility of the common law. And if it were insufficiently detailed, as Zander (2004) points out, it would need to be interpreted by the courts, so creating a new body of case law around it, which would defeat the object of codification and make the law neither more accessible nor more certain. It may be that the Law Commission's failure to codify the law signifies a problem with codification, not with the Law Commission.

Instead of proceeding with large-scale codification, the Law Commission has chosen to clarify areas of law piece by piece, with the aim of eventual codification if possible. Family law in particular has been significantly reformed in this way, even if the results are, as Zander points out, a 'jumble of disconnected statutes rather than a spanking new code'.

As far as general law reform is concerned, as well as the major family law reforms, the Commission has radically changed contract law by recommending control of exclusion clauses which led to the passing of the Unfair Contract Terms Act 1977. Its report, *Criminal Law: Conspiracy and Criminal Law Reform* (1976), helped shape the Criminal Law Act 1977 and its working paper, *Offences Against Public Order* (1982), was instrumental in creating the Public Order Act 1986. Following its recommendations, the Computer Misuse Act 1990 introduced new criminal offences relating to the misuse of computers; and the Family Law Act 1996 changed the law on domestic violence and divorce.

In recent years, however, there has been a major problem with lack of implementation of Law Commission proposals. By 1999, 102 law reform reports had been implemented, which represented two-thirds of their final reports. There is a better chance of proposals from the Law Commission becoming legislation if the subject concerned comes within the remit of the Ministry of Justice; there is less chance if they concern other departments, particularly the Home Office. In any case, it has been pointed out that implementation of proposals is not the only benefit of a permanent law reform body. Stephen Cretney (1998), a legal academic who has been a Law Commissioner, suggests that one of its most important contributions has simply been getting law reform under discussion and examination, and drawing attention to the needs of various areas of law.

In its White Paper, *Governance of Britain: Constitutional Renewal* (2008), the Labour Government laid out plans to strengthen the Law Commission's role. The Law Commission Act 2009 has now been passed which places a statutory duty on the Lord Chancellor to report annually to Parliament on the Government's intentions regarding outstanding Law Commission recommendations. The 2009 Act has been supplemented by a protocol agreed between the Government and the Commission designed to ensure closer collaboration between the two. In 2008, the House of Lords introduced an accelerated procedure for legislating uncontroversial Law Commission recommendations. Parliament's annual report, published in 2013, on the progress of Law Commission reform proposals, noted that the new House of Lords procedure for Law Commission Bills is proving to be effective in implementing uncontroversial changes to the law.

Royal Commissions

These have had mixed success. The 1978 Royal Commission on Civil Liability and Compensation for Personal Injury produced a report that won neither public nor Government support, and few of its proposals were implemented.

The Royal Commission on Criminal Procedure had most of its recommendations implemented by the Police and Criminal Evidence Act 1984 (PACE), but subsequent criticisms of PACE mean this is less of a success than it appears. The Royal Commission stated that the aim behind its proposals was to secure a balance between the rights of individuals suspected of crime, and the need to bring guilty people to justice. PACE has, however, been criticised by the police as leaning too far towards suspects' rights, and by civil liberties campaigners as not leaning far enough.

Perhaps the most successful Royal Commission in recent years has been the Royal Commission on Assizes and Quarter Sessions, which reported in 1969. Its proposals for the reorganisation of criminal courts were speedily implemented.

As regards the 1993 Royal Commission on Criminal Justice, this has met with mixed results. Some of its recommendations were introduced in the Criminal Justice and Public Order Act 1994 and the Criminal Appeal Act 1995, which created the Criminal Cases Review Commission in response to the Commission's criticism of the criminal appeals system. On the other hand, the Government has ignored some of its proposals and has proceeded to introduce changes that the Royal Commission was specifically opposed to, for example the abolition of the right to silence.

Public inquiries and other temporary committees

These rely to a great extent on political will, and the best committees in the world may be ineffective if they propose changes that a Government dislikes. Lord Scarman's investigation into the Brixton riots is seen as a particularly effective public inquiry, getting to the root of the problem by going out to ask the people involved what caused it (his Lordship, then retired, shocked his previous colleagues by taking to the streets of Brixton and being shown on television chatting to residents and cuddling their babies). His proposals produced some of the steps towards police accountability in PACE. But the subsequent inquiry into the case of Stephen Lawrence shows that the progress made was not sufficient. The Civil Justice Review was also instrumental in bringing about reform, though views on the success of the changes are mixed and the area has subsequently been tackled again by Lord Woolf.

Photo 9.4 Scene outside the Lawrence Inquiry, Elephant and Castle, London
Source: © Tony Harris/Press Association Images

Public inquiries are often set up after a major disaster or matter of controversy, where there is suspicion on the part of the community involved. For example, an inquiry was set up into the fire of the Grenfell Tower. Another inquiry was that of Harold Shipman, who was convicted of murdering a large number of his elderly patients. People demanding an inquiry are usually looking for an independent and open examination of the facts to determine what exactly happened and to prevent this happening again. In practice, public inquiries can put forward a large number of recommendations that the Government may appear to accept but then nothing is done to implement these recommendations, so that the risks of reoccurrence remain. For example, Dame Janet Smith's inquiry into the Shipman case made many recommendations that have not been acted upon.

Governments can refuse to hold a public inquiry which they feel may prove politically embarrassing. The parents of four soldiers killed in Iraq wanted there to be a public inquiry into whether the war in Iraq was illegal. The Labour Government refused to establish such an inquiry and the families sought a judicial review of this decision, arguing that they had a right to a public inquiry under Art. 2 of the European Convention on Human Rights which guarantees the right to life: **R (on the application of Gentle)** *v* **Prime Minister** (2008). Their application was rejected by the House of Lords, which held that Art. 2 could not restrict a nation's decision to go to war. Ultimately, the decision as to whether or not to hold a public inquiry is normally a political one, not a legal one. An exception to this is where there is a potential breach of the right to life and the right not to be subjected to torture, inhuman or degrading treatment where the European Convention imposes an obligation on the state to investigate. Following accusations of abuse by British soldiers of Iraqi prisoners, the Defence Minister had set up an internal inquiry. However, this inquiry was being carried out by a unit of the army which was itself implicated in the abuse. As a result, in **R (on the application of Mousa)** *v* **Secretary of State for Defence** (2011) the Court of Appeal held that this inquiry was inadequate to satisfy the Convention obligation and the Government Minister was instructed to look at the matter again.

Streamlining public inquiries

The Labour Government was concerned by the inefficiency and cost of recent public inquiries. For example, the inquiry into Bloody Sunday in Ireland took twelve years and is reported to have cost £195 million. By contrast, Lord Hutton's inquiry into the death of Dr David Kelly cost £2.5 million and lasted six weeks. The Government decided to introduce legislation to improve the inquiry process, partly in an attempt to keep costs down. In 2004, a consultation paper was issued on the subject called *Effective Inquiries*. Following this consultation process, the Inquiries Act 2005 was passed. The stated aim of the legislation was to modernise procedures, control costs and give more effective powers to those chairing the inquiries. Despite this, the legislation has been criticised; Amnesty International has claimed that any inquiries established under this legislation would be a 'sham' and urged judges to refuse appointments to them. It is worried that the legislation fails to allow adequate public scrutiny and 'undermines the rule of law, the separation of powers and human rights protection'. The Act arguably gives too much

▶

power to the executive, as the executive will be able to decide whether or not to publish the final report of any inquiry, whether to exclude evidence if this is deemed 'in the public interest', and whether the inquiry, or part of it, will be held in public or private.

The first inquiry to be set up under this legislation looked at allegations of state collusion in the murder of Patrick Finucane, who was an outspoken human rights lawyer in Northern Ireland. Amnesty International was concerned that this inquiry was ineffective because of the limitations of the Inquiries Act 2005.

Problems with law reform agencies

Lack of power

There is no obligation for Government to consult the permanent law reform bodies, or to set up Royal Commissions or other committees when considering major law reforms. Mrs Thatcher set up no Royal Commissions during her terms of office, despite the fact that important and controversial legislation – such as that abolishing the Greater London Council – was being passed.

Political difficulties

Governments also have no obligation to follow recommendations, and perfectly well-thought-out proposals may be rejected on the grounds that they do not fit in with a Government's political position. An example was the recommendation of the Law Commission in 1978 that changes be made to the rule that interest is not payable on a contract debt unless the parties agreed otherwise. The idea was supported by the House of Lords in **President of India v La Pintada** (1984), but the Government was persuaded not to implement the proposals after lobbying from the Confederation of British Industry and consumer organisations.

Even where general suggestions for areas of new legislation are implemented, the detailed proposals may be radically altered. The recommendations of law reform agencies may act as justification for introducing new legislation yet, as Zander (2004) points out, often when the Bill is published it becomes clear that the carefully constructed proposal put together by the law reform agency 'has been unstitched and a new and different package has been constructed'.

Lack of influence on results

Where proposals are implemented, ideas that are effective in themselves may be weakened if they are insufficiently funded when put into practice – a matter on which law reform bodies can have little or no influence. The 1981 Royal Commission on Criminal Procedure's recommendations were largely implemented in the Police and Criminal Evidence Act 1984, and one of them was that suspects questioned in a police station should have the right to free legal advice, leading to the setting up of the duty solicitor scheme. While the idea of the scheme was seen as a good one, underfunding has brought it close to collapse, and meant that in practice relatively small numbers of suspects actually get advice from qualified, experienced solicitors within a reasonable waiting time. This has clearly frustrated the aims of the Royal Commission's recommendation.

Too much compromise

Royal Commissions and temporary committees have the advantage of drawing members from wide backgrounds, with a good spread of experience and expertise. However, in some cases this can result in proposals that try too hard to represent a compromise. The result can be a lack of political support and little chance of implementation. It is generally agreed that this was the problem with the Pearson Report, the report of the Royal Commission on Civil Liability and Compensation for Personal Injury.

Influence of the legal profession

Where temporary law reform committees have a high proportion of non-lawyers, the result can be more innovative, imaginative ideas than might come from legally trained people who, however open-minded, are within 'the system' and accustomed to seeing the problems in a particular framework. However, this benefit is heavily diluted by the fact that the strong influence of the legal profession on any type of reform can defeat such proposals even before they reach an official report.

An example was the suggestion of the Civil Justice Review in its consultation paper that the County Courts and High Court might merge, with some High Court judges being stationed in the provinces to deal with the more complex cases there. Despite a warm welcome from consumer groups and the National Association of Citizens Advice Bureaux, the proposals were effectively shot down by the outcry from senior judges who were concerned that their status and way of life might be adversely affected, and the Bar, which was worried that it might lose too much work to solicitors. In the event the proposal was not included in the final report.

Waste of expertise

Royal Commissions and temporary committees are disbanded after producing their report, and take no part in the rest of the law-making process. This is in many ways a waste of the expertise they have built up.

Lack of ministerial involvement

There is no single ministry responsible for law reform so that often no Minister makes it his or her priority.

Answering questions

1 To what extent is the English Law Commission effective?

Here you are basically being asked how well the Law Commission has done its job. Your introduction might state what the Commission was set up to do, and then the rest of your essay can consider whether it has fulfilled that function and thereby given an important impetus to law reform. You could start by explaining that the Law Commission is a permanent body drawing personnel from the judiciary, the legal professions and academia. It puts forward proposals for:

- codification;
- the removal of anomalies;
- repealing obsolete laws;
- consolidation;
- simplification; and
- modernisation.

With regard to how effective the Law Commission has been, its original ambitions of codifying the law – particularly criminal, family, contract, landlord and tenant and evidence law – has not been achieved. Zander has suggested that this failure is due to conservatism and that codification fits uneasily into the English legal system. More recently the Law Commission has been dogged by a lack of resources and it has focused upon draft Bills addressing relatively narrow topics, such as unfair contract terms.

Finish by summing up what you think the Commission's contribution has been – it has certainly managed to promote discussion of law reform and drawn attention to the need to amend certain areas of law.

2 Critically evaluate the agencies of law reform in England and Wales.

Note that this question can apply not only to the official bodies such as the Law Commission, but also to informal ones such as pressure groups, and you need to discuss both types. It may be a good idea to divide your answer into official and unofficial law reform bodies: taking each in turn, you can describe how they operate and assess their effectiveness, pointing out any problems in the way they work. Do not forget that what is needed is a critical account – just listing the bodies and what they do will get you very few marks. What the examiners want to know is not just what the bodies do, but how well they do it.

Your discussion of the formal bodies of law reform could include the Law Commission, Royal Commissions and public inquiries. Your discussion of the informal bodies of law reform could include pressure groups, the media, academics through their research showing how the law is working in practice and the judiciary who might highlight problems with the law in their judgments in the hope that Parliament might take note.

Your conclusion might generally sum up the effect of these multiple bodies, saying whether, taken together, you feel they do an adequate job in reforming the law. The success of these agencies depends essentially upon the parliamentary willingness to accept their findings and act thereon.

3 Despite the influence of, for example, pressure groups, public opinion and the media, numerous problems with law reform agencies have resulted in a lack of implementation of reform proposals, especially those advanced by the Law Commission. What factors have contributed towards this lack of implementation?

You could start by setting out what influence pressure groups, public opinion and the media do have on proposed reforms to the law (p. 135). The main part of your answer should then concentrate on the material contained in the section entitled 'Problems with law reform agencies' (p. 146), explaining why reform proposals are often not implemented.

You could also note that, although there has been a lack of implementation of Law Commission proposals in recent years, those proposals do nonetheless perform the useful function of highlighting areas of law needing reform (p. 141).

Summary of Chapter 9: Law reform

The law needs to change to reflect the changes in society. Changes in the law can be made through the process of case law or by Parliament. The four ways in which Parliament can change the law are:

- repeal;
- creation;
- consolidation; and
- codification.

Pressures for reform

The inspiration for reform may come from a variety of sources, including:

- pressure groups;
- political parties;
- the civil service;
- treaty obligations; and
- public opinion and media pressure.

Agencies of law reform

There are a number of agencies set up to consider the need for reform in areas referred to them by the Government. These agencies are:

- the Law Commission;
- Royal Commissions;
- public inquiries; and
- other temporary inquiries.

The level of success of these agencies has varied considerably. Governments have no obligation to follow their recommendations. Some of the recommendations involve too many compromises and, where lawyers dominate, the resulting reforms may be under-ambitious.

Reading list

Auld, Sir R. (2001) *Review of the Criminal Courts*. London: HMSO.

Cretney, S. (1998) *Law, Law Reform and the Family*. Oxford: Clarendon Press.

Halliday, J. (2001) *Making Punishment Work: Report of the Review of the Sentencing Framework for England and Wales*. London: Home Office.

Home Office (2001) *Criminal Justice: The Way Ahead*. Cm 5074. London: Stationery Office.

Hutton, Lord (2004) *Report of the Inquiry into the Circumstances Surrounding the Death of Dr David Kelly CMG*. London: Stationery Office.

Law Commission (1976) *Criminal Law: Report on Conspiracy and Criminal Law Reform.* London: HMSO.

(1982) *Offences against Public Order.* London: HMSO.

Marsh, N. (1971) Law reform in the United Kingdom: a new institutional approach. *William and Mary Law Review,* 13: 263.

Williams, G. (1983) *Textbook of Criminal Law.* London: Stevens and Sons.

Zander, M. (1988) *A Matter of Justice.* Oxford: Oxford University Press.

(2004) *The Law-Making Process.* London: Butterworths.

On the internet

www   The Law Commission's website is:
https://www.lawcom.gov.uk/

10

Introduction to human rights

This chapter discusses:

- the European Convention on Human Rights;
- the Human Rights Act 1998;
- recent developments in human rights law; and
- whether the UK needs a Bill of Rights.

Introduction

Most democratic countries have a written Bill of Rights, which lays down the rights which, by law, can be enjoyed by citizens of that country. These rights have to be respected by the courts, Parliament, the police and private citizens, unless the Bill of Rights allows otherwise (for example, some rights may be suspended in times of war or when it is necessary in the interests of national security). Such a Bill may form part of a written constitution or sit alongside such a constitution: either way, it will usually have a status which is superior to that of ordinary law, in that it can only be changed by a special procedure. This will vary from country to country, but might involve holding a referendum, or securing a larger than usual majority in Parliament. Legislation which is protected in this way is said to be entrenched.

Britain is unusual among democratic countries in having, to date, neither a Bill of Rights nor a written constitution. In this country, our rights and freedoms are traditionally considered to be protected by a presumption that we are free to do whatever is not specifically forbidden by either legislation or the common law. Anyone prevented by the state from doing something which they are legally entitled to do should have a remedy against the state – an example is that a person wrongly detained in a police station can sue for false imprisonment. Citizens' rights in the UK were described as residual, in that they consisted of what was left after taking into account the lawful limitations.

The system of residual freedoms had shown itself to be seriously flawed over the past couple of decades. The idea that a person is free to do anything not specifically prohibited by law also applies to the state, so that the Government may violate individual freedom even though it is not formally empowered to do so, on the ground that it is doing nothing which is prohibited. An example of this is **Malone** *v* **Metropolitan Police Commissioner** (1979). Mr Malone's telephone had been tapped, and he was able to prove that this was done without any lawful authority – that is, there was no law which allowed the Government or its agencies to tap his phone. But equally, there was no law which forbade them to do so as English law gives no general right to privacy. Therefore, Mr Malone's action failed.

A significant change in the British position was made by the Human Rights Act 1998. This came into force in October 2000. The Act makes the European Convention on Human Rights (ECHR) part of the law of the UK. While the Convention had been part of the international law that is recognised by the UK, it had never been integrated as part of our domestic law. While the Human Rights Act represents a major shift in approach to civil liberties it still fails to give the UK a Bill of Rights. A Bill of Rights is the supreme authority on human rights in a country and is entrenched, which means that it cannot be changed by legislation and amounts to a significant limitation on the powers of the elected legislature. The Human Rights Act and the European Convention are not entrenched in the UK, though there is some debate as to how exactly the Human Rights Act could be repealed. Lord Justice Laws stated in **Thoburn** *v* **Sunderland City Council** (2002) that the Human Rights Act was a constitutional Act which could only be repealed by express provisions of an Act of Parliament (and not by implication). This could be described as a 'soft' form of entrenchment.

Even before the passing of the Human Rights Act 1998, English law was being influenced by the European Convention. With the passing of the 1998 Act this process has gathered momentum. The Act has raised the importance of human rights law in the UK, provides a clear legal basis for human rights challenges and has led to greater scrutiny of such matters during the progress of Bills through Parliament.

The European Convention on Human Rights

The ECHR was drawn up by the Council of Europe, which was established after the Second World War when countries tried to unite to prevent such horrors from ever happening again. The Council now has 47 members, including the 28 members of the EU. Signed in Rome in 1950, the Convention was ratified by the UK in 1951 and became binding on those states which had ratified it in 1953.

A special court, known as the European Court of Human Rights, was set up to deal with claims concerning breaches of the ECHR. The Court sits in Strasbourg, and handles claims made by one state against another and by individuals against a state. It only hears individual claims where the relevant state has accepted the right of individuals to bring such cases; not all states accept this right of individual petition, though the UK Government agreed to this in 1966.

The fact that a state has ratified the Convention does not mean it has to incorporate Convention provisions into its domestic law: each state can choose whether or not to do this, and about half have done so. In these cases, citizens can claim their rights under the Convention through domestic courts and the national parliaments cannot usually legislate in conflict with the Convention.

The UK refused for many years to incorporate the Convention and so it was not recognised by the national courts as part of English law. UK citizens who believed that their rights under the Convention had been breached could not bring their claim through the normal domestic courts, but had to take their case to the European Court of Human Rights; if they succeeded there, the UK Government was expected to amend whatever aspect of domestic law caused the problem. But such litigation is slow and expensive and the eventual remedies often inadequate. As with any other international treaty, British courts could take the Convention into account when interpreting UK legislation, and presume that Parliament did not intend to legislate inconsistently with it. Where a statute was ambiguous, they could use the Convention as a guide to its correct interpretation; an example of this is provided by **Waddington _v_ Miah** (1974), where the House of Lords referred to Art. 7 of the Convention to support its view that s. 34 of the Immigration Act 1971 could not be interpreted as having retrospective effect. Where the words of a statute were clear, domestic courts had to apply them, even if they obviously conflicted with the Convention. This position has changed radically with the passing of the Human Rights Act 1998 incorporating the Convention into domestic law.

The scope of the Convention

The rights protected by the ECHR include: the right to life (Art. 2); freedom from torture, inhuman or degrading treatment (Art. 3); freedom from slavery or forced labour (Art. 4); the right to liberty and security of the person (Art. 5); the right to a fair trial (Art. 6); the prohibition of retrospective criminal laws (Art. 7); the right to respect for a person's private and family life, home and correspondence (Art. 8); freedom of thought, conscience and religion (Art. 9); freedom of expression (Art. 10); freedom of peaceful assembly and association, including the right to join a trade union (Art. 11); and the right to marry and have a family (Art. 12).

The Convention provides that people should be able to enjoy these rights without discrimination (Art. 14). Some additions, known as Protocols, have been made to the ECHR since it was first drawn up. The First Protocol was written in 1952 and provides three new rights: the right to peaceful enjoyment of one's possessions (Art. 1); the right to education (Art. 2); and the right to take part in free elections by secret ballot (Art. 3). The other important Protocol is the fourth, concluded in 1963, which guarantees freedom of movement within a state and freedom to leave any country; it precludes a country from expelling or refusing to admit its own nationals. This Protocol has not been ratified by the UK and, in the past, some citizens from Northern Ireland have been excluded from mainland Britain.

Many of the rights provided under the Convention contain specific restrictions and exemptions. For example, Art. 10 allows restrictions on freedom of expression where they are:

> necessary in a democratic society, in the interests of national security, territorial integrity or public safety, for the prevention of disorder or crime, for the protection of health or morals, for the protection of the reputation or rights of others, for preventing the disclosure of information received in confidence, or for maintaining the authority and impartiality of the judiciary.

Member states may decline to carry out most of their obligations under the Convention in time of war or some other national emergency if this is strictly required by the situation. The UK has done so in respect of Northern Ireland. In such cases a state must inform the Secretary-General of the Council of Europe with its reasons (Art. 15). There are some rights, most importantly freedom from torture, inhuman or degrading treatment, from which states are never permitted to derogate. The Convention does not cover the whole field of human rights. It omits general economic and social rights, such as a right to housing, a minimum income and free health care, which some would argue should be guaranteed in a civilised society. This is because there is less agreement between different countries on such issues than there is on the traditional freedoms currently protected by the ECHR.

The administration

The European Court of Human Rights (ECtHR) has the same number of judges as contracting states, which is currently 47. The court is divided into four Sections, there are Committees of three judges and Chambers of seven judges. There is also a Grand Chamber of 17 judges. Any contracting state or individual claiming to be a victim of a violation of the Convention by a contracting state may lodge an application directly with the court in Strasbourg. Each individual application is assigned to a Section and a judge, called a rapporteur, makes a preliminary examination of the case and decides whether it should be dealt with by a three-member Committee or by a Chamber. A Committee may decide, by unanimous vote, to declare an application inadmissible or strike it out. Cases are admissible only after the applicant has exhausted all available domestic remedies and makes the

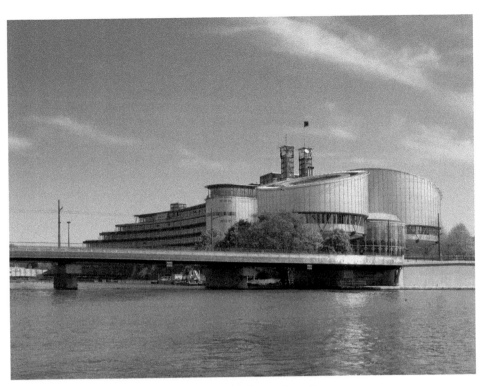

Photo 10.1 European Court of Human Rights in Strasbourg
Source: © Thinkstock/Getty Images

application no more than six months after the final national decision (Art. 26). The Committee will also reject as inadmissible any petition which is outside the scope of the Convention or manifestly ill-founded (Art. 27). Apart from those cases that are struck out by a Committee, all the other cases are heard by a Chamber. Chambers may at any time relinquish jurisdiction in favour of a Grand Chamber where a case raises a serious question of interpretation of the Convention or where there is a risk of departing from existing case law, unless one of the parties objects to this transfer.

Within three months of delivery of the judgment of a Chamber, any party may request that a case be referred to the Grand Chamber if it raises a serious question of interpretation or application or a serious issue of general importance. Such requests are examined by a panel of judges of the Grand Chamber. If the panel accepts the request the case will be heard by the Grand Chamber of 17 judges. The decision of the Grand Chamber is final. As well as deciding whether a state is in breach of the Convention, the court can award compensation or other 'just satisfaction' of the complaint (Art. 50). Responsibility for supervising the execution of judgments lies with the Committee of Ministers of the Council of Europe.

Unfortunately, the ECtHR has become a victim of its own success – in 2011 it had a backlog of 120,000 cases. In order to reduce this backlog, the 47 member nations of the Council of Europe agreed a package of reforms at a conference in Brighton in 2012. These reforms were published in the Brighton Declaration. Following this agreement the introduction to the European Convention on Human Rights (known as the preamble) has been amended to include the principle of subsidiarity, a principle developed in the ECtHR's case law and which under these reforms is expressly mentioned in the Convention. There is some disagreement about what exactly is meant by the 'principle of subsidiarity', but the Brighton Declaration refers to a shared responsibility between State Parties and the European Court of Human Rights for realising the effective implementation of the Convention and the fact that State Parties may choose how to fulfil their obligations under the Convention. This reflects the fact that the Convention system is subsidiary to the safeguarding of human rights at national level and that national authorities are in principle better placed than an international court to evaluate local needs and conditions.

The Preamble has also been amended to expressly lay down that State Parties enjoy a margin of appreciation in how they apply and implement the Convention, depending on the circumstances of the case and the rights and freedoms engaged.

The Brighton Declaration has led to reforms to the court process to try and reduce the backlog of cases. Applicants may be charged a fee to bring a case to the court, and a tighter admissibility test will be applied to filter out weak cases. An application will be rejected as manifestly ill-founded 'unless the Court finds that it raises a serious question affecting the interpretation or application of the Convention'. The time limit for bringing claims has been reduced from six to four months. As a result of these reforms, the backlog of the Court has fallen considerably, and at the end of 2013 fell below 100,000. Further reforms have been initiated with the purpose of reducing the backlog of cases, which has seen some success although the crises occurring in Europe have impacted on the number of cases, which has started to increase again and saw just under 80,000 cases pending at the close of 2016. The Court has taken the approach of joining certain claims which raise similar legal questions by considering them together to increase its efficiency.

The Human Rights Act 1998

The Human Rights Act 1998 incorporated the ECHR (and its first Protocol) into domestic law. The effect of this is to strengthen the protection of individual rights by UK courts and provide improved remedies where these are violated. The Convention is now applicable directly in the UK courts (s. 7), so that it is no longer necessary to go all the way to Strasbourg, though it is still possible. Under s. 2 of the Human Rights Act, the domestic judiciary 'must take into account' any relevant Strasbourg jurisprudence, although they are not bound by it (see p. 13).

The UK courts are required to interpret all legislation in a way which is compatible with Convention rights 'so far as it is possible to do so' (s. 3). This goes much further than the previous position of allowing ambiguities to be interpreted in favour of the Convention.

It is unlawful for public authorities to act in a way which is incompatible with Convention rights (s. 6). A public authority includes central and local government, the police and the NHS. In addition, a private body can be regarded as a public authority for the purposes of the Human Rights Act if, under s. 6(3)(b), it performs 'functions of a public nature'. Such a body is described as a hybrid public authority. The obligation on such hybrid bodies to observe Convention rights attaches only to functions which are of a public nature; other work that it carries out will not be affected.

There has been some debate as to whether the Act allows individual citizens to enforce Convention rights in proceedings against other individuals (known as 'horizontal effect').

Table 10.1 The European Convention on Human Rights

Article	Rights and freedoms
2	The right to life
3	Freedom from torture or inhuman or degrading treatment
4	Freedom from slavery and forced labour
5	The right to liberty and security of the person
6	The right to a fair trial
7	Protection from the criminal law having retrospective effect
8	The right to respect of one's private and family life
9	Freedom of thought, conscience and religion
10	Freedom of expression
11	Freedom of assembly and association
12	The right to marry
14	The right to enjoy Convention rights without discrimination on the grounds of sex, race, colour, language, religion, political or other opinion, national or social origin, association with a national minority, property, birth or other status.
The First Protocol	
1	The right to peaceful enjoyment of one's possessions
2	The right to education
3	The right to free elections.

KEY CASE

The application of s. 6(3)(b) of the Human Rights Act was considered by the House of Lords in **YL v Birmingham City Council** (2007). It did not lay down a single test to be applied to determine this issue, but said that the question had to be decided on a case-by-case basis, though it identified the sort of factors that would be taken into account. The case involved an appeal of an 84-year-old lady suffering from dementia. Under the National Assistance Act 1948, Birmingham City Council had a statutory obligation to make residential arrangements for elderly people in need of care. She had been placed by the council in a private care home operated by a company called Southern Cross Healthcare Ltd. Unfortunately, the relationship between some of the elderly lady's family and the care home's management deteriorated, and Southern Cross gave notice that she would have to leave the home. The House of Lords had to decide whether Southern Cross was required to respect Convention rights when exercising its powers in relation to the elderly lady. The majority of the Law Lords concluded that it was not. It noted that in determining the scope of s. 6 it should reflect the extent of the UK Government's liabilities before the European Court of Human Rights, as the section aimed to allow UK citizens remedies in the UK to avoid the need for them to go to Strasbourg to get a remedy. Section 6, therefore, is designed to mirror the scope of state responsibility at

▶

Strasbourg. The fact that public funding was used to pay Southern Cross was not decisive, as on the facts this was equivalent to a payment for services. The greater the powers given to the private body, the more likely that it is exercising a public function. For example, a private prison has the power to detain individuals and, therefore, is exercising a public function, whereas Southern Cross had no such power. The House concluded that Southern Cross was not carrying out a public function and its state-funded residents, therefore, could not benefit from Convention rights. The House of Lords observed that a finding to the contrary would have created rights which sat uneasily with the ordinary private law freedom of contract enjoyed in the private sector.

Legal principle

A private body can be regarded as a public authority for the purposes of the Human Rights Act 1998 under s. 6(3)(b), if it performs functions of a public nature, and this will be determined on a case-by-case basis.

Section 6 states that public authorities cannot breach Convention rights. It is therefore clear from s. 6 that citizens can rely on their Convention rights against the state (known as 'vertical effect'). The reference primarily to 'public authorities' would suggest that individual citizens can breach the Convention with impunity. But the courts are public authorities. It is therefore arguable that if a civil court failed to apply a Convention right in legal proceedings between private parties it would be in breach of the Human Rights Act. Academic opinion on this issue has been sharply divided.

The courts appear to have accepted that the Convention has a limited form of horizontal effect. Thus, in **Douglas *v* Hello!** (2001) photographs of the marriage of the Hollywood celebrities Michael Douglas and Catherine Zeta-Jones had been published without their authority by the popular magazine *Hello!* The legal proceedings were between private parties, but all the judges treated the Convention as relevant to the case because of the Human Rights Act 1998.

In **R (on the application of Al-Skeini) *v* Secretary of State for Defence** (2007) the House of Lords considered whether Iraqi civilians arrested and detained by British soldiers had the protection of the 1998 Act. It concluded that the Act has a potentially wide geographical application, beyond the physical boundaries of the United Kingdom itself, to places where the UK has effective control. The Supreme Court extended this extraterritorial application of the 1998 Act in **Smith *v* Ministry of Defence** (2013), when it held that the Act also applies to British soldiers serving abroad. Given that the House of Lords in **Al-Skeini** held that civilians detained by soldiers abroad were covered by the 1998 Act, it only makes sense that the Act also applies to soldiers.

Under s. 19 Government Ministers have to publish a written statement as to whether or not a Bill is compatible with the Convention. The House of Lords Parliamentary Committee has issued a report *Relations between the executive, the judiciary and Parliament* (2007) in which it has suggested that there have been cases where Ministers had adopted a 'far too optimistic view' about the compatibility of provisions in Bills with the European Convention. It recommended that in cases of doubt about compatibility, Ministers should seek the involvement of the Law Officers to ensure that the Bill is compatible.

While the Human Rights Act represents an important advance for civil liberties in the UK, there are still significant limitations on the impact that the Act will have. In particular, legislation which is incompatible with the Convention is still valid; judges do not have the power to strike down offending statutes as unconstitutional. Thus, the principle of parliamentary sovereignty remains intact. If a higher court does find that legislation is incompatible with the Convention, then it can choose to make a declaration to this effect (s. 4) and a Minister can subsequently amend the offending legislation by a fast-track procedure which avoids the full parliamentary process (s. 10). An early example of a declaration of incompatibility is provided by the case of **Wilson** *v* **First County Trust Ltd** (2003) where the House of Lords declared that a provision of the Consumer Credit Act 1974 violated the Convention. The Ministry of Justice report *Responding to Human Rights judgments* notes that as of July 2016, 34 declarations of incompatibility have been made, of which eight were overturned on appeal, four are subject to appeal and 22 have become final. Of these 22:

- 13 have been remedied by a subsequent Act of Parliament or secondary legislation;
- four related to provisions that had already been remedied by primary legislation at the time of the declaration;
- three have been remedied by a remedial order provided for by s. 10 of the Act;
- the Government has notified the Joint Committee on Human Rights that it intends to address one declaration of incompatibility through a remedial order; and
- one is under consideration as to how to remedy the incompatibility.

The judiciary has a lot of power in determining the impact and success of the Human Rights Act 1998. The Convention rights are very loosely drafted and through their interpretation the judges could easily dilute them and render them ineffective. The Government is clearly aware of the central role of the judges in the success or failure of the Act. It spent £4.5 million training the judges, magistrates and tribunal chairpersons ready for the implementation of the Act. The Lord Chancellor wrote directly to all the judges pointing out their vital role. The letter stated:

> With proper training and planning, I am confident that all courts and tribunals will be able to give full effect to the rights recognised by the Convention and to make their distinctive contribution to fostering a culture of awareness of, and respect for, human rights throughout the whole of society. I hope you look forward to playing your part in making those rights real, as do I.

The Human Rights Act 1998 appears to have been successfully implemented and has engendered a stronger human rights culture in the courts. Research has been carried out by Raine and Walker (2002) into the impact of the Act in its first 18 months. Their research points to 'the comparative success with which the courts managed the implementation process and the ways in which they have adapted their practices'. Prior to the Act's implementation, there had been fears that the courts would be overrun with speculative human rights claims. This has not in fact happened. The report states that:

> . . . the general picture from the research was one of relatively limited impact of the Human Rights Act in terms of challenges and additional workload for the courts, although it had invoked a number of significant and specific policy and practice changes.

A statistical analysis has been published of the first effects of the Human Rights Act 1998 on the work of the civil courts. In the last three months of the year 2000, 76 claims for damages were issued in the civil courts relying wholly on the Human Rights Act 1998, out of a total of 467,000 claims.

One of the first cases to seek to rely on the Human Rights Act 1998 was **Procurator Fiscal** *v* **Brown** (2000), which started in the Scottish courts. Under the road traffic legislation, Ms Brown had been required to inform the police of the identity of the person driving her car on the evening she was questioned. It would have been a criminal offence for her not to have answered the question. She admitted that she had been driving her car and was prosecuted for drink-driving. She claimed at her trial that her confession should not be admissible as evidence as she had been forced to incriminate herself in breach of her right to a fair trial in Art. 6 of the European Convention. The High Court in Scotland accepted this argument. This decision was highly controversial as it threatened the credibility of the Human Rights Act. It appeared to justify fears that the Act would create a large amount of litigation and give people rights that went against the general interests of society. However, on appeal the Privy Council ruled that the road traffic legislation did not breach the European Convention and the evidence was admissible at her trial. Reviewing the case law of the European Court of Human Rights, Lord Bingham concluded:

> The jurisprudence of the European Court very clearly established that while the overall fairness of a criminal trial cannot be compromised, the constituent rights comprised, whether expressly or implicitly, within Art. 6 [such as freedom from self-incrimination] are not themselves absolute.

The privilege against self-incrimination was not absolute, but had to be balanced against the wider interests of the community, in particular public safety. The Privy Council found that the obligation to state who was driving the vehicle represented a proportionate response to the serious social problem of death and injury on the roads. The case was distinguished from **Saunders** *v* **UK** (1997) (discussed at p. 162) where the UK legislation had allowed prolonged questioning, as opposed to the answering of a single question in this case. The decision shows that the courts will not tolerate attempts to misuse provisions of the Convention in ways which are contrary to the public interest.

KEY CASE

In **Wilson v Secretary of State for Trade and Industry** (2003) the House of Lords took a slightly more flexible view as to whether the Human Rights Act could have retrospective effect. It cited with approval a statement of Staughton LJ in **Secretary of State for Social Security v Tunnicliffe** (1991) on the presumption that Acts of Parliament will not have retrospective effect:

> [T]he true principle is that Parliament is presumed not to have intended to alter the law applicable to past events and transactions in a manner which is unfair to those concerned in them, unless a contrary intention appears. It is not simply a question of classifying an enactment as retrospective or not retrospective. Rather it may well be a matter of degree – the greater the unfairness, the more it is to be expected that Parliament will make it clear if that is intended.

Thus, some of the provisions of the Human Rights Act 1998 could have retrospective effect if that would not be unfair to the parties in a particular case.

Legal principle

Provisions of the Human Rights Act 1998 can have retrospective effect if it would not be unfair to the parties in a particular case.

Retrospective effect?

The Human Rights Act 1998 was brought into force in October 2000. In **R** *v* **Lambert** (2001) the House of Lords ruled that the Act did not have retrospective effect.

Commission for Equality and Human Rights

When preparing the Human Rights Act, the Labour Government considered establishing a Human Rights Commission, but then rejected this idea. However, in 2004, the Labour Government announced that it intended to establish a Commission for Equality and Human Rights. A consultation paper, *Fairness for All: A New Commission for Equality and Human Rights,* was published in 2004 by the Department for Trade and Industry. Following this consultation process, the Equality Act 2006 was passed by Parliament which contained provisions for the creation of the new Commission. It has replaced the Commission for Racial Equality, the Disability Rights Commission and the Equal Opportunities Commission, which had fought against racism, disability discrimination and sexism. The Commission is responsible for promoting both human rights and equality of opportunity. It seeks to prevent a wider range of discriminatory behaviour, including discrimination on the grounds of religion, age and sexual orientation. The new body was launched in October 2007. Its functions include:

- providing advice and guidance to people wishing to assert their rights;
- conducting inquiries;
- bringing legal proceedings;
- monitoring the operation of the ECHR in domestic law;
- scrutinising new legislation; and
- publishing regular reports on the state of the nation.

Advantages of the Human Rights Act 1998

Improved access

Bringing a case to Strasbourg can take up to six years and can be very expensive. Through incorporation, UK citizens are now able to enforce their rights under the Convention directly before the domestic courts (though applications to Strasbourg are still possible as a last resort).

Remedies

The remedies available from the European Court of Human Rights are inadequate. Also, the long delays mean that the remedies awarded can be too late to be effective. The national courts are able to provide quicker and more effective remedies.

Tried and tested

The ECHR has already been tried and tested over the last 60 years. The UK courts have developed some knowledge of its provisions as their decisions have been challenged in Strasbourg. The Privy Council has also developed case law in relation to similar provisions to be found in the written constitutions of Commonwealth countries, which were often drafted with the Convention in mind. It is therefore likely to prove easier to incorporate the Convention into domestic law than a completely new Bill of Rights.

Avoid conflict between domestic and international law

Problems were highlighted in the case of **R** v **Saunders** (1996). In this case, evidence obtained by Government inspectors under s. 177 of the Financial Services Act 1986 was used against Saunders in criminal proceedings for insider dealing. The English courts ruled that in English law this evidence was admissible at a criminal trial. The court in Strasbourg ruled that this evidence had been obtained by an unfair procedure and should have been excluded from the trial – **Saunders** v **UK** (1997). Evidence obtained in the same way was accepted by the trial court in **R** v **Morrissey** and **R** v **Staines** (1997). The Court of Appeal stated that it was 'an unsatisfactory position' that it was obliged to follow the domestic decision, which had held Saunders's evidence was admissible, despite the fact that the European Court had subsequently ruled that this breached the Convention. Now, under ss. 2 and 3 of the Human Rights Act 1998 a court would be able to take into account the Strasbourg jurisprudence and interpret relevant legislation in a way which is compatible with Convention rights 'so far as it is possible to do so'.

Encouraging conformity

While there are many instances of UK Governments changing the law as a result of losing cases in the European Court of Human Rights, they are not always keen to do so. In **Brogan** v **United Kingdom** (1988) the provisions of the Prevention of Terrorism (Temporary Provisions) Act 1984, allowing detention of suspects for up to seven days without judicial authority, were found to violate Art. 5, protecting freedom of the person. The Government responded by declaring that the power was necessary on security grounds and by depositing at Strasbourg a limited derogation under Art. 15 from the Convention to the extent that the legislation violated Art. 5.

In **Abdulaziz** v **United Kingdom** (1985) the Government technically complied with the European Court of Human Rights' decision, but in such a way as to decrease rather than increase rights. The case alleged that British immigration rules discriminated against women, because men permanently settled in the UK were allowed to bring their wives and fiancées to live with them here, but women in the same position could not bring their husbands and fiancés into the country. The European Court agreed, but the Government was determined not to increase immigration rights. Instead of allowing husbands and fiancés to settle here, they removed the right of wives and fiancées to do so, thereby ending the sexual discrimination but making the immigration laws even more restrictive.

Incorporation has reduced the problem of bringing domestic law into line with the ECHR. The courts are contributing to this process in every case where a conflict arises between the Convention and domestic law. But tensions can still arise between the European Court of Human Rights and the British Government, and on occasion the British Government is still prepared to ignore a decision of the European Court. In 2008, two men, Faisal Al-Saadoon and Khalaf Mufdhi were being held prisoner by UK soldiers in Iraq, accused of being responsible for the deaths of two British soldiers. The UK

Government wished to transfer these men to the Iraqi Government as part of the process of handing back power in Iraq in accordance with a United Nations mandate. The two prisoners objected to the handover, claiming that the Iraqi Government tortured prisoners and if they were convicted they faced the death penalty. They took their case to the European Court of Human Rights and before the Court had time to give a final judgment it issued an injunction ordering the UK Government not to hand over the men until the Court had heard the case. The UK Government was concerned that if it continued to detain the men after 1 January 2009 it would be in breach of the UN mandate. It therefore went ahead and handed over the men to the Iraqi Government in breach of the European Court's injunction.

International image

It is not good for the UK's image abroad frequently to be found in error by a 'foreign' court, as it has been many times.

Clarity and accessibility

The law on civil rights has been complex and disorderly. For example, there has been no clear definition of the right to freedom of expression, only a collection of statutes and cases which state when and how such a freedom can be restricted. The ECHR provides a comprehensive and easily accessible statement of rights and freedoms enforceable in the UK.

Education

The ECHR sets out for citizens, Government and the judiciary the basic rights and freedoms we are all entitled to expect. This should lead to better awareness by citizens of their legal rights, and to legislation and judicial decisions which take those rights as their starting point, rather than just one of many things to be considered.

Disadvantages of the Human Rights Act 1998

Judicial power

Politicians have been unhappy with some of the decisions handed down by the judges relying on the Human Rights Act, which undermine national policies. While Members of Parliament have been elected to make and change law, judges are not elected and are supposed to apply the law, not make it. For example, the High Court ruled that the Government of the day had breached the human rights of some Afghan nationals who had hijacked an aircraft in order to escape to the UK. The High Court held that the Home Secretary had behaved unlawfully when he had denied the applicants leave to enter the UK after they had already successfully claimed before the courts that it would be in breach of their human rights to return them to Afghanistan. Instead, the Home Secretary had sought to delay granting the men leave to enter so that the rules could be changed and the men refused leave to enter. The High Court considered this to amount to an abuse of power. Following this case, the then Prime Minister described the judgment as an 'abuse of common sense' and announced that he would consider restricting the rights granted in the Human Rights Act.

Problems arise when politicians refuse or delay changing domestic law to bring it into line with Convention rights where problems have been identified by judges. For example, in **Greens and MT** *v* **UK** (2010) the European Court of Human Rights ruled that a blanket ban on prisoners voting in elections breached the European Convention. In **R (on the application of Chester)** *v* **Secretary of State for Justice; McGeoch** *v* **The Lord President of the Council** (2013) the Supreme Court acknowledged that s. 2 of the 1998 Act meant that they had to 'take into account' decisions of the European Court of Human Rights, but that did not mean they necessarily had to follow them. Here, two prisoners were unsuccessful in overturning the ban on prisoner voting as a draft Bill had been prepared by the Government which would allow certain prisoners the right to vote. However, to date this Bill has not been introduced for debate in Parliament.

Legal status

Incorporation of the ECHR would have had more impact if it had been entrenched. Any legislation which did not comply with it would have been struck down by the courts, and the ECHR itself could only have been changed in domestic law by special procedures, such as a referendum or an increased parliamentary majority. The American constitution is entrenched and as a result the American Supreme Court can strike down legislation which conflicts with the constitution. The Human Rights Act 1998 does not give UK citizens a Bill of Rights.

Many experts believe it would be constitutionally impossible to make the ECHR an entrenched Bill of Rights. This is because the doctrine of parliamentary sovereignty provides that no sitting Parliament can bind a future one: in other words, every Parliament is free to unmake laws made by their predecessors. This means that a future Parliament could simply abolish a Bill of Rights and any arrangements for entrenchment could be legislated away.

Not everybody agrees that such entrenchment would be impossible. Many Commonwealth countries which have inherited ideas of parliamentary sovereignty from the UK have enacted entrenched Bills of Rights without any constitutional problems arising. Alternatively, the ECHR could have been partially entrenched so that it was treated in the same way as EU law is today.

As the Labour Government decided not to entrench or partly entrench the ECHR into domestic law, so the legal protections provided by it are limited. Real weight would be given to the Convention both if it was entrenched and if a constitutional court were created.

Because the Convention is not entrenched into domestic law, the UK Government can derogate from it (which means they can obtain permission to breach a provision of the Convention with impunity). It has chosen to do this in order to be able to detain terrorist suspects without trial for indefinite periods under the Anti-Terrorism, Crime and Security Act 2001. To enable the above legislation to be passed, the Government obtained a derogation from Art. 5 of the European Convention which guarantees the right to liberty of the person. This piece of legislation followed the attacks on the US on 11 September 2001 and constitutes a significant violation of an individual's human rights. By January 2002, 11 individuals had been detained under these powers. Investigators from the European Committee for the Prevention of Torture and Degrading Treatment or Punishment visited the UK amid concerns over the treatment of these suspects. The Committee raised a number of concerns, including the fact that the detainees were being denied access to their family and lawyers for long periods of time.

Limited scope

The ECHR is over 60 years old and, since its creation, new rights have become important – for example, the Convention makes limited provision for preventing racial discrimination and none at all for preventing discrimination on the basis of disability or sexual orientation. Some people feel that a UK Bill of Rights should be broader, including environmental, economic and social rights.

The Convention is proving to be totally ineffective in the face of international violations of human rights. UK citizens and residents were held by the US at Camp X-Ray on Guantanamo Bay in Cuba for years, with no effective human rights.

A Bill of Rights for the UK?

It has been observed that the ECHR does not constitute a Bill of Rights for the UK because it has not been entrenched. Many people feel that while the Human Rights Act 1998 is a first step in the right direction, ultimately the UK needs a properly entrenched Bill of Rights to protect its citizens. Among developed Western countries, Israel and the UK are the only ones without such a Bill.

Arguments in favour of a Bill of Rights

Curbs on the executive

A Bill of Rights provides an important check on the enormous powers of the executive (the Government of the day and its agencies, such as the police, the army and Government departments). Constitutional writers of the nineteenth century, such as Dicey, made much of the role of Parliament as a watchdog over the executive, ensuring that oppressive legislation could not be passed. Since Dicey's time, the growth of a strong party system has fundamentally altered the nature of Parliament; in the vast majority of cases, a Government can expect its own members to obey party discipline, so that Government proposals will almost invariably be passed – during the 1980s, for example, only one Government Bill was defeated. Not only do those in opposition lack the numbers to prevent this, but the pressures of parliamentary time may even curtail a detailed scrutiny of proposed legislation. This can result in Governments being able to legislate against individual rights and freedoms almost at will.

The movement in favour of a Bill of Rights gained considerable support during the later years of the Thatcher regime, when the Government showed itself willing to compromise many important civil liberties. Many commentators were alarmed as they watched the banning of trade unions at Government Communications Headquarters (GCHQ), the attempts to ban the publication of *Spycatcher* (the memoirs of a retired security service agent) and the use of the Official Secrets Act 1911 to prosecute civil servants Sarah Tisdall and Clive Ponting who leaked official information the Government had wished to keep secret.

The fact that, given a decent majority in Parliament, Governments can make whatever law they like, means that they can simply legislate freedoms away, secure in the knowledge that the courts cannot refuse to apply their legislation, as they can in countries which have a Bill of Rights or written constitution. The Public Order Act 1986 and the Criminal Justice and Public Order Act 1994, for example, severely restrict rights of peaceful protest, of assembly and of movement, but English courts must apply this legislation nevertheless.

Supporters of a Bill of Rights claim it would curb executive powers, since the courts could simply refuse to apply laws which conflicted with it. This in turn would be a powerful incentive for a Government to avoid introducing such legislative provisions in the first place.

While the provision in s. 19 of the Human Rights Act 1998, requiring Ministers to state whether a Bill conforms with the 1998 Act, will discourage the executive in some circumstances from introducing legislation that breaches the ECHR, they are still able to do so.

Attitude of the judiciary

Even where the constitution does allow for judicial protection of civil rights, British judges have frequently proved themselves unequal to the task. As Griffith (1997) has famously pointed out, they show a tendency to view the public interest as the maintenance of established authority and traditional values. Though exceptions can always be found, the overall result has been that the maintenance of 'order' and the suppression of challenges to established authority – whether of trade unions or terrorists – have taken precedence over the kind of liberties a Bill of Rights might seek to protect. For example, in **R v Secretary of State for the Home Department,** *ex parte* **Brind** (1989), the judiciary upheld a broadcasting ban on members of a legitimate political party in Northern Ireland; in **Council of Civil Service Unions v Minister for the Civil Service** (1984), the ban on trade unions at GCHQ was accepted; and in **Kent v Metropolitan Police Commissioner** (1981) a blanket ban on protest marches through an area of London was allowed.

The numerous miscarriages of justice suggest there is little protection of the right to a fair trial, nor, given the treatment of some of those involved while in police custody, to freedom from torture and inhuman treatment. The wide powers of surveillance permitted under statute to the police and security services prove the right to privacy a fallacy.

The Human Rights Act 1998 only requires the UK courts to interpret legislation in a way which is compatible with Convention rights 'so far as it is possible to do so' (s. 3). If a judge decides that the Act breaches a Convention right, the Act prevails.

Arguments against a Bill of Rights

Unnecessary

The previous Conservative Government was among those who asserted that civil liberties were already adequately protected in this country. However, the present Conservative Government has gone from debating leaving the ECHR altogether to adopting a Bill of Rights in its place which will remain faithful to protecting fundamental rights. This debate now stands in abeyance until the details for Brexit are negotiated and focus can return to the need for a Bill of Rights.

Increased power for the judiciary

Among those who oppose a Bill of Rights, mistrust of the judiciary and constitutional objections to taking power from Parliament and giving it to judges, are perhaps the most frequent reasons given. There is no doubt that such a Bill would considerably increase judicial power. Unlike British statutes, the language of a Bill of Rights is typically open and imprecise, setting out broad principles rather than detailed provisions. This gives judges a wide discretion in interpretation – so wide that in the US, for example, the provisions against racial discrimination in the American Bill of Rights were once held to allow a form of apartheid, yet since 1954 such a system has been held to violate the Bill. Even within recent decades, the US Bill of Rights has been interpreted to allow discrimination against minorities. Thus, in the Supreme Court's decision in **Bowers** *v* **Hardwick** (1986), the constitutional right of privacy was effectively denied to homosexuals. However, it should be noted that **Bowers** was overruled by the Supreme Court in 1996, and in recent years the court has given much wider protections to homosexuals. More recently, in **United States** *v* **Windsor** (2013), the court held that it was unconstitutional to define 'marriage' as being between one man and one woman, meaning that the United States Government must recognise same-sex marriages which have taken place in specific States (such as California) as valid.

A Bill of Rights also calls upon judges to decide the relative importance of protected rights where two of them clash. Should, for example, the right to free expression of members of the British National Party override or give way to that of ethnic minorities to be free of racial harassment? Does a foetus have a right to life which overrides its mother's right to liberty and security of the person? There are no obvious right or wrong answers to questions like these and nor are there always obvious legal answers, even where there is a Bill of Rights. In many such cases the real problem is not what the law is, but what the law should be. Many people believe that is not a question which should be answered by judges, who are not elected but appointed from a narrow social elite by a secretive procedure. As Griffith (1997) has pointed out, these questions are political and political questions should, as far as possible, be answered by politicians elected to do so.

Supporters of such a Bill argue that the problems associated with greater judicial power could be dealt with by reforming judicial selection and drawing judges from a wider spread of the population. While this is clearly desirable in itself, it would not remove the fundamental objection that judges are not elected and nor, whatever the reforms, is it likely to avoid the fact that, by virtue of their education and their lifestyle, judges would be unrepresentative of the mass of the population. Commentators like Griffith, who oppose a Bill of Rights, argue that what is needed is not so much reform of the judiciary, but political reforms that would allow a democratically elected legislature genuinely to supervise the acts of the executive and to fetter the exercise of executive discretion. The protection of fundamental freedoms and rights should not be for the individual to establish in court, but for the legislature to safeguard as part of its job.

Inflexibility

Supporters of our current constitutional arrangements argue that, without a written constitution, our system can adapt over time, meeting new needs as they arise. They contend that a Bill of Rights would lack this flexibility. Two responses to this are that, first, the open and imprecise language of a Bill of Rights allows flexibility; and, secondly, the Bills can be changed when necessary: the arrangements for entrenchment will usually set down a special procedure that can be used to make amendments. The fact that these procedures may be long and difficult simply protects those rights originally laid down from rash or unpopular change; it does not set them in stone.

Too much flexibility

Ironically, it is also argued that the imprecise language typical of a Bill of Rights would lead to uncertainty about the law, leading to increased litigation with no clear objectives as to how general principles might emerge and policies be interpreted. This is clearly linked to the problem of mistrust of the judiciary.

Rights are not powers

A more fundamental problem is the idea that merely granting rights is not enough to secure individual freedom and empowerment. It is all very well to grant rights but, unless they are underpinned by economic and social provision, they may prove to be useless. Freedom of labour is effectively useless in times of high unemployment, when it becomes nothing more than the freedom to live in poverty. Freedom of movement fails to help disabled people who cannot use public transport or afford their own. Freedom of association offers little advantage if employers refuse to recognise trade unions, and liberty of the person means nothing for the battered wife or abused child who has neither the personal nor the practical resources to escape.

Where there are huge imbalances in power in society, giving equal rights to all may be of limited use because those who have the most power can use it to find a way round the rights of those who are less powerful. For example, recent compensation payments made to women sacked for being pregnant have led to speculation that as a result employers may simply become even less keen than before to employ women; cases on racial discrimination may have had similar effects on the employment prospects of members of ethnic minorities. While it should not be denied that this kind of provision helps people, it can be argued that in focusing on individual rights, rather than social duties, a Bill of Rights might detract attention from any real commitment to a just society. The point is not that a Bill of Rights is undesirable but that, on its own, it cannot make the kind of changes sought by its supporters.

There is also the question of whether the same Bill of Rights would be appropriate for all parts of the UK. Northern Ireland may require special treatment given the intensity of religious and political animosity.

Drafting style

The ECHR follows the more general, looser European style of legislative drafting, in contrast to the more tightly worded legislation our courts are used to applying – though, British courts are gaining more experience of this approach.

TOPICAL ISSUE

A British Bill of Rights

The Conservative Party has pledged to repeal the Human Rights Act 1998 and replace it with a British Bill of Rights. It is also considering withdrawing from the European Convention on Human Rights. The Government is concerned that the Human Rights Act is hindering the fight against crime and terrorism and undermines national sovereignty. It was particularly angered by the European Court of Human Rights temporarily blocking the deportation of Abu Qatada, a Muslim cleric who was suspected of having terrorist links. The European court was concerned that, if deported, evidence obtained by torture was likely to be relied on in a subsequent trial in Jordan. This would amount to a breach of his Art. 6 right to a fair trial: **Othman (Abu Qatada)** v **UK** (2012). As regards national sovereignty, the Conservatives oppose the influence of European human rights law over UK law, through the incorporation of the European Convention on Human Rights. The European Court has been accused of 'mission creep', by expanding its jurisdiction beyond that contemplated by the member states. Its supporters have counter-argued that the Convention is a living instrument which must be constantly re-interpreted to take into account social change; and that sovereignty is not surrendered merely by entering into international commitments. Lord Lester has observed that:

> The political commitment to an enduring system is fragile and uncertain because of constant challenges to the legitimacy of the Human Rights Act. From its birth, powerful sections of the British media have attacked the Human Rights Act on a daily basis, because they oppose its protection of personal privacy against media intrusion on private lives and because they wish the UK to withdraw from the European Convention and the European Union.

The Government established a Commission to look at whether the Human Rights Act should be repealed and a British Bill of Rights created in its place. The Commission published its final report in 2012, entitled *A UK Bill of Rights? The Choice Before Us.* The majority of its members recommended establishing a UK Bill of Rights, because of the 'lack of ownership by the public' of the Human Rights Act 1998 and the European Convention. This problem would be overcome if a home-grown Bill of Rights was produced which would not be entrenched to respect the principle of the sovereignty of Parliament. A minority opposed this recommendation, fearing it could lead to the diminution of rights and be the first step towards withdrawing from the European system altogether.

In its manifesto for the 2015 elections, the Conservative Party pledged to repeal the Human Rights Act and establish a UK Bill of Rights. This Bill of Rights would re-enact the Convention rights but with clarification and more precise definition, in order, for example, to prevent foreign nationals from using human rights to resist deportation. It would remove the UK courts' obligation to 'take account' of decisions of the Strasbourg Court and remove the requirement to interpret domestic legislation compatibly with Convention rights. The new Bill would also require UK courts to strike out 'trivial' rights cases. Judgments of the European Court of Human Rights would be 'advisory', becoming binding only if Parliament agreed to them. The Conservative Party is also considering withdrawing from the European Convention on Human Rights. The only country to withdraw from the Convention to date was Greece in 1970 when it was governed by military colonels who had been found to have tortured political opponents in breach of the European Convention. It rejoined the Convention when democracy was restored to the country. The momentum for withdrawing from the ECHR has slowed down considerably after the decision was made to withdraw from the EU. The Conservative Party has said that it does not want there to be any distractions while negations for Brexit are underway and that withdrawal from the ECHR will firmly be on their 2020 election campaign agenda.

Those in favour of retaining the Human Rights Act argue it has been the victim of a sustained campaign of misinformation. If the Act was repealed the UK would return to its previous position of being a signatory to the Convention, giving individuals merely a right to take cases to the European Court of Human Rights. Individuals in UK courts would have to rely on the new Bill of Rights, rather than being able to rely on the European Convention. The international reputation of the UK as a liberal democracy could be damaged. A complication in trying to 'nationalise' human rights, is that the European Union has now established its Charter of Rights which is based on the Convention. The Charter will not have any effect in the UK when it officially withdraws from the EU. A former Conservative Attorney General considered that it was an incoherent policy to remain a signatory to the European Convention but refuse to recognise the rulings of the court which enforces it. The former Lord Chancellor, Kenneth Clarke, has commented: 'Modern government is big, powerful and bureaucratic. It interferes with every aspect of our lives. We need the ECHR more now than we did when it was created.'

Due to opposition by some Conservative Members of Parliament, these reforms were not included in the first Parliamentary session under the new Conservative Government because of concerns it would be difficult to get these changes passed in Parliament. Instead the Government has simply stated it will 'bring forward proposals for a British Bill of Rights'.

The European Court of Human Rights and the CJEU

The European Court of Human Rights in Strasbourg is often confused with the Court of Justice of the European Union (CJEU) in Luxembourg, but these are quite separate institutions, as are the Commission of Human Rights and the Commission of the European Union. The phrase 'taking your case to Europe' tends to be used broadly, but the process and grounds for bringing an action to the CJEU are quite distinct from those for the European Court of Human Rights.

There are, however, growing links between the ECHR and European Union law. Article 164 of the Treaty of Rome provides that one of the functions of the CJEU is to ensure observance of the general principles of law contained in that treaty. In recent cases the CJEU has suggested that respect for human rights is one of these principles, and that for guidance in understanding the scope of this principle they can look to the Convention. For example, in **P v S and Cornwall County Council** (1996) P was dismissed from her employment because she was a transsexual. Her application to the UK courts for sex discrimination was rejected. When the case was heard by the CJEU the Court referred to the European Court of Human Rights' judgment in **Re Rees** (1986). It concluded that the European Equal Treatment Directive had been breached, as this directive encapsulated the fundamental principle of equality.

The European Charter of Fundamental Rights

The European Union looks set to become more involved in the protection of human rights within Europe. Article 6 of the Lisbon Treaty came into force in 2009 and recognises the rights and freedoms set out in the European Charter of Fundamental Rights. Thus the treaty provides for the incorporation of the Charter into EU law. It also states that the fundamental rights guaranteed by the European Convention on Human Rights 'constitute general principles of the Union's law'.

Where the Charter lays down rights contained in the European Convention, these rights will be interpreted in accordance with the Convention right, even if the Charter is worded slightly differently. Thus, Art. 53(2) of the Charter states:

> so far as this Charter contains rights which correspond to rights guaranteed by the [Convention], the meaning and scope of those rights shall be the same as those laid down by the said Convention.

The Charter lays down more extensive rights than those contained in the European Convention because, as well as containing civil and political rights, it lays down social and economic rights, such as freedom of information, freedom of the arts and sciences and rights for children and the elderly. The Charter also extends some of the existing Convention rights to a more modern context. Thus it includes the established right to life and prohibition of torture, but also prohibits more modern problems of human trafficking, forced labour, human cloning and the sale of body parts. The rights in the Charter are divided into six sections:

- Dignity
- Freedoms
- Equality
- Solidarity
- Citizens' rights
- Justice.

In the section on 'justice' it explicitly requires criminal sentences to be proportionate to the offence and lays down a right not to be tried twice for the same offence (known as the double jeopardy rule). The section entitled 'solidarity' deals with workers' rights, including a right to consultation, protection from unjustified dismissals, fair and just working conditions, parental leave and, most importantly, the right to strike (a right which has never been recognised in this country).

The Charter applies to the acts of EU institutions and member states when implementing EU law (Art. 51 of the Charter). It is not clear whether the Charter can be relied on between private citizens (horizontal effect) or whether it can only be relied on against member states and EU institutions.

McB *v* **E** (2011) is the first case in which the European Court looks at the impact of the Charter. It noted that 'it is called upon to interpret, in the light of the Charter, the law of the European Union within the limits of the powers conferred on it'. So the Charter would only be looked at for the purposes of interpreting the European Regulation that was relevant to the case, and would not be used to assess the national law as such. On the facts of the case, the Charter did not actually affect the Court's interpretation of the Regulation. In the subsequent case of **Volker und Markus Schecke** *v* **Land Hessen** (2012) the European Court used the Charter to strike down a piece of EU legislation.

The UK has obtained a legally binding protocol, which states that no court can rule that UK laws or practices are inconsistent with the principles laid down in the Charter and the Charter will not therefore create new legal rights in the UK.

The European Union has established a Fundamental Rights Agency. There has been some criticism of this organisation on the basis that the new agency might simply duplicate much of the work being done by existing bodies, particularly the European Court of Human Rights. However, with the current backlash to terrorist activity, greater involvement of the EU in the protection of human rights might be desirable.

Today's debates

Responding to the threat of terrorism

If one person extends their rights, it tends to be at the expense of another person's rights. For example, when a newspaper exercises its right to freedom of expression, this will frequently be to the detriment of another person's right to privacy. Thus careful controls need to be in place to make sure that one person or organisation does not extend their rights too far at the expense of another. This is particularly the case where a Government is seeking to extend its rights over its citizens. In recent years there has been particular concern that in its fight against terrorism the Government has not been respecting human rights. After the bombing of the public transport system in London in July 2005, Tony Blair stated that the 'rules of the game have changed' and outlined some of his ideas for amending the law in the UK to tackle this threat to our society. At the same time, civil liberties organisations are concerned that the Government might respond to these attacks in a way that amounted to a significant attack on an individual's human rights, while at the same time proving to be counter-productive in the fight against terrorism. In 2008, the Labour Government was forced to drop its provision in the Counter-Terrorism Bill to allow the detention of suspected terrorists for 42 days without charge, but the judges will still be placed in a very sensitive position when interpreting this piece of legislation.

Following the 11 September 2001 attacks on the United States, there was international concern about terrorism. This led the UK Government to pass the Anti-Terrorism, Crime and Security Act 2001, which allowed it to detain in prison suspected terrorists without trial. This was in breach of their right to freedom of movement which is guaranteed under Art. 5 of the European Convention. The UK Government therefore gained permission from the European Council to not comply with this article on the basis that there was a national emergency under Art. 15.

Under this legislation, nine foreign nationals were certified as suspected terrorists and detained without trial. The legality of the detention was challenged through the courts in **A and X and others** *v* **Secretary of State for the Home Department** (2004). Some of the applicants had been detained in a high security prison for three years, with no prospect of release or a trial. Because the case was so important, nine judges in the House of Lords heard the case instead of the usual five. The House held that the detentions were unlawful. It accepted that there was a national emergency justifying derogation under Art. 15, but the measures taken were not strictly required. Indefinite detention without trial was not strictly required because it was being imposed only on foreign nationals unable to leave Britain and not on foreign nationals who could leave for another country or on British nationals. The legislation also therefore discriminated against foreign nationals and so breached Art. 14 of the Convention.

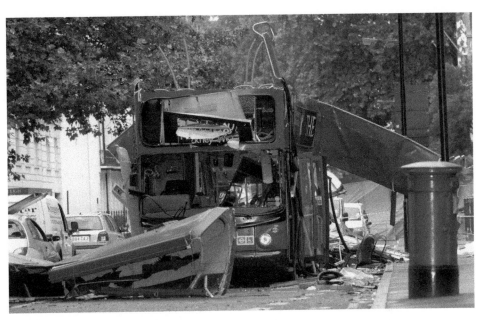

Photo 10.2 Bus bombed in London on 7 July 2005
Source: © Eddie Mulholland/Rex Features

As a result, the legislation was repealed and replaced by the Prevention of Terrorism Act 2005. This established control orders (sometimes called 'gag and tag orders'), which can potentially amount to house arrest – the first time we have seen this measure in the UK. The people who had been detained without trial were released and were allowed to return home, but they were placed under control orders (not amounting to house arrest). Up to 16 different restrictions can be placed on an individual who is subjected to a control order, such as the use of electronic tagging, surveillance, permission to search their premises and a curfew. The order is usually made by the High Court following an application by the Home Secretary. It will be imposed where the individuals are suspected of having been involved in terrorism-related activity but it is thought that, due to the sensitivity surrounding Security Service involvement, evidence demonstrating suspicions against the person, and the high standard of proof required in criminal trials, a criminal conviction cannot be obtained. Breach of a control order without reasonable excuse is a criminal offence punishable by up to five years' imprisonment.

In **Secretary of State for the Home Department** *v* **JJ** (2007) control orders had been imposed on six suspects, under which they were electronically tagged, required to remain at home for 18 hours a day and have all visitors vetted by the Home Office. The House of Lords concluded that these orders amounted to a deprivation of liberty in breach of Art. 5 of the Convention. As a result of this decision, the Home Office has amended the restrictions imposed on the complainants under the control orders and they are currently subjected to a 16-hour curfew.

In **Secretary of State for the Home Department** *v* **MB** (2007), the High Court described control orders as an 'affront to justice'. MB is a British Muslim who was arrested when trying to leave the country in March 2005. The judge concluded that he could not quash the order due to the 'one-sided information' available to the court. However, he criticised the control orders for allowing a suspect's rights to be determined by 'executive decision-making, untrammelled by any prospect of effective judicial supervision'.

> To say that the [Prevention of Terrorism] Act does not give the respondent in the case . . . a 'fair hearing' . . . would be an understatement. The court would be failing in its duty under the Human Rights Act, a duty imposed upon the court by Parliament, if it did not say, loud and clear that the procedure under the Act whereby the court merely reviews the lawfulness of the Secretary of State's decision to make the order upon the basis of the material available to him at the early stage is conspicuously unfair.

An appeal against the High Court decision was subsequently successful before the Court of Appeal, which held that the control order procedures did not breach a right to a fair trial under Art. 6 of the Convention. MB appealed to the House of Lords, which held that a control order review hearing would only be fair if the Home Office disclosed the allegation against the individual along with enough information for the person to have sufficient knowledge of the case against them to be able to contest the allegation. The House sent the case back to the High Court to consider whether the control order was fair in the light of this ruling. Forty-eight control orders had been issued by 2011, with eight people remaining under a control order in that year and seven people who were placed under a control order having disappeared altogether.

In 2006, Lord Carlile, the Government's independent terrorism watchdog, issued his first annual review of the Prevention of Terrorism Act 2005. With access to secret security service papers, he made clear that '[t]he nature of the activities is sufficiently alarming for me to re-emphasise . . . the real and present danger of shocking terrorism acts involving suicide bombers'. He considered that further suicide bombings in the UK must be expected and that in his view such an ongoing threat meant that 'as a last resort (only), in my view the control order system as operated currently in its non-derogating form is a justifiable and proportionate safety valve for the proper protection of civil society'.

The coalition Government set up a review to look at the impact of anti-terrorist legislation on civil liberties. The review published its final report in 2011: *Review of Counter-Terrorism and Security Powers*. In light of the review's recommendations, the coalition Government abolished control orders and replaced them with terrorism prevention and investigation measures (TPIMs). These new measures are contained in the Terrorism Prevention and Investigation Measures Act 2011. They look very similar to control orders, but suspects under these measures are allowed to leave home for longer periods; they can only be required to stay at home at night for 8 hours (instead of 16 hours); they can no longer be asked to move to another part of the country away from their family and friends; and internet and phone use can be restricted but not banned altogether. The similarities with control orders has led to the suggestion that this reform amounts to little more than rebranding.

The former Labour Government planned to introduce compulsory identity cards into the UK and the Identity Cards Act 2006 was passed by Parliament. The justification for ID cards is that they would help to fight terrorism, organised crime, illegal immigration, identity fraud and benefit fraud. On the other hand, ID cards can be a dangerous tool for controlling a population and their absence in this country has to date been seen as a sign of our freedom. The coalition Government scrapped the identity cards scheme by passing the Identity Documents Act 2010, after deciding that the arguments against identity cards outweighed their perceived benefits.

The right to privacy

Another very different area that has given rise to considerable debate is whether the European Convention protects the right to privacy of celebrities. While the courts are recognising that the Convention does provide a right to privacy they are anxious to balance this against the right to freedom of expression. In April 2005, the celebrities Victoria and David Beckham tried to prevent the publication by the *News of the World* of revelations by their former nanny about their private lives. The court allowed the newspaper to publish, pointing to the public interest in the publication of the stories, despite the fact that the story was merely trivial information primarily about the state of their marriage and Victoria's cosmetic surgery.

The courts are prepared to recognise that the European Convention protects the right to privacy and has sought to seek a balance between this right and the right to freedom of expression. This has caused particular tensions where newspapers have wanted to publish details of celebrities' sex lives and the celebrities have sought to prevent publication. The approach that the court seems to be taking is that there needs to be a public interest in details being published. The very well-publicised controversy of topless photos of the Duchess of Cambridge, Kate Middleton, being published by the magazine *Closer* in France ended in the magazine having to pay out significant sums to the Duke and Duchess of Cambridge. The pair were holidaying in a private chateau owned by the Queen's nephew, Viscount Linley, and the waiting paparazzi used long lens cameras to be able to take intrusive photos of the couple. Prince William has remarked that this intrusion of privacy is particularly shocking because it reminded him of the harassment that led to the death of his mother, Diana, Princess of Wales. The case was heard in France and the court held that the taking of such photos was an unjustified intrusion of the couple's privacy. Some critics have argued, however, that knowing all about the royals and the strength of their marriage, is in fact in the public interest.

The approach of the courts has been that there is no public interest in the public knowing details of, for example, a footballer's extra-marital affairs. **CTB** *v* **News Group Newspapers Ltd** (2011) concerned a case brought against a newspaper company which was seeking to publish a story about an affair between the *Big Brother* TV programme contestant, Imogen Thomas, and a footballer (who was named by an MP in Parliament). The High Court stated that in determining whether to allow publication the court had to consider whether publication would contribute to a debate of general interest – for instance, whether it would help achieve a social purpose, such as the prevention or detection of crime or whether it would in some way prevent the public from being seriously misled. On the facts of the case, the High Court concluded that no public interest would be served by allowing publication.

TOPICAL ISSUE

Your rights in school and university

Young people are actually quite vulnerable members of our society and it is important that they realise they benefit from human rights as well as adults. The Equality Act 2006 gives children the right not to be discriminated against, Art. 9 of the European Convention protects the rights to freedom of religion and Art. 2 of Protocol 1 to the Convention protects the right to education.

▶

English schools often require pupils to wear a school uniform. They also frequently lay down rules about how the children should wear their hair, known as a 'hair policy'. The schools have to be careful that in setting the rules about uniform and hair that they respect the rights of all the children in the school. Discrimination can take different forms: it can be direct (for example, banning black children from a school) or indirect (where there may be no racist intent, but a rule has a greater impact on black children). In **SG** v **St Gregory's Catholic Science College** (2011) a school's hair policy banned boys from having cornrows (traditional plaits). The High Court ruled that this ban was illegal because it indirectly discriminated against black boys. While the policy theoretically applied to all children in the school, in practice black boys were being treated differently from white boys because the policy had a greater impact on them, as their cultural traditions included wearing plaits. The legal principle in this case will equally apply to an afro and neatly shaved black hair. A boys' school cannot, therefore, have a policy stating all hair must be between 1 and 3 cm long, because this amounts to indirect discrimination. Instead, schools have moved to having hair policies that simply require a boy's hair to be cut above the collar. Some people might argue that a hairstyle is a very trivial issue and the courts should not waste their time on this. But actually this is a very important issue because racism stems from a person looking physically different from the majority: black children do not just have a different skin colour but they also often have different hair. A British multicultural society celebrates these differences, it does not try to repress them.

In **R (on the application of Shabina Begum)** v **Headteacher and Governors of Denbigh High School** (2006) a Muslim schoolgirl, Shabina Begum, wanted to wear a jilbab (a full-length gown) to school instead of the agreed school uniform, because of her religious beliefs. In 2002, she had arrived at school wearing a jilbab, but she was told to go home and change. Because of her continued refusal to wear a school uniform, she was excluded from school for two years. Pupils at the school were allowed to wear a shalwar kameez (trousers and tunic) but not a jilbab. The House of Lords concluded that the school's conduct did not amount to a breach of her right to freedom of religion or right to education. She had not attended school for two years, but her school was entitled to exclude her while she refused to comply with the uniform and she could have attended another local school where the jilbab was allowed. But this case is not

Photo 10.3 *Source*: © Yuri Arcurs/Shutterstock.com (l); © Ivonne Wiernek/Shutterstock.com (c); © Sophie Bluy/Pearson Education Ltd (r)

necessarily the final word on this issue. In **Eweida v UK** (2013) the ECtHR accepted that simply because a person could go elsewhere did not in itself prevent there being a breach of a human right. Instead, the possibility of going elsewhere would be one factor that could be taken into account when deciding whether the restriction was proportionate.

In **Ali v Head Teacher and Governors of Lord Grey School** (2006) the House of Lords held a pupil's exclusion from school for eight months did not amount to a breach of his right to education. Following the exclusion, the 13-year-old pupil had access to educational facilities outside the school (including homework and tuition in a pupil referral unit) and failed to attend a meeting to re-integrate him back into the school. Schools can insist on compliance with rules: as long as alternative educational facilities are made available to excluded pupils, their Convention rights have not been breached. The House of Lords said that the right to education would only be breached in extreme cases, where virtually no education had been provided.

The process of excluding a pupil from school does not amount to criminal proceedings, so Art. 6 does not apply guaranteeing the right to a fair hearing. In **R (on the application of LG) v Independent Appeal Panel for Tom Hood School** (2010), a boy had been excluded from school because he had threatened a teacher with a knife. Article 6 did not apply because this was a disciplinary case, not a criminal case.

Answering questions

1 Critically evaluate the impact of the Human Rights Act 1998 upon the English legal system.

A strong answer would explain the position prior to the introduction of the Convention into UK law by the Human Rights Act 1998, emphasising the lack of directly enforceable rights in the UK and the need to proceed to the ECtHR to enforce Convention rights. Changes in domestic law following a successful application to the ECtHR were not inevitable and there are several cases where such a change was not effected – see, for example, **Brogan v UK** and **Abdulaziz v UK**.

This historical discussion could be followed by a description of the principal rights contained in the European Convention. It should be mentioned that the Convention itself contains some restrictions on the rights it protects.

You could discuss how the Convention has been implemented into the UK by the Human Rights Act 1998, and in particular the requirement of a statement of compatibility when legislation is introduced and the means by which an individual can assert rights under the Convention in the national courts.

Finally, you could point out that the 1998 Act has increased the power of the judiciary to protect human rights, but the Act does not enjoy an enhanced status and so could, at least in theory, be repealed by Parliament.

2 **What has been the effect of s. 2 of the Human Rights Act 1998 on the exercise of precedent by UK judges?**

You need to begin by explaining what precedent is and what it means (refer back to Chapter 1). Then briefly explain the relevant background to the Human Rights Act 1998, in particular that, although the European Convention on Human Rights was ratified by the UK in 1951, it did not become part of UK law until it was incorporated therein by the 1998 Act. The Act does, however, have the status of any other piece of domestic legislation in the sense that it is not entrenched.

You should set out the provisions of s. 2 and its effect. Sections 3 and 4 are also relevant (p. 156). You could also compare the obligation under s. 2 to s. 3 of the European Communities Act 1972, noting that the latter gives the judges less power. As judges are building up a familiarity with loosely drafted European legislation, it can be argued that they are adopting a more purposive approach to interpretation in general (see Chapter 3).

To conclude, you could say that, contrary to fears, the Human Rights Act has not led to an excess of speculative human rights claims and that it has succeeded in creating a stronger human rights culture in the courts (p. 159). However, judges are likely to encounter problems in deciding how to implement, for example, new terrorist legislation which restricts human rights (see the section entitled 'Today's debates' on p. 172).

3 **To what extent would a Bill of Rights provide additional protection of human rights in the United Kingdom?**

While the Human Rights Act 1998 applies the European Convention on Human Rights in the UK, those provisions are not entrenched. A Bill of Rights would entrench human rights into national law and empower the courts to refuse to apply legislation inconsistent with the entrenched rights. It would thereby provide some additional protection against a strong executive with a large parliamentary majority. However, such a step would effect a significant shift of power from an elected Parliament to an unelected judiciary. Moreover, a Bill of Rights is usually expressed in wide terms that may not provide sufficient certainty, and give the judges too much discretion as to how to interpret it. Rights are meaningless without an effective means of enforcement, and a Bill of Rights without a pro-liberty judiciary would offer only nominal protection.

Summary of Chapter 10: Introduction to human rights

Introduction
Most democratic countries have a written Bill of Rights. Britain is unusual among democratic countries in having, to date, neither a Bill of Rights nor a written constitution. In this country, our rights and freedoms are traditionally considered to be protected by a presumption that we are free to do whatever is not specifically forbidden either by legislation or by the common law. A significant change in the British position was made by the Human Rights Act 1998, which makes the European Convention on Human Rights (ECHR) part of the law of the UK.

The European Convention on Human Rights
The ECHR was drawn up by the Council of Europe, which was established after the Second World War. A special court, known as the European Court of Human Rights, was set up to deal with claims concerning breaches of the ECHR.

The Human Rights Act 1998

The Convention is now applicable directly in the UK courts under s. 7 of the Human Rights Act. Under s. 2 of the Act, the domestic judiciary 'must take into account' any relevant Strasbourg jurisprudence, although they are not bound by it. The UK courts are required to interpret all legislation in a way which is compatible with Convention rights 'so far as it is possible to do so' (s. 3). It is unlawful for public authorities to act in a way which is incompatible with Convention rights (s. 6).

Retrospective effect?

Following the case of **Wilson v Secretary of State for Trade and Industry** (2003) some provisions of the Human Rights Act 1998 could have retrospective effect if that would not be unfair to the parties in a particular case.

The scope of the Convention

The rights protected by the ECHR include the right to life (Art. 2); freedom from torture, inhuman or degrading treatment (Art. 3); freedom from slavery or forced labour (Art. 4); the right to liberty and security of the person (Art. 5); the right to a fair trial (Art. 6); the prohibition of retrospective criminal laws (Art. 7); the right to respect for a person's private and family life, home and correspondence (Art. 8); freedom of thought, conscience and religion (Art. 9); freedom of expression (Art. 10); freedom of peaceful assembly and association, including the right to join a trade union (Art. 11); and the right to marry and have a family (Art. 12).

A Bill of Rights for the UK?

It has been observed that the ECHR does not constitute a Bill of Rights for the UK because it has not been entrenched. Many people feel that while the Human Rights Act 1998 is a first step in the right direction, ultimately the UK needs a properly entrenched Bill of Rights to protect its citizens. Among developed Western countries, Israel and the UK are the only ones without such a Bill.

Reform

The European Union is becoming more involved in the protection of human rights within Europe.

Reading list

Clayton, R. (2015) The empire strikes back: common law rights and the Human Rights Act [2015]. *Public Law*, 3.

Department for Trade and Industry (2004) *Fairness for All: A New Commission for Equality and Human Rights*, Cm 6185. London: Stationery Office.

Griffith, J.A.G. (1997) *The Politics of the Judiciary*. London: Fontana.

Hoffmann, Lord (2009) The universality of human rights. *Law Quarterly Review*, 125: 416.

Laws, J. (1998) The limitations of human rights. *Public Law*, 254.

Raine, J. and Walker, C. (2002) *The Impact on the Courts and the Administration of Justice of the Human Rights Act 1998*. London: Lord Chancellor's Department, Research Secretariat.

Tickell, A. (2015) More 'efficient' justice at the European Court of Human Rights: but at whose expense? *Public Law*, 206.

Wright, J. (2009) Interpreting section 2 of the Human Rights Act 1998: towards an indigenous jurisprudence of human rights. *Public Law*, 595.

On the internet

www   The Human Rights Act 1998 is available on the legislation.gov.uk website at:
www.legislation.gov.uk/ukpga/1998/42/contents

The website of the European Court of Human Rights is:
http://www.echr.coe.int

The Ministry of Justice report *Responding to Human Rights judgments* (2016) is available at:
https://www.gov.uk/government/uploads/system/uploads/attachment_data/file/570754/responding-to-human-rights-judgments-2014-to-2016-print.pdf

The *Review of Counter-Terrorism and Security Powers* (2011) has been published on the Home Office website at:
http://www.homeoffice.gov.uk/publications/counter-terrorism/review-of-ct-security-powers/report-by-lord-mcdonald?view=Binary

The report of the Commission on a Bill of Rights entitled *A UK Bill of Rights? The Choice Before Us* (2012) is available at:
http://webarchive.nationalarchives.gov.uk/20130206065653/https://www.justice.gov.uk/downloads/about/cbr/uk-bill-rights-vol-1.pdf

A useful source of information on human rights in England is:
http://www.direct.gov.uk/en/Governmentcitizensandrights/index.htm

The European Court of Human Rights' Annual Report 2016 can be found at:
http://www.echr.coe.int/Documents/Annual_report_2016_ENG.pdf

11

Remedies for infringement of human rights

This chapter discusses the different remedies available when a person's human rights have been breached, including:

- judicial review;
- *habeas corpus*;
- civil proceedings;
- compensation paid by the state;
- criminal proceedings;
- the Criminal Injuries Compensation Scheme;
- the European Court of Human Rights;
- disciplinary proceedings against the police;
- the exclusion of evidence from the criminal courts;
- the right to use force in self-defence; and
- parliamentary controls.

Introduction

Rights are only worthwhile if there are adequate remedies for their enforcement. The fact that we do not yet have a Bill of Rights, but only a collection of laws detailing what we may not do, has inevitably meant that remedies are similarly scattered. Some of the main remedies available in English law for unlawful infringement of basic rights are the subject of this section.

Judicial review

Where a public body – such as a local authority, the police, or a Government department – acts illegally, the result will often be an infringement of an individual's rights, and in some cases the remedy for this is a procedure known as judicial review.

Habeas corpus

Personal liberty is regarded as the most fundamental of all freedoms, and where individuals are wrongfully deprived of their liberty, the fact that, on release, they can sue their captor for damages under the ordinary civil law is not regarded as sufficient. *Habeas corpus* is an ancient remedy which allows a person detained to challenge the legality of detention and, if successful, get themselves quickly released. It does not punish the person responsible for the detention, but once the detainee is set free, they can still pursue any other available remedies for compensation or punishment.

Habeas corpus may be sought by, among others, convicted prisoners; those detained in custody pending trial or held by the police during criminal investigations; those awaiting extradition; psychiatric patients; and those with excessive bail conditions imposed on them. Application is made to the Divisional Court, and takes priority over all other court business.

Civil action for negligence

Where a public body breaches a person's rights in such a way as to amount to a tort, that body may be sued in the same way as a private citizen would be; since the Crown Proceedings Act 1947, this includes the Crown.

As far as civil rights are concerned, this remedy is of particular importance in relation to illegal behaviour by the police: possible actions include assault, malicious prosecution, false imprisonment, wrongful arrest and trespass to property or goods. Exemplary damages may be awarded against the police even where there has been no oppressive behaviour or other aggravating circumstances. These cases are usually heard by a jury.

In the past the police have benefited from an effective immunity from liability for negligence in their investigations. This immunity stems from the case of **Hill** *v* **Chief Constable of West Yorkshire** (1989). The case looked at whether the police owed a duty of care to a victim of Peter Sutcliffe, known as the Yorkshire Ripper. The House of Lords ruled that public policy prevented any action for negligence lying in respect of police strategies for the investigation and prevention of crime.

In **Osman** *v* **UK** (1998) the European Court of Human Rights threw into doubt the future of this immunity. In that case, a teacher had developed a fixation with a 14-year-old boy at his school. He gave him money, took photographs of him and sometimes followed him home. Graffiti of a sexual nature appeared in the neighbourhood and the parents' house and car suffered criminal damage but the teacher denied any involvement. The teacher changed his name by deed poll to include the boy's name. He was suspended from his position as a teacher and he indicated that he was thinking of 'doing a Hungerford' by which it was assumed he meant he might use firearms to kill the deputy headmaster and other victims at random. In December 1987, the police sought to interview the man in connection with allegations of criminal damage but he had disappeared. Two months later he went to the boy's home, shot and wounded him and killed his father. He also went to the home of the deputy headmaster and shot and wounded him and killed his son. He was convicted of manslaughter and placed in a psychiatric hospital.

The pupil with whom he had had an obsession and the mother brought a civil action against the Metropolitan Police for negligence. They claimed that the police had been negligent in not apprehending the man before the incident that led to the killing. Relying on **Hill** *v* **Chief Constable of West Yorkshire** the Court of Appeal upheld a ruling to strike out the case as disclosing no cause of action. The Court of Appeal treated that case as laying down a watertight defence. It was contended before the European Court of Human Rights that the rule of public policy preventing the action for negligence breached the European Convention on Human Rights. The European Court ruled that Art. 6 of the Convention, which guarantees the right to a fair trial, had been violated. It considered that the exclusionary rule formulated in the **Hill** case should not be used as a blanket immunity, but that the existence of competing public policy issues had to be considered. The approach of the Court of Appeal had amounted to an unjustifiable restriction on the right of access to a court to have a claim determined on its merits.

In **Brooks** *v* **Metropolitan Police Commissioner** (2005) the House of Lords clarified that **Hill** was laying down a rule of substantive law (that the police did not owe a duty of care on the facts), rather than a rule of procedure (which is associated with an 'immunity' from proceedings). The right to a fair trial in Art. 6 is restricted to rules of procedure and should not interfere with the substantive law in a country. In **Z** *v* **UK** (2001) the European Court acknowledged it had not fully understood the English law as laid down in **Hill** because it had thought it was laying down a procedural immunity that was covered by Art. 6.

The policy aims which underlie the decision in **Hill** are that the police should make their operational decisions on the basis of what is best to provide protection to the community at large. But the absolute rule that the House of Lords seemed to have laid down in **Hill** has been subject to some modest backtracking by the courts in subsequent years. In **Brooks** the House of Lords did accept that the court in **Hill** may have overstated the position to some degree. There was one circumstance in which the police may have a duty to individuals in relation to their role in the investigation and suppression of crime and that was where there was an assumption of responsibility by the police to that individual. In addition, even where no negligence liability may be imposed, the courts may be prepared to impose liability on the basis that there has been a separate breach of the European Convention following the Human Rights Act 1998.

The Human Rights Act 1998

Claimants may be entitled to compensation for breach of the European Convention under the Human Rights Act 1998. For example, a woman may be the victim of domestic abuse over a number of years to the knowledge of the police. If she rings the police telling them she is about to be stabbed by her partner and the police do not respond appropriately and she is killed, then her family may be entitled to compensation for breach of her right to life under Art. 2 of the European Convention. On the basis of the leading case of **Osman** *v* **UK,** Art. 2 applies where the authorities knew or ought to have known of the existence of a 'real and immediate risk to the life of an identified individual . . . from the criminal acts of a third party'.

The number of actions against the London Metropolitan Police has risen considerably over the years, reaching 5,836 in 2017. In 1995/96, £2,014,000 was paid out in damages and settlements; 1996 saw a number of very high awards of damages in civil actions by the courts of first instance. For example, in **Goswell** *v* **Commissioner of Police for the Metropolis** (1998) Mr Goswell was waiting in his car for his girlfriend when PC Trigg approached. Mr Goswell complained about the police failure to investigate an arson attack on his home. He was handcuffed to another officer, struck by PC Trigg (causing injuries which required stitches and left a permanent scar) and then arrested for assault and threatening behaviour. His prosecution for these charges failed and when he brought a civil action he was awarded £120,000 damages for assault, £12,000 for false imprisonment and £170,000 exemplary damages for arbitrary and oppressive behaviour.

Appeals were lodged against the more substantial payments in damages and they were reduced by the Court of Appeal to £47,600. Strict guidelines were laid down for future allocations of damages by a jury, including figures as a starting point in their deliberations for different types of cases. For example, basic damages for false imprisonment should be between £500 for one hour and £3,000 for 24 hours with an upper limit of £50,000 on exemplary damages. Their Lordships claimed to be at pains to establish a proper balance between the need to add teeth to the damages paid by the defendant and the fact that this money has to be drawn from public funds. Lawyers have taken issue with the likely impact of a £50,000 award on an institution with an annual budget in excess of £3 billion.

Compensation

Compensation should be paid to a person whose conviction has been reversed or whom has been pardoned on the grounds that 'a new or newly discovered fact shows beyond reasonable doubt that there has been a miscarriage of justice' (s. 133 of the Criminal Justice Act 1988). There has been a miscarriage of justice 'if and only if the new or newly discovered fact shows beyond reasonable doubt that the person did not commit the offence'.

The sums awarded were reduced in 2006 and the maximum payable is now £1 million. Controversially, when calculating the award, the House of Lords confirmed in **R (on the application of O'Brien)** *v* **Independent Assessor** (2007) that deductions can be made to take into account the fact that the claimant did not have to pay for food and lodging while in prison, and previous criminal convictions and conduct leading to their wrongful imprisonment. Under the Criminal Justice and Immigration Act 2008, deductions can be made from an award of compensation to take into account the claimant's conduct that contributed to their wrongful conviction and any previous convictions.

In the past, discretionary payments could also be awarded by the Home Secretary where there had been gross misconduct that fell outside the statutory scheme. This discretionary scheme was abolished in 2006, on the pretext that the money should be spent on the victims of crime, ignoring the fact that people who have been wrongly held in prison are themselves victims.

Criminal proceedings

Criminal proceedings may be brought for false imprisonment or assault, if necessary by means of a private prosecution. In 2003, 195 police officers were convicted of a criminal offence; of these, 61 were for non-traffic offences. Sadly, not one police officer accused of malpractice arising from the many high-profile miscarriages of justice put right by the Court of Appeal since 1989 has been convicted of a criminal offence.

TOPICAL ISSUE

The shooting of Jean Charles de Menezes

Following the fatal shooting by a police officer of Jean Charles de Menezes, who was mistaken for a suicide bomber, the Metropolitan Police was found guilty of breaching Health and Safety Rules and fined £175,000. Section 3 of the Health and Safety at Work etc. Act 1974 provides that it is:

the duty of every employer to conduct his undertaking in such a way as to ensure, so far as reasonably practicable, that persons not in his employment who may be affected are not thereby exposed to risks to their health and safety.

Members of the de Menezes family would have preferred to have seen a prosecution for a homicide offence, but this would have been unlikely to succeed. No individuals were prosecuted for the death and no disciplinary proceedings were brought against those involved in the surveillance and shooting. At the inquest into Jean Charles's death, the coroner controversially instructed the jury that they could not find that the death was an unlawful killing.

Criminal Injuries Compensation Scheme

The Criminal Injuries Compensation Scheme (CICS) aims to compensate innocent victims of violent crime. Compensation is awarded by the Criminal Injuries Compensation Authority according to a tariff system. The CICS currently pays £170 million each year in compensation to about 40,000 victims, which is more than all the other equivalent schemes in Europe put together. Two-thirds of the awards are for less than £3,000. The maximum that can be awarded is £500,000. The award seeks to provide financial assistance while at the same time showing solidarity for the victim from the community.

These arrangements for compensation were subject to some criticism following the 7 July 2005 bombing in Central London. Many of the victims of the bombing had to wait a considerable amount of time before receiving any compensation and when they did receive compensation this was considered inadequate for those who had been more seriously injured. Where a person was killed, their families were only eligible for £11,000 compared to the £1.13 million paid to the victims of the 9/11 bombing in America.

Proposals for reforming the scheme have been published in a consultation paper, *Rebuilding Lives, Supporting Victims of Crime* (2005). One of the proposals in the consultation paper is that if an employee is assaulted while at work, and sustains injury, it should be the employer rather than the state that compensates the victim. The paper considers removing the maximum limit for compensation awards to allow very serious cases to receive adequate financial support, while giving no financial compensation for minor injuries, about two-thirds of cases. Instead, such victims would receive more practical and emotional help (such as professional counselling and help with insurance claims). But for victims the crime is always serious and a denial of compensation on the basis that the injury was not serious will be adding insult to injury. One benefit of the proposed arrangements is that those people with more serious injuries should receive compensation more swiftly.

The Independent Police Complaints Commission

In the past, complaints against the police could be made to the Police Complaints Authority. Following persistent criticism of this organisation both by the public and the police, the Police Reform Act 2002 abolished this body and replaced it with the Independent Police Complaints Commission (IPCC). It was hoped this body would be more accessible, open and independent than its predecessor.

The primary responsibility for recording complaints against the police and civilian staff remains with the police. Certain complaints can be handled informally (called 'local resolution'). There are three situations in which a complaint must be referred to the Commission. These are where:

- the conduct complained of is alleged to have resulted in death or serious injury;
- the complainant falls into a specified category of people; or
- the Commission requires the complaint to be referred to it.

There is a discretion to refer a complaint to the Commission due to the gravity of the subject matter, or exceptional circumstances. These provisions have been criticised as too narrow, as, for example, complaints of assault, corruption and racism will not automatically be referred to the Commission.

The Commission has the power to determine, according to the seriousness of the case and the public interest, the form the investigation should take. There are four options:

- a police investigation on behalf of the appropriate authority;
- a police investigation supervised by the Commission;
- a police investigation managed by the Commission; or
- an investigation by the Commission, independent of the police.

Investigations by the Commission are carried out for the most serious complaints. The investigators have the same powers as the police. The most high-profile case to be the subject of such an investigation is the fatal shooting in 2005 by a police officer of Jean Charles de Menezes, who was mistaken for a suicide bomber at Stockwell tube station. Initially, the Metropolitan Police were reluctant to allow an independent investigation to take place and there were clear tensions between the police and the Commission during the course of the investigation.

Misconduct by the police can be punished by internal disciplinary procedures. The Home Office report, *Police Complaints and Discipline* (Cotton and Povey, 2004) found that, in 2003, disciplinary misconduct charges were brought against 1,529 police officers and these led to 115 police officers being dismissed or required to resign.

Complainants have a right to appeal against a decision taken concerning the handling of a complaint.

The IPCC has itself been the subject of some criticism, as being ineffective and too close to the police. The Legal Action Group produced a damaging report on the subject in 2007. In 2008 a hundred lawyers refused to continue to work with the organisation because they were concerned the IPCC was not handling complaints effectively. It was criticised by a report of the Home Affairs Select Committee in 2013 for being 'woefully under-equipped' and lacking the investigative resources necessary to get to the truth, which was harming public confidence in the police.

Further reforms to the complaints system have been introduced by the Police Reform and Social Responsibility Act 2011. The police are no longer required to record every complaint they receive. Instead, they have an unfettered discretion to determine which complaints they wish to record. While the aim is to reduce bureaucracy, there is a risk that the complaints system will be undermined.

The admissibility of evidence

Where police officers commit serious infringements of a suspect's rights during the investigation of an offence, the courts may hold that evidence obtained as a result of such misbehaviour is inadmissible in court, the idea being to remove any incentive for the police to break the rules.

Under s. 76(2) of the Police and Criminal Evidence Act 1984 (PACE), confession evidence is inadmissible where it was obtained by oppression or in circumstances likely to render it unreliable and, if the defence alleges that this is the case, the onus is on the prosecution to establish otherwise (s. 76(1)). Oppression is defined as including 'torture, inhuman or degrading treatment, and the use or threat of violence (whether or not amounting to torture)' (s. 76(8)). The definition of 'oppression' was considered in **R** *v* **Fulling** (1987). In that case, the police had persuaded a woman to make a confession by telling her that her lover was being unfaithful. The court held that this did not amount to oppression, and stated that the term should carry its ordinary meaning, that of unjust treatment or cruelty, or the wrongful use of power. Excluding evidence is potentially a powerful safeguard against oppressive treatment by the police, since there is little point in pressurising a suspect to confess if that confession cannot be used to obtain a conviction. However, the extent of this protection is diluted by s. 76(4), which states that, even if a confession is excluded, any facts discovered as a result of it may still be admissible. Parts of an excluded confession may also be allowed if relevant to show that the defendant speaks or writes in a particular way. This means that the police can use oppressive treatment to secure a confession which will help them find other evidence.

Section 78 provides that in any proceedings the court may refuse to admit evidence 'if it appears to the court that, having regard to all the circumstances, including the circumstances in which the evidence was obtained, the admission of the evidence would have such an adverse effect on the fairness of the proceedings that the court ought not to admit it'. This provision covers all types of evidence, not just confessions. It is generally invoked only if the police have committed serious breaches of PACE, such as refusing a suspect access to legal advice over a long period.

The right to exercise self-defence

Any citizen may use reasonable force to prevent unlawful interference with their person or property, or to protect others from such interference. This can affect both civil and criminal liability.

Parliamentary controls

One of the basic functions of Parliament is to act as a watchdog over the rights of citizens, protecting them from undue interference by Government. A number of methods are available, from questions directed to Ministers in Parliament, to committees designed to scrutinise legislation. However, this function has suffered as a result of the strength of party discipline, which means that many MPs appear to put loyalty to their party above loyalty to the citizens they represent. The result is that even measures which clearly restrict fundamental rights can be voted through if the Government has a clear majority.

The Ombudsman

The Parliamentary Commissioner for Administration, known as the Ombudsman, has a role in protecting individual rights.

Answering questions

1 Critically discuss the effectiveness of remedies available to individuals for infringement of human rights by the police.

Note the question is limited to discussing police infringements only. There is a variety of remedies available to individuals whose rights are breached:

- the police force is a public body, so s. 6 of the Human Rights Act 1998 applies and judicial review may be available;
- *habeas corpus* (p. 182);
- civil proceedings (you could discuss **Hill** (1989); **Osman** (1998); and **Z v UK** (2001) here (p. 183));
- criminal proceedings (p. 185);
- disciplinary procedures against the police (p. 187); and
- prevention of disclosure of previous evidence (p. 187).

2 Mary had been convicted in the past of theft and burglary, but had no convictions for violence. One Friday afternoon the police received an urgent telephone call telling them that someone had been stabbed in a car park. Two young women had been seen running away from the car park and the description of one of the women bore similarities to Mary's appearance. Police officer Percy saw Mary walking down the street with her friend Kelly two miles away from the car park. He grabbed hold of Mary's arm and said that she had to empty her pockets so that he could check whether she was carrying a knife. Mary refused to do so and Kelly kicked Percy to help her friend run away, but was unsuccessful and ran off herself. Percy then pushed Mary against a wall and carried out a thorough search of her person. He found that she was carrying nothing suspicious, but told Mary that she had to give her friend's name and address or she would have to go down to the police station. Mary gave him the details and together they went round to Kelly's house. Percy told Mary to pretend she was alone so that Kelly would open the door. When Kelly opened the door, Percy rushed inside and searched the house. He found a number of televisions with their serial numbers rubbed out and seized them all, despite Kelly's claims that she was just a lodger and the televisions were in the homeowner's bedroom and she had no knowledge of them. Mary and Kelly were then taken down to the police station where they were detained for 28 hours. They were only allowed to see a duty solicitor briefly on one occasion and were subjected to lengthy questioning about the stabbing and the televisions. They were finally released without charge when two other women were arrested for the stabbing and Kelly's landlady provided a satisfactory explanation for the presence of the televisions in her bedroom.

Consider whether the police were legally entitled to act as they did and whether Mary and Kelly have any remedies for their ordeal.

Your answer should be divided into two halves, first looking at the police powers and secondly the remedies available. On the first issue of the police powers, Percy may have had reasonable grounds to suspect that he would find offensive weapons or blades on Mary because of the information he had received. Thus, stop and search under s. 1 of PACE may have been justified. However, the search was carried out in breach of Code provisions.

It is unclear whether Mary was placed under arrest at any point before the discovery of the televisions. If she was, the grounds are unclear and it would almost certainly be unlawful. The entry into Kelly's house is unlawful as it was not carried out with Kelly's genuine consent and there are no other grounds to make it lawful (such as to arrest, consequent on arrest or to prevent breach of the peace). Thus, seizure of the televisions is also unlawful. However, the presence of the televisions did give rise to a reasonable suspicion that an offence had been or was being committed (either theft or handling stolen goods) with the involvement of Kelly, and possibly Mary. As a result, Percy could reasonably believe that an arrest at this stage was necessary.

The detention and questioning of Mary and Kelly may have contravened the time limits imposed by the Code of Practice requirements about breaks and refreshments, and the restricted access to the solicitor may contravene the requirements of s. 58.

On the second half of the essay concerning the remedies available, breach of the Code provisions in the carrying out of the search and questioning do not give rise to any rights under civil or criminal law, but can be the subject of a complaint to the Independent Police Complaints Commission. The violations of PACE could give rise to civil actions for unlawful arrest, trespass to premises and false imprisonment. Criminal proceedings in relation to the unlawful detention and excessive use of force could be brought and disciplinary proceedings would be possible.

3 **Explain how people can obtain a remedy when they consider that the state has breached one of their human rights.**

Civil proceedings can be brought for breach of the Human Rights Act 1998 either independently or as part of more traditional civil or administrative court proceedings. The High Court has a number of inherent powers to control abusive state conduct. It can hear judicial review applications and may quash executive decisions that have been wrongly taken. The High Court can also examine the legality of any detention (and order release) through an application of *habeas corpus*.

Civil actions are possible for assault, false imprisonment and trespass. In **Hill v Chief Constable of West Yorkshire** the House of Lords suggested that a police authority effectively enjoyed an immunity from liability for negligence, although **Osman v UK** has now questioned this immunity. Criminal proceedings could be brought against the police, an application could be made to the Criminal Injuries Compensation Scheme, a complaint could be issued to the Independent Police Complaints Commission and disciplinary proceedings could be taken against individual police officers. In addition, a court has the power to hold as inadmissible in criminal proceedings evidence obtained contrary to PACE.

Summary of Chapter 11: Remedies for infringement of human rights

Introduction
Rights are only worthwhile if there are adequate remedies for their enforcement. Some of the main remedies available in English law for unlawful infringement of basic rights are the subject of this chapter.

Judicial review
Where a public body acts illegally a remedy may be available through the procedure of judicial review.

Habeas corpus

Habeas corpus is an ancient remedy which allows people detained to challenge the legality of their detention and, if successful, get themselves quickly released.

Civil action for negligence

Where a public body breaches a person's rights it may be sued in the civil courts.

Compensation

If there has been a miscarriage of justice an award of compensation can be made by the state under s. 133 of the Criminal Justice Act 1988.

The Human Rights Act 1998

Claimants may be entitled to compensation for breach of the European Convention.

Criminal proceedings

Criminal proceedings may be brought for false imprisonment or assault, if necessary by means of a private prosecution.

The Independent Police Complaints Commission

Misconduct by the police can be punished by internal disciplinary procedures. Complaints against the police can be made to the Independent Police Complaints Commission (IPCC).

The admissibility of evidence

Where police officers commit serious infringements of a suspect's rights during the investigation of an offence, the courts may hold that evidence obtained as a result of such misbehaviour is inadmissible in court.

The right to exercise self-defence

Any citizen may use reasonable force to prevent unlawful interference with their person or property, or to protect others from such interference. This can affect both civil and criminal liability.

Parliamentary controls

One of the basic functions of Parliament is to act as a watchdog over the rights of citizens, protecting them from undue interference by Government.

The Ombudsman

The Parliamentary Commissioner for Administration, known as the Ombudsman, has a role in protecting individual rights.

 ## Reading list

Cotton, J. and Povey, D. (2004) *Police Complaints and Discipline*. London: Home Office.

Ormerod, D. (2003) ECHR and the exclusion of evidence: trial remedies for article 8 breaches? *Criminal Law Review*, 61.

Spencer, J. (2010) Compensation for wrongful imprisonment. *Criminal Law Review*, 803.

On the internet

www The consultation paper, *Rebuilding Lives – supporting victims of crime* (2005), looking at the future of the Criminal Injuries Compensation Scheme, is available at:

http://www.official-documents.gov.uk/document/cm67/6705/6705.pdf

The website address of the Independent Police Complaints Commission is:

http://www.ipcc.gov.uk

12

Law and rules

This chapter looks at the distinction between legal rules and other types of rules by examining different academic theories on the subject. In particular it considers:

- the command theory developed by John Austin in the seventeenth century;

- Professor Hart's distinction between primary and secondary rules;

- Professor Dworkin's emphasis on legal principles;

- the natural law theory; and

- the importance that some writers have placed on the function of law.

Introduction

What is law? What do we mean when we say that something is the law? One answer is that a law is a type of rule, but clearly there are many rules which are not law: for example rules of etiquette, school or club rules and moral rules. One way to understand more about what law is, is to look at what distinguishes legal rules from other types of rules.

Austin: the command theory

The nineteenth-century writer John Austin, in his book *The Province of Jurisprudence Determined,* argued that law differed from other rules because it was the command of a sovereign body, which the state could enforce by means of punishment. The relevant sovereign body would vary in different countries; in Britain it was the Queen in Parliament, but in other countries it might be the monarch alone, or an emperor or president.

Austin's definition has fairly clear application to some areas of law, most obviously criminal law, where we are told we must do or not do certain things, with penalties for disobedience. But there are large areas which fall outside it. Contract law, for example, details the sanctions which can be imposed when contracts are broken, but it does not command us to make contracts in the first place. The law concerning marriage does not order anyone to marry; it simply sets out the conditions under which people may do so if they wish, the procedure they should follow to make the marriage legally valid, and the legal consequences of being married. The rules about marriage and contracts could be described as rules giving power, in contrast to the rules imposing duties which comprise criminal law; they have different functions, but both types are legal rules. As Professor Hart and other legal philosophers have pointed out, there are an enormous number of legal rules which neither make commands, nor impose sanctions. The complexity and variety of legal rules make it impossible to cover them all with the proposition that laws are commands.

Hart: primary and secondary rules

In his influential book *The Concept of Law* (1994, first published in 1961), Professor Hart attempted to link types of rules with types of legal systems. He divided legal rules into primary rules and secondary rules, and argued that the existence of secondary rules was a mark of a developed legal system.

Primary rules were described as those which any society needs in order to survive. These rules forbid the most socially destructive forms of behaviour – typically murder, theft and fraud – and also cover areas of civil law, such as tort. According to Hart, simple societies, which generally have a high degree of social cohesion, can survive with only these basic rules but, as a society becomes more complex, it will require what he described as secondary rules.

Secondary rules confer power rather than impose duties, and can be divided into three types: rules of adjudication, rules of change and rules of recognition.

Rules of adjudication

In simple societies, the primary rules can be applied and enforced by means of informal social pressures within the group; this works because the community is close-knit, and individuals rely on each other. As societies become larger and more complex, these bonds are broken, and social pressures will not be enough to shape behaviour. Therefore the community needs some means of giving authority to its rules, and the secondary rules of adjudication are designed to provide this. They enable officials (usually judges) to decide disputes, and to define the procedures to be followed and the sanctions which can be applied when rules are broken. Examples of secondary rules in our society are those which lay down what kind of issues can be decided by courts, who is qualified to be a judge and sentencing legislation for criminal cases; there are many more.

Rules of change

The second type of secondary rule is concerned with making new rules, both primary and secondary. A developed society will need these to respond to new situations – perhaps the clearest example in our society is the huge number of laws introduced over the last century as a result of the invention of motorised transport and the laws introduced to regulate the use of the internet. Rules of change lay down the procedure to be followed in making new rules or changing old ones. In our system, the main rules of change are those concerning how legislation is made and how judicial decisions become part of the common law.

There are also rules of change concerning the power of individuals to produce changes in the legal relationships they have with others.

Rules of recognition

The fact that in simple forms of society rules are enforced by social pressure means that they are only binding if the community as a whole accepts them. Within a small-scale, close-knit community it will generally be obvious to all what the accepted rules are. In a more complex society, this is not the case; there may be many rules, some of them complex, and individuals cannot be expected to know them all. To minimise uncertainty, the developed society, according to Hart, develops rules of recognition, which spell out which of the many rules that govern society actually have legal force. As Hart explains, in the simpler form of society we must wait and see whether a potential rule gets accepted as a rule or not; in a system with a basic rule of recognition we can say before a rule is actually made that it will be valid if it conforms to the requirements of the rule of recognition.

Hart described the UK as having a single rule of recognition: what the Queen in Parliament enacts is law. This leaves out the issue of judge-made law; the difficulties in pinpointing exactly how precedent works mean that a rule of recognition is more difficult to specify here, but it would certainly be inaccurate to say that only what the Queen in Parliament enacts is law.

Dworkin: legal principles

Professor Dworkin (1986) rejects Hart's analysis of law as consisting purely of rules. He argues that the rich fabric of law contains not just rules, but also a set of principles on which all legal rules are based. Dworkin defines rules as operating in an all or nothing manner, stating a particular answer to a particular question. Legal principles, on the other hand, are guidelines, giving a reason that argues in one direction, but does not dictate a decision. Take, for example, a hypothetical murder of a father by his son. One of the legal principles Dworkin advances is that no one should benefit from their own wrong, and this should clearly be taken into account in deciding this dispute. But it does not dictate a particular answer; there may be other aspects to the dispute which make other principles a stronger influence (perhaps the son killed in self-defence). By contrast, a rule that no one can inherit property from a person they have murdered is clear-cut and straightforward in application: the son cannot inherit from his father regardless of his motive.

Other differences between principles and rules, according to Dworkin, are that principles have a dimension of weight or importance – a suggestion of morality – that rules lack. Conflicts between principles can be weighed up by a judge, and the background guidance they give means that, even in hard cases, they should provide a fairly clear answer: if rules clash, a further rule will be needed to establish which should prevail (for example, the rule that if law and equity conflict, equity prevails). Finally, the strength of a principle can become eroded over time, whereas rules stand until they are removed.

The natural law theory

The theories of Austin (1954) and Hart (1963) attempt to define what law is, without examining what it says: they could be said to look at the outside appearance of law, rather than defining it by its content. This approach is called positivism. Another school of thought, the natural law theory, defines law by its content: only laws which conform to a particular moral code, seen as a higher form of law, can genuinely be called law. (This natural law theory is discussed in Chapter 13.)

The function of law

Some writers have taken the view that law is best understood by looking at the role it plays in society: what is it for? The following are some of the key theories in this area.

Social cohesion

The nineteenth-century French sociologist Emile Durkheim (see Lukes and Scull, 1983) looked at the issue of social cohesion, searching for what keeps a society together, and concluded that law played an important role in this area. He looked at the role of law in two contrasting types of society: the first a relatively simple, technologically undeveloped society; the second highly developed in terms of technology and social structure.

Durkheim argued that in the first type of society, the whole group would have clearly identifiable common aims, and would all work to achieve them: the interests of any individual within the group would be exactly the same as those of the group as a whole. A moral and legal code based on these aims would be recognised and accepted by all, and would keep the group working together. Durkheim called this mechanical solidarity. An individual who deviated from this code would be punished, and their punishment would reinforce the code by reflecting the group's disapproval of the wrongdoing.

According to Durkheim's analysis, as social groups become larger and more complex, developing links with other social groups, the interests of individual members become less closely linked to those of the group as a whole. To take a simple example, members of a forest tribe might hunt together to provide food for everyone, whereas in a developed society individuals and families look after their own interests. Social solidarity does not disappear but becomes based on increasing interdependence, which itself stems from the division of labour. Whereas, for example, in the small-scale society, each family would make its own bread, in the developed society this task is shared between farmer, flour mill, bakery and retailer, all dependent on each other and the consumer. This interdependence means that the individual has social importance in their own right, rather than occupying a social position simply as one member of the group.

Durkheim argued that these changes would be accompanied by a corresponding change in the type of law present in the society. Penal law would become less important and would increasingly be replaced by compensatory law, where the object is not to punish but to resolve grievances by restoring the injured party to the position they were in before the dispute arose. There would be less need for resolution of disputes between the individual and society, and more for those between individuals.

Durkheim's analysis has been criticised for overestimating the extent to which criminal law would decline and give way to compensatory law in an industrialised society: if anything, industrialised societies have increased the application of criminal law and, indeed, industrialisation has created new crimes, such as corporate manslaughter and pollution. Anthropological studies have shown that he also underestimated the degree to which compensatory or civil law already exists in simple societies.

Survival

Professor Hart argues that the main function of law is simply to allow human beings to survive in a community. He suggests that there are certain truths about human existence which, without rules guiding our behaviour, would make life excessively dangerous. Each member of society has, more or less, the same physical strength and intelligence, and both our powers of self-restraint and willingness to help others are limited. We therefore all face the danger of attack from the others and competition for such resources as are available. Knowing this, any group of humans will soon recognise that it needs rules curbing individual desires and impulses. We realise that, if we attack people or take their goods when they are weak, the same could easily happen to us. To protect ourselves we must accept limitations on our behaviour. The alternative would be a degree of conflict that would make it impossible for the group to stay together, yet individual members might be even less safe if they had to face the world alone.

The realisation that we are not safe in the world alone and can only be safe in a community if there are rules of self-restraint, leads to the development of such rules, protecting the property and person of others. It also leads to acceptance of the idea that observance of the rules must be guaranteed by some kind of penalty directed against the rule-breaker. Hart maintains that such rules are the minimum necessary content of law in any society.

The maintenance of order

The German sociologist Max Weber (1979) argues that the primary role of law is to maintain order in society. Law makes individuals accept the legitimacy of their rules, and gives them the power to make law and coerce individuals into obeying it. Without this coercive power, argues Weber, order could not be maintained.

This idea has enjoyed much political support as political parties, from either side of the spectrum, are keen to present themselves as promoting law and order. But Weber's view can be criticised as overestimating the role of law in keeping order. If he is to be believed, a relaxation of law would result in the immediate degeneration of society into chaos and disorder; but this ignores the many other factors which make our society relatively orderly. In many cases we obey the law not because it is the law, but because of social or moral pressures – we do not steal, for example, because we have been brought up to think stealing is wrong, not because we might be caught and punished for it. Similarly, we may obey moral or social rules as strictly as we obey legal ones – we are unlikely to find ourselves in court for swearing at the vicar, but few of us would do it because of strong social and moral pressures.

Critics argue that Weber's theory fails to allow for the fact that societies are not just a loose group of independent individuals; they have clear patterns of behaviour, relationships and beliefs, which differ from society to society. These are what hold society together and, while law is one aspect of them, it is not the only force for social cohesion. Other social institutions which promote cohesion include the family and schools, which transmit social standards to new generations; political institutions (such as Parliament and political parties); economic and commercial institutions (such as trade unions, manufacturers' associations, patterns of production and trade); and religious and cultural institutions (such as literature and the arts, the press, television and radio). All of these play a part in establishing social rules.

The importance of these social rules can be seen if we compare a human society to a group of animals. Like animals, we have instincts to eat, sleep and mate. But whereas animals do all these things in response only to instinct and opportunity, our behaviour is controlled, directly and indirectly, through moral standards, religious doctrines, social traditions and legal rules. For example, like animals we are born with a mating instinct but, unlike animals, human societies attempt to channel this instinct into a form of relationship which has traditionally been seen as offering benefits for society: heterosexual marriage. As we have said, there are no legal rules commanding people to marry, but there are a great many social and moral pressures upholding heterosexual marriage as the desired form of relationship; the predominant religion in our history upholds it, and alternatives, such as homosexual relationships or heterosexual couples living together without marriage, have traditionally been seen as immoral and socially unacceptable. It can be argued that these pressures have, in the past, operated just as forcefully as laws do in other areas, though they now appear to be breaking down.

Balancing different interests

The US jurist Roscoe Pound (1968) saw law as a social institution, created and designed to satisfy human wants, both individual and social. Pound identified different interests in society, including individual, domestic, property, social and public interests. He argued that the law's main aim was to secure and balance these different and often competing interests.

Where interests on a different level conflicted – such as individual interests conflicting with social interests – they could not be weighed against each other, but where there is a conflict between interests on the same level, they must be weighed against one another with the aim of ensuring that as many as possible are satisfied.

'Law jobs'

Karl Llewellyn (1962) was a member of the US realist school of thought which, like the positivists, is concerned with what law is, rather than what it ought to be. Working with Hoebel, an anthropologist, Llewellyn studied Native American groups and, from this research, constructed a theory of 'law jobs' to explain the social functions of law.

Llewellyn's theory is that every social group has certain jobs which need to be done for it to survive, and law is one of the main ways in which these jobs are done. The jobs include preventing disruptive disputes within the group; providing a means of resolving disputes which do arise; allocating authority and providing mechanisms for constructing relationships between people, including ways of adjusting to change. Although these jobs are common to all societies, the ways in which the jobs are done will vary from society to society. For example, the allocation of authority in a simple society might be done by basic rules on electing or appointing a chief while, in a more complex society, this job can be done by a constitution.

Robert Summers (1992) has also looked at law in terms of the various jobs it does for society, and identified five main uses of law: putting right grievances among members of a society; prohibiting and prosecuting forbidden behaviour; promoting certain defined activities; conferring social and governmental benefits, including education and welfare; and giving effect to private arrangements, such as contracts. Although their theses are different, both Llewellyn and Summers look at law in its social context, in contrast to writers such as Austin who believe rules, including legal rules, can be analysed without reference to their settings.

Exploitation

A radical alternative to the views of writers such as Durkheim and Weber is put forward by Karl Marx (1933). Durkheim and Weber disagreed about the precise functions of law, but they accepted the idea that law must in some way be of benefit to society as a whole. Marx, however, rejected the idea that there was a common interest in society which law could serve. He argued that society was composed of classes whose interests were fundamentally opposed to each other. Law, Marx maintained, was not made in the interests of society as a whole, but in the interests of the small group which dominates society; through law (and other social institutions, such as religion), this group is able to exploit the working class, which Marx called the proletariat.

Later Marxist writers, such as Althusser and Gramsci, have developed this thesis. They argue that the ruling class controls the ideology of society, including the beliefs and ideas which shape it. This ideology is expressed through social institutions such as the school, the family, religion and the law. By shaping the way in which people see the world around them, the ruling class is able to ensure that the working class see their exploitation as natural, as the only way things could be, rather than as the oppressive state of affairs that Marxists see. This minimises their resistance.

Law is seen as an important part of this process. Because, for example, the law protects private property, we come to view private property and all its implications as natural and inevitable. Take, for example, the acceptance of profit. If someone pays £100 for a set of raw materials, and pays an employee £100 to turn those materials into goods which they then sell for £600, it is quite acceptable in our society for the employer to keep the profit, because they purchased both the raw materials and the employee's labour. Clearly, an acceptance of people making a profit out of another's labour is fundamental to acceptance of the capitalist system as a whole, and the legal doctrine of private property is the basis of this acceptance. But Marxists point out that the situation can be looked at in another way, as the employer stealing from the worker the added value their labour gives to the raw materials. The fact that we would not usually think to see it this way is, Marxists say, because we see it through a capitalist ideology, and law plays a fundamental role in upholding this ideology.

Marx believed that law was only needed because of the fundamental clash of interests between those of the ruling class and those of the proletariat; once society was transformed by communism, these divisions would no longer exist, and law would wither away.

Why are laws obeyed?

Austin thought laws were obeyed because of the threat of sanction and out of a habit of obedience to the state. Hart rejects this explanation, arguing that acceptance of a rule is more important than possible sanctions. As well as the external aspect of obedience – recognition of the validity of the rule, and a potential sanction – Hart argues that there is an internal process, which inclines us to obey because we consider it right and proper to do so. Hart suggests that if a law is not internalised, an individual will feel no obligation to obey it. In our system there are many examples of laws which for some reason widely fail this internalisation test: parking offences, speeding, use of mobile phones whilst driving, tax evasion and drug legislation are obvious examples of laws which large numbers of people apparently feel no real compulsion to follow. He suggests that in order for law to promote social cohesion in a simple society with only primary rules, members must not only obey those rules, but also consciously see them as common standards of behaviour, breaches of which can legitimately be criticised: in other words, they internalise all the rules, following them not just because they are rules, but because they consider it right to do so. But, in a more developed legal system like ours, Hart believes individuals need not internalise every rule. It is clearly desirable for them to internalise as many as possible, but, failing this, the necessary functions can be served by officials internalising the rules and, thereby, becoming committed to their maintenance.

Fear and internalisation

If we obey laws because we internalise them, what makes us internalise some rules and not others? One theory, put forward by Professor Karl Olivecrona (1971), suggests that fear is a strong motivation. He points out that we are all aware from childhood of the consequences of breaking rules and, as a result, we experience a tension between temptation to break rules and fear of punishment. Olivecrona suggests that the human mind cannot accommodate such tension indefinitely, and so we gradually adjust psychologically to accept conformity to rules as a means of getting rid of the fear of punishment; eventually we do not believe we are acting out of fear at all, we have just become used to keeping the rules.

Perhaps because of the efficacy of this process, many writers have suggested that law can be used to shape moral and social ideas. Aristotle suggested that law could be used to educate citizens, commenting that 'Legislators make citizens good by forming their habits.' On the other hand, social pressures can often bring about changes in conduct which legal rules have been unable to do. A recent example is that of drink-driving. At one time this offence was seen as being in a similar category to speeding or parking offences; it was against the law, but many still saw it as acceptable. Now, as a result of social pressures, partly driven by public information campaigns, it is viewed as highly anti-social behaviour, and the law is apparently more widely obeyed.

Answering questions

1 '. . . a law is a type of rule, but clearly there are many rules which are not law.' Discuss.

In essence, this simply requires an analysis of what rules are and what law is (possibly by reference to its functions (p. 206)), referring to the authors mentioned in this chapter (in other words, Austin, Hart and Dworkin). It will also require knowledge of the natural law theory (see Chapter 13) in order to discuss the quotation comprehensively.

2 Is it possible to live in a society without law?

This type of question allows many different approaches, all of which could be very successful. One approach would be to use the material under the heading 'The function of law' above (at p. 196). You could consider each theory in turn and consider whether, if that theory is right, there would be a society without law. For example, Durkheim suggests that law achieves social cohesion – without law you could only have a primitive society and not a technologically advanced society – while Karl Marx considers that law is merely a tool for exploitation and that without law we could enjoy a much healthier society.

Summary of Chapter 12: Law and rules

One way to understand more about what law is, is to look at what distinguishes legal rules from other types of rules.

Austin: the command theory
The nineteenth-century writer John Austin argued that law differed from other rules because it was the command of a sovereign body, which the state could enforce by means of punishment.

Hart: primary and secondary rules
Professor Hart divided legal rules into primary rules and secondary rules, and argued that the existence of secondary rules was a mark of a developed legal system. Primary rules were described as those which any society needs in order to survive. Secondary rules confer power rather than impose duties, and can be divided into three types:

- rules of adjudication;
- rules of change; and
- rules of recognition.

Dworkin: legal principles
Professor Dworkin argues that the rich fabric of law contains a set of principles on which all legal rules are based. Legal principles are guidelines, giving a reason that argues in one direction, but does not dictate a decision.

The natural law theory
The natural law theory defines law by its content: only laws which conform to a particular moral code, seen as a higher form of law, can genuinely be called law.

The function of law
Some writers have taken the view that law is best understood by looking at the role it plays in society.

Social cohesion
The nineteenth-century French sociologist Emile Durkheim looked at the issue of social cohesion, searching for what keeps a society together, and concluded that law played an important role in this area.

Survival
Professor Hart argues that the main function of law is simply to allow human beings to survive in a community.

The maintenance of order
The German sociologist Max Weber argued that the primary role of law is to maintain order in society.

Balancing different interests
The US jurist Roscoe Pound saw law as a social institution, created and designed to satisfy human wants, both individual and social.

'Law jobs'

Karl Llewellyn's theory is that every social group has certain jobs which need to be done for it to survive, and law is one of the main ways in which these jobs are done.

Exploitation

Karl Marx argued that society was composed of classes whose interests were fundamentally opposed to each other. Law, Marx maintained, was not made in the interests of society as a whole, but in the interests of the small group which dominates society; through law (and other social institutions, such as religion), this group is able to exploit the working class.

Why are laws obeyed?

Austin thought laws were obeyed because of the threat of sanction and out of a habit of obedience to the state. Hart argues that there is an internal process, which inclines us to obey because we consider it right and proper to do so.

Fear and internalisation

If we obey laws because we internalise them, what makes us internalise some rules and not others? One theory, put forward by Professor Olivecrona, suggests that fear is a strong motivation.

Reading list

Austin, J. (1954) *The Province of Jurisprudence Determined*. London: Weidenfeld & Nicolson.

Dworkin, R. (1977) *Taking Rights Seriously*, London: Duckworth.

(1986) *Law's Empire*. London: Fontana.

Hart, H.L.A. (1963) *Law, Liberty and Morality*. Oxford: Oxford University Press.

(1994) *The Concept of Law*. Oxford: Clarendon.

Llewellyn, K. (1962) *Jurisprudence: Realism in Theory and Practice*. Chicago: University of Chicago Press.

Lukes, S. and Scull, A. (eds) (1983) *Durkheim and the Law*. Oxford: Robertson.

Marx, K. (1933) *Capital*. London: J.M. Dent.

Olivecrona, K. (1971) *Law as Fact*. London: Stevens.

Pound, R. (1968) *Social Control Through Law*. Hamden: Archon Books.

Summers, R. (1992) *Essays on the Nature of Law and Legal Reasoning*. Berlin: Duncker & Humblot.

Twining, W. and Miers, D. (1991) *How To Do Things With Rules*. London: Weidenfeld & Nicolson.

Weber, M. (1979) *Economy and Society*. Berkeley: University of California Press.

13

Law and morals

This chapter discusses:

- the relationship between law and morality;
- the evolution of law and morality;
- differences between law and morality;
- whether law and morality should be separate; and
- the impact of morality on law as seen through the work of the Human Fertilisation and Embryology Authority.

Introduction

Morals are beliefs and values which are shared by a society, or a section of a society; they tell those who share them what is right or wrong. In our society, moral values have been heavily influenced by the dominant religion, Christianity, though this is not our only source of moral values.

Debates about morals and morality often centre around sexual issues, such as sex outside marriage, homosexuality and pornography. The passing of the Marriage (Same Sex Couples) Act 2013, which legalised gay marriages, was the subject of considerable public discussion. But moral values also shape attitudes towards money and property, gender roles, friendship, behaviour at work – in fact it is difficult to think of any area of our lives where morality has no application. Mary Warnock (1986), an academic who has been involved in inquiries into issues of moral concern, says: 'I do not believe that there is a neat way of marking off moral issues from all others; some people, at some time, may regard things as matters of moral right or wrong, which at another time or in another place are thought to be matters of taste, or indeed to be matters of no importance at all.' However, she points out that in any society, at any time, questions relating to birth and death and to the establishing of families are regarded as morally significant. These can perhaps be regarded as core moral issues.

As Warnock has observed, moral attitudes tend to change over time. It is only within recent decades, for example, that the idea of couples living together without marriage has become widely accepted; even now acceptance is not total, but a generation or so ago it would have been unthinkable. Similar shifts have taken place with regard to homosexuality and women's liberation.

The French sociologist Durkheim (see Lukes and Scull, 1983) has highlighted the fact that in a modern, developed society it is difficult to pinpoint a set of moral values shared by all. In less developed societies, such as small tribal groups, Durkheim argued that all the members of the group are likely to share a moral code; but, in a technologically advanced society such as our own, where individuals differ widely in social status, income, occupation, ethnic background and so on, its members are unlikely to share identical moral values, even if they largely agree on some basic points. For example, most people in the UK agree that it is usually wrong to kill or steal, but there is much less consensus on whether it is wrong to take drugs, have abortions, experiment on animals or help a terminally ill person to die. Even on the basic crimes of theft and murder, some people will see these as always wrong, while others will believe there are situations in which they may be justified; among the latter, there will be disagreement as to what those situations are.

Criminologist Jock Young (1971) has pointed out that much depends on the standpoint of the observer, and how they see the norms of society. Looking at attitudes to illegal drug use, Young has observed that to those who see society's rules as based on a moral consensus, drug-taking was against that moral consensus, so those who indulged in it were therefore maladjusted and sick. But, if society's rules on deviant behaviour are seen simply as a yardstick of what that particular society considers normal, drug-taking is neither necessarily deviant nor necessarily a social problem: it is merely deviant to groups who condemn it and a problem to those who wish to eliminate it. What is being made is simply a value judgement, and values vary between people and over time.

Law and morality

Both law and morals are normative; they specify what ought to be done, and aim to mark the boundaries between acceptable and unacceptable conduct. While moral rules tend not to be backed by the obvious sanctions which make some legal rules enforceable, they are often reinforced by pressures which in some cases may be as strong, if not stronger: the disapproval of family and friends, loss of status and being shunned by the community are powerful disincentives against immoral conduct. Of course, many types of undesirable behaviour offend against both moral and legal rules – serious crimes are obvious examples.

Both law and morals are often presented as if they were the only possible responses to social or political problems and crises, yet both vary widely between societies. For example, in our society, private property is such a basic doctrine that we readily condemn any infringement of our rights – legal and moral – to acquire, possess and enjoy our personal property. Stealing is seen as immoral as well as illegal. But in a society where property is held communally, any attempt by one individual to treat property as their own private possession would be regarded as every bit as immoral as we would consider stealing. The idea of private property is not a basic part of human nature, as it is often presented, but a socially constructed value. Our society has for centuries been based on trade, and this requires a basis of private property.

Some areas of law are explicitly presented as raising moral issues and, when these areas arise in Parliament, MPs are allowed to vote according to their own beliefs, rather than according to party policy. This is called a vote of conscience and was used, for example, when the issue of capital punishment was debated. However, the kinds of issue on which a vote of conscience would be allowed are not the only ones to which moral values apply: when MPs vote on tax changes, the welfare state, employment or any number of issues before Parliament in every session, they are voting on moral issues, because they are voting on the way a Government treats its citizens, and the way in which citizens are allowed to treat each other.

Similarly, some areas of law, such as criminal law, have obvious moral implications, but these are also present in areas where morality is less obvious. Tort law, for example, and especially negligence, is built around the principle that those who harm others should compensate for the damage done; that, as Lord Atkin noted in the famous case of **Donoghue v Stevenson** (1932), the biblical principle of 'love thy neighbour' must include 'do not harm your neighbour'. Similarly, contract, as Atiyah (1979) has pointed out, is based around the principle that promises should be kept. Even land law which, on the surface, appears to consist of technicalities far removed from elevated questions of morality, has enormous moral importance because it is upholding the whole notion of property and ownership. Take the question of squatting: the property owner has all the rights to begin with but, if the squatting continues for long enough, the squatter can gain some rights. Is it moral that the property owner should lose rights to someone acting illegally? On the other hand, is it moral that some should be homeless while others have property they can afford to leave empty?

In **Re A (Children) (Conjoined Twins: Surgical Separation)** (2000), the Court of Appeal expressly stated that it was 'not a court of morals but a court of law and our decisions have to be taken from a solid base of legal principle'. But, in reality, law and morals were closely interlinked in that case. It concerned the legality of an operation to separate conjoined twins. The operation would inevitably lead to the death of the weaker twin, but was the sole chance of saving the life of the stronger twin. The judgment of the court is based on the principle of the sanctity of life, which itself is a moral commitment.

Changes in law and morality

As we have observed, the moral values of a society tend to change over time; the same applies to its laws. In the UK, legal changes have tended to lag behind moral ones, coming only when the process of moral acceptance is well advanced. Thus, the law was changed in 1991 to make rape within marriage a crime, the House of Lords stating that the change was necessary because marriages were now seen as equal partnerships, in which the husband could no longer enforce rights to sex. This shift in attitude had taken place long before 1991, but the time-lag between moral change and legal change was fairly typical. Often it is the possession of effective political power which finally determines which and whose definition of morality is reflected in the law.

On the other hand, law can sometimes bring about changes in social morality. Troy Duster, in *The Legislation of Morality* (1970), traced the history of drug use and its legal control in the US from the end of the nineteenth century. At that time, drug addiction was commonly restricted to the middle and upper classes, who had become dependent on morphine through the use of patented medicines; despite the fact that these contained morphine, it was perfectly legal to buy and sell them. Addiction carried no social stigma. However, when certain drugs were made illegal under the Harrison Act 1914, such drugs began to be supplied by the criminal underworld. Dependency on drugs became associated with this underworld and with the lower classes who had most contact with it. This in turn led to social stigma. Interestingly, this stigma, which was in a sense created by legal controls, was partly responsible for the calls for greater legal controls on drug-taking which have been heard over the last two decades, as more and more young people become involved in the drug culture.

Academics from the Scandinavian realist standpoint, such as Olivecrona (1971), argue that our morality is created by the law, rather than the law emerging from our morality. Olivecrona suggests that law has an influence on us from our earliest days, helping to mould our moral views. From the start, parents and teachers tell us what we must and must not do and we quickly learn the consequences of disobedience.

Differences between law and morality

Although law and morality are clearly closely linked, there are certain ways in which they differ. Many types of behaviour exist which may be widely considered to be immoral, yet we would be very surprised to find laws against them: telling lies, for example. Equally, some forms of behaviour are illegal, but would not usually be described as immoral, such as parking on a yellow line. Then there are areas where the law shares morality's disapproval, but not so far as to prohibit the relevant behaviour. Adultery, for example, is not illegal in this country, but it has long constituted grounds for a divorce, an important legal step for individuals.

KEY CASE

The problem for the law in deciding whether to respond to appeals to morality is that there are very often conflicting moral views in a given situation. We can see this in the case of **Gillick v West Norfolk and Wisbech Area Health Authority** (1985). The claimant, Mrs Victoria Gillick, was a Roman Catholic. She objected to guidance given to doctors from the Department of Health and Social Security that, in exceptional cases, they could offer contraceptive advice and treatment to girls under 16, without parental consent. Mrs Gillick sought a declaration that these guidelines were illegal because they encouraged under-age sex.

Mrs Gillick lost at first instance, won in the Court of Appeal and lost by a majority in the House of Lords. The House held that the guidelines were lawful because they concerned what were essentially medical matters. In this field, girls under 16 had the legal capacity to consent to a medical examination and treatment, including contraceptive treatment, as long as they were sufficiently mature and intelligent to understand the nature and implications of the proposed treatment. The majority, in reaching this conclusion, stressed they were merely applying the law as it stood rather than taking a moral standpoint; the minority referred to the kind of moral arguments Mrs Gillick had advanced. This does not mean that, in rejecting Mrs Gillick's view, the majority ignored morality, even though they claimed to be making an objective decision. It could be argued that if teenage girls were likely to have sexual intercourse anyway, preventing doctors from giving contraceptive help would simply increase the chances of unwanted pregnancies and it would, therefore, be moral to protect girls from that. Neither approach is objectively wrong or right; in this, as in many areas, there are opposing moral views.

Legal principle

Children have the legal capacity to consent to medical treatment if they are sufficiently mature and intelligent to understand the nature and implications of the proposed treatment.

Should law and morality be separate?

The view taken by Mrs Gillick would seem to suggest that if something is immoral it should also be illegal and, to the person who holds strong moral opinions, this may seem a natural conclusion. But there are problems with it. First, moral opinions, however strongly held, are just that: moral opinions. Mrs Gillick believes under-age girls should not be given contraception and many people agree with her, but many others disagree. Which group's moral opinions should be adopted by the law?

Even if there were complete consensus, the logistics of enforcing as legal rules all the moral rules of our society would present enormous problems. How would we pay for the necessary manpower, both for policing and prosecutions? What sanctions would be severe enough to compel obedience, yet not too severe for the nature of the offences? Making every immoral act also illegal seems both impossible and undesirable, yet law with no connection to morality might find it difficult to command much respect. There is still much debate as to how far law should reflect morality; the following are some of the key suggestions.

Natural law

Natural law theorists argue that law should strongly reflect morality. Though their specific theories differ, their shared premise is that there is a kind of higher law, known as the natural law, to which we can turn for a basic moral code: some, such as St Thomas Aquinas, see this higher law as coming from God, others see it as simply the foundations of a human society. The principles in this higher law should be reflected in the laws societies make for themselves; laws which do not reflect these principles cannot really be called law at all, and in some cases need not be obeyed. The campaign, during the 1980s, against payment of the Poll Tax on the grounds that it was unfair might be seen as an example of this kind of disobedience.

Different natural law theorists disagree as to the actual content of natural law, but it is usually felt to embody basic human rights which governments should respect. Bills of Rights, like that in the US Constitution, could be seen as embodying natural law principles. Professor Fuller, in *The Morality of Law* (1969), talked about law's inner morality which he formulated in terms of eight procedural requirements of a legal system:

1 Generality: there should be rules, not *ad hoc* judgments.
2 Promulgation: the rules should be made known to all those affected by them.
3 Non-retroactivity: rules should not have retrospective effect.
4 Clarity: rules should be understandable.
5 Consistency: rules should not conflict.
6 Realism: people should not be required to do the impossible.
7 Constancy: rules should not be changed so frequently that people cannot use them to guide their behaviour.
8 Congruence: the actual administration of the rules should coincide with the information available to the public about them.

Fuller claims that a legal system which fails in any one of these areas is not just a bad system, it is not a legal system at all. As an example, he gives the legal system of Nazi Germany: although laws were made by recognised methods, in Fuller's view the system's failure to meet the above criteria meant that those laws were not really law at all.

Utilitarianism

During the nineteenth century, the rise of science and the beginning of the decline in the social importance of religion meant that natural law theories declined. In their place the theory of utilitarianism grew up, apparently offering a rational and scientific theory of law. One of the best-known exponents of this theory is John Stuart Mill (1859). He argued that rather than society imposing morality on individuals, individuals should be free to choose their own conduct, so long as in doing so they did not harm others or, if they did, that the harm done did not outweigh the harm which would be done by interfering with individual liberty.

The view that people should be left alone to do what they like so long as they do not harm others remains influential today, but it is open to criticism. First, the fact that someone's actions do not cause another direct and physical harm, in the way Mill envisaged, does not necessarily mean they do no harm at all. For example, opponents of pornography claim that while looking at pornography may not directly inspire individual users to rape, the fact that pornography is available and, to a degree, accepted, promotes the view that women are sexual objects which, in turn, promotes sexual violence against women.

Secondly, who counts as 'another'? This issue is clearly at the heart of debates over abortion and experimentation on embryos: does harming an unborn child count as harming another person, and from what point? The fact that abortion is legal up until a certain stage in pregnancy suggests that the law sees this as the moment at which the foetus becomes another: many people believe that point is reached earlier in pregnancy, and those opposed to abortion believe it is at the time of conception. On the other hand, many people who support the law on abortion nevertheless disapprove of experiments on embryos, even though their views of abortion might suggest that the embryo is not another at this point.

Crimes without victims

Modern theories which subscribe, at least partly, to Mill's view of individual liberty have tended to focus on what are often called victimless crimes. Using the examples of drug use, homosexuality and abortion, all of which were illegal at the time in which he was writing, in *Crimes without Victims* (1965) the academic Schur observes that the common characteristics of such crimes are that they involve no harm to anyone except the participants; they occur through the willing participation of those involved; and, as a result, there is no victim to make a complaint, rendering the law difficult to enforce. Schur argues that there is a social demand for these activities, which continues to be met despite illegality, through such means as back street abortions and black market drug supply. There is no proof that prohibition of such activities brought greater social benefits than decriminalisation, therefore there is no good reason to prohibit them.

As with John Stuart Mill, the main criticism of Schur's theory is his assertion that these activities harm no one who has not willingly taken part in them. Anti-abortionists would certainly dispute this as far as abortion is concerned. A further criticism is directed at the suggestion that participants join in these activities of their own free will; in the case of drug-taking, for example, that may be so at first, but can we really say that, once addicted, drug users take drugs of their own free will?

The Hart–Devlin debate

The issue of whether or not law should follow morality was hotly debated during the late 1950s, when there was public concern about what was perceived to be a decline in sexual morality. The Government of the day set up a commission to look at whether the laws on homosexuality and prostitution should be changed, and much debate was triggered by publication of the commission's findings, known as the Wolfenden Report (1957). Central to this debate were the writings of the leading judge, Lord Devlin, who opposed the report's findings, and Professor Hart who approved of them.

The Wolfenden Committee recommended that homosexuality and prostitution should be legalised, with some restrictions. Its reasoning was based on the notion that some areas of behaviour had to be left to individual morality, rather than being supervised by the law. The purpose of the criminal law, said the report, was:

> to preserve public order and decency, to protect the citizen from what is offensive and injurious and to provide sufficient safeguards against exploitation and corruption of others

especially the vulnerable, that is the young, weak in body or mind, inexperienced or those in a state of physical, official or economic dependence. The law should not intervene in the private lives of citizens or seek to enforce any particular pattern of behaviour further than necessary to carry out the above purposes.

The reasoning is very like that of Mill: leave people to make their own choices, so long as they do not harm others. The Committee therefore recommended that prostitution itself should not be an offence, since the individual ought to be allowed to choose whether to take part in it, but activities associated with prostitution which could cause offence to others (such as soliciting in the street) were still to be regulated by the law.

Lord Devlin was opposed to this approach. He argued that some form of common morality, with basic agreement on good and evil, was necessary to keep society together. This being the case, the law had every right – and in fact a duty – to uphold that common morality. He compared contravention of public morality to treason, in the sense that it was something society had to protect itself against. How are we to know what this public morality consists of? Devlin argued that we can judge immorality by the standard of the right-minded person, who could perhaps be thought of as the person in the jury box. Opinions should be reached after informed and educated discussion of all relevant points of view and, if there is still debate, the majority view should prevail, as it does in the ordinary legislative process.

In addition, said Devlin, there was a set of basic principles which should be followed by the legislature. First, individuals should be allowed the maximum of freedom consistent with the integrity of society, and privacy should be respected as much as possible. Secondly, punishment should be reserved for that which creates disgust among right-minded people, and society has the right to eradicate any practice which is so abominable that its very presence is an offence. Law-makers should be slow to change laws which protect morality. Thirdly, the law should set down a minimum standard of morality; society's standards should be higher.

Reaction to Devlin's thesis was mixed. Those who felt the Wolfenden Report had gone too far agreed with him, and there were many of them – the commission's recommendations seem rather tame now, but at the time they were ground-breaking. Others felt that his approach was out of step with the times. Hart, who was influenced by John Stuart Mill and, therefore, approved of the commission's approach, led this opposition. Hart argued that using law to enforce moral values was unnecessary, undesirable and morally unacceptable: unnecessary because society was capable of containing many moral standpoints without disintegrating; undesirable because it would freeze morality at a particular point; and morally unacceptable because it infringes the liberty of the individual. Devlin's response was that individual liberty could only flourish in a stable society: disintegration of our society through lack of a shared morality would, therefore, threaten individual freedom.

Hart pointed out that the standard of the right-minded person is a tenuous one. When people object to unusual behaviour, the response is not always prompted by rational moral objections, but often by prejudice, ignorance or misunderstanding. He gave four basic reasons why moral censure should not necessarily lead to legal sanctions. First, punishing the offender involves doing some harm to them, when they may have done no harm to others. Secondly, the exercise of free choice by individuals is a moral value in itself, with which it is wrong to interfere. Thirdly, this exercise of free choice can be valuable in that it allows individuals to experiment and learn. Finally, as far as sexual morality is concerned, the suppression of sexual impulses affects the development or balance of the individual's emotional life, happiness and personality and, thus, causes them harm. He objects strongly to the idea that the law should punish behaviour which does not harm others, but merely causes them distress or disgust by its very existence, even when conducted out of their sight: recognition of individual liberty as a value involves, as a minimum, acceptance of the principle that individuals may do what they want, even if others are distressed when they learn what it is that they do, unless, of course, there are other good grounds for forbidding it.

Judicial support for Devlin's view – and perhaps reaction against liberalising legislation – can be seen in some of the more high-profile cases which arose in its aftermath. In **Shaw** *v* **Director of Public Prosecutions** (1961), Shaw had published a booklet entitled *The Ladies' Directory,* which contained advertisements by prostitutes, featuring photographs and descriptions of the sexual practices they offered. He was convicted of the crime of conspiring to corrupt public morals, an offence which had not been prosecuted since the eighteenth century. The House of Lords upheld the conviction and, defending the court's power to uphold the recognition of such an antiquated offence, Viscount Simonds said: 'In the sphere of criminal law I entertain no doubt that there remains in the courts of law a residual power to enforce the supreme and fundamental purpose of the law, to conserve not only the safety and order but also the moral welfare of the State.' As an example of offences against this moral welfare, Viscount Simonds said:

> Let it be supposed that at some future, perhaps early, date homosexual practices between consenting adult males are no longer a crime. Would it not be an offence if, even without obscenity, such practices were publicly advocated and encouraged by pamphlet and advertisement?

This proved to be an uncannily accurate prediction: in 1967 the Sexual Offences Act was passed, which stated that homosexual acts between consenting adult males in private were no longer a criminal offence.

In **Knuller Ltd** *v* **Director of Public Prosecutions** (1972), the defendants were prosecuted for having published in their magazine, *International Times,* advertisements placed by readers inviting others to contact them for homosexual purposes. Once again, the charge was conspiracy to corrupt public morals and the court convicted. Lord Reid (who had dissented from the majority decision in **Shaw**'s case, but felt that **Shaw** should still apply to avoid inconsistency) recognised that the 1967 Act legalised homosexual acts, but said:

> I find nothing in that Act to indicate that Parliament thought or intended to lay down that indulgence in these practices is not corrupting. I read the Act as saying that, even though it may be corrupting, if people choose to corrupt themselves in this way that is their affair and the law will not interfere. But no licence is given to others to encourage the practice.

More recent decisions still show judicial support for the Devlin viewpoint that some acts are intrinsically immoral, regardless of whether they harm others. In **R** *v* **Gibson** (1990), an artist exhibited earrings made from freeze-dried foetuses of three to four months' gestation. A conviction for the common law offence of outraging public decency was upheld. The appellants in **R** *v* **Brown** (1992) were homosexual men who had willingly participated in the commission of acts of sado-masochistic violence against each other, involving the use of, among other things, heated wires, stinging nettles, nails, sandpaper and safety-pins. Evidence showed that all the men involved had consented; although the activities were videotaped by the participants, this was not for any profit or gain; none of the injuries was permanent and no medical attention had been sought; the activities were carried out in private; and none of the victims had complained to the police. They were convicted of committing a range of offences against the person and appealed to the House of Lords, arguing that, since all the participants had consented and the activities took place in private, the law had no reason to intervene. Their convictions were upheld; by a majority, the House held that public policy demanded such acts be treated as criminal offences. This decision was subsequently approved by the European Court of Human Rights.

The Warnock Committee

Despite the debate between Devlin and Hart, their two views are not always as opposed as they may seem, and in practice both are influential: a Government commission, the Warnock Committee, incorporates features of both approaches in its reasoning. The Committee was set up by the Government of the day to consider issues relating to scientific advances concerning conception and pregnancy. With the advent of *in vitro* fertilisation (the technique used to create test-tube babies) and other technological advances, new scientific possibilities have arisen. These include the possibility of creating embryos for use in medical experiments, sperm, egg and embryo donation by fertile men or women to those who are infertile, and the use of surrogate mothers – women who bear a child for another couple, using their own egg and the father's sperm. These practices raised a number of moral issues, including that of payment for surrogacy, and the parentage of children born from donated eggs and sperm.

The Committee's report, published in 1984, advised the setting up of an independent statutory body to monitor, regulate and license infertility services and embryo experiments. On the specific issues before them, they recommended that experiments on embryos up to 14 days old should be lawful; and that sperm, egg and embryo donation should be facilitated in that the babies born could be registered as the legitimate children of the non-contributing parent(s) on the birth certificate, and donors should be relieved of parental rights and duties in law. But surrogacy arrangements met with disapproval by the majority, who recommended that surrogacy agencies should be criminally prohibited, and private surrogacy arrangements between individuals should be illegal and unenforceable in the courts – although no criminal sanction would be imposed as it would be against the child's interests to be born into a family threatened by imprisonment. Many of the Committee's conclusions became law in the Human Fertilisation and Embryology Act 1990.

If we look at the reasoning behind the Committee's findings, we can see aspects of both Hart's utilitarian approach, and Devlin's upholding of common morality. In its conclusions on embryo research, it points out:

> We do not want to see a situation in which human embryos are frivolously or unnecessarily used in research but we are bound to take account of the fact that the advances in the treatment of infertility, which we have discussed in the earlier part of this report, could not have taken place without such research; and that continued research is essential, if advances in treatment and medical knowledge are to continue. A majority of us therefore agreed that research on human embryos should continue.

But this utilitarian approach is balanced against issues of morality.

A strict utilitarian would suppose that, given procedures, it would be possible to calculate their benefits and their costs. Future advantages, therapeutic or scientific, should be weighed against present and future harm. However, even if such a calculation were possible, it could not provide a final or verifiable answer to the question whether it is right that such procedures should be carried out. There would still remain the possibility that they were unacceptable, whatever their long-term benefits were supposed to be. Moral questions, such as those with which we have been concerned are, by definition, questions that involve not only a calculation of consequences, but also strong sentiments with regard to the nature of the proposed activities themselves.

As the report shows, issues of law and morality cannot easily be separated into distinct theoretical approaches like those of Hart and Devlin; legislators in practice have to tread an uneasy path between the two.

TOPICAL ISSUE

Infertility treatment

Modern science has made major developments in helping women who in the past would have been unable to have children, but these developments have themselves given rise to fundamental moral dilemmas. A case that caused some controversy is that of **R v Human Fertilisation and Embryology Authority, *ex parte* Blood** (1997). The husband of Diane Blood contracted meningitis and lapsed into a coma. Diane Blood asked for samples of his sperm to be collected for future use in artificial insemination. The samples were entrusted to a research trust for storage. The husband died and the Human Fertilisation and Embryology Authority prevented the research trust from releasing the samples from storage, on the ground that the written consent of the donor to the taking of his sperm had not been obtained as required by the relevant statute. The applicant sought judicial review of the Authority's decision. The Court of Appeal ruled that the applicant could have the sperm samples and undergo treatment for an artificially assisted pregnancy, provided she went abroad for the fertility treatment. The Authority's decision had been lawful under the terms of the statute but the circumstances were exceptional and had not been foreseen by Parliament when passing the regulatory legislation. Judicial discretion was sufficiently flexible to grant the remedy which the compassionate circumstances demanded, particularly as the legal situation had never before been explored.

In **Evans v Amicus Healthcare Ltd** (2004) Natalie Evans and her partner had no children and attended a fertility clinic for IVF treatment. During the course of treatment, it was discovered that Natalie had cancer in both her ovaries. Before her ovaries were removed, Natalie had some of her eggs fertilised with her partner's sperm and the resulting six embryos frozen. She and her partner had been engaged to be married, but they later split up and her partner wrote to the clinic stating that the embryos should now be destroyed. Natalie went to court to try to stop the embryos being destroyed as they were her only chance of having her own biological child. The Court of Appeal rejected her application. While it accepted that the destruction of the embryos was an interference with Natalie's private life under Art. 8 of the European Convention, it considered that this interference was necessary to respect the rights of her former partner. This seems quite a tough decision, as her former partner was able to have children with a future partner, but Natalie would not be able to, so perhaps the interference with her ex-partner's rights should have been justified to prevent the much greater interference with Natalie's rights.

Natalie took her case to the European Court of Human Rights, but again the European Court held there had not been any breach of the European Convention and rejected her application (**Evans v United Kingdom** (2007)).

The Human Fertilisation and Embryology Authority

The Human Fertilisation and Embryology Authority (HFEA) was set up in 1990. Areas of debate on morality and the need for law to prevent immorality have centred in recent years around scientific developments that the HFEA has to regulate. In the field of human genetics it is difficult for the law to keep up with the changes in scientific knowledge and the moral dilemmas to which these can give rise. The birth of Dolly, the cloned sheep, caused particular concern when it was announced in 1997. In January 1998 the Human Genetics Advisory Commission and the HFEA jointly published a consultation paper inviting views on various issues raised by cloning technology. The most troubling questions focused on the legality, ethics and practical consequences of human and reproductive cloning. The Authority's policy at the moment is not to license any research having reproductive cloning as its aim. The Human Reproductive Cloning Act 2001 was passed confirming this position.

The Human Genetics Advisory Commission has now recommended that controlled research using embryos (which are eggs that have been fertilised) should be allowed in order to increase understanding about human disease and disorders, and their treatment. It has recommended that reproductive cloning of human beings should remain a criminal offence. The Government has accepted these recommendations.

Another area of scientific activity that raises difficult moral questions concerns research which mixes human and animal tissue. This can take various forms:

- cybrids (where the nucleus of an animal egg is replaced with that from a human cell) – the resulting inter-species embryo is 99.9 per cent human;
- human transgenic embryos where a human embryo is altered by the introduction of animal genetic material;
- human–animal chimeras where a human embryo has been altered by the introduction of animal cells – chimeras can be made by fertilising an animal egg with human sperm.

There is public anxiety about such scientific developments, as these experiments evoke images of mad scientists creating half human/half animal monsters, such as the Minotaur – a half human/half bull monster from Greek mythology. There is also concern that these experiments fail to respect the moral status of human beings, including human embryos. HFEA has approved the creation of cybrids for research purposes by scientists at London University and the University of Newcastle. The creation of a cybrid involves the same cloning procedure that was used to create Dolly the sheep, but, instead of using cells from two animals of the same species, cells are used from two different species. The eggs are likely to come from farmyard animals, such as cows and sheep, since thousands of these animals are killed each day to be eaten. A key reason for using these eggs is simply that they are more easily available than human eggs. Two hundred and seventy sheep eggs were needed before the successful creation of Dolly the sheep.

Cybrid embryos will enable scientists to create cells useful for research into genetic diseases. It is hoped that this research could enable scientists in the future to grow tissues or organs that could replace damaged parts of the body of people suffering from such illnesses as spinal muscular atrophy, Alzheimer's disease or motor neurone disease. The recipient's immune system would not reject these transplants because they would be tissue compatible with the patient's body.

Another contentious issue is how far parents should be allowed to have 'designer babies' to provide living tissue to help cure a sibling. A high-profile case on this subject was that of **R (on the application of Quintavalle) v Human Fertilisation and Embryology Authority** (2005). The case concerned a young boy, Zain Hashmi, who had been born with a rare blood disorder. He would have died if he had not received stem cells from a compatible donor. These stem cells were taken from the umbilical cord of his healthy sibling, who had been conceived for this purpose. HFEA had licensed the procedure by which a genetically compatible embryo was selected for implantation in the body of the boy's mother. A pro-life campaigning organisation, Comment on Reproductive Ethics (CORE), had challenged the legality of HFEA's conduct, arguing that the procedure was opening the door to parents selecting 'designer babies' according to such criteria as sex, hair and eye colour. CORE's action succeeded in the High Court but the mother's appeal was successful before the Court of Appeal and the House of Lords. The House gave a purposive interpretation to the legislation containing HFEA's powers rather than a narrow literal reading, and thereby found that the Authority had the power to issue the licence. Zain Hashmi's life was saved both by the Law Lords and his 'saviour sibling', but CORE felt the medical procedure had been immoral.

In 2005, the House of Commons Science and Technology Select Committee published a review of the Human Fertilisation and Embryology Act 1990. The Department of Health issued a White Paper on the subject in 2006 and the Human Fertilisation and Embryology Act was passed in 2008. This Act replaces the provisions in the 1990 Act, updates and rationalises the law in this field to reflect developments in research and recent case law, and enshrines in the law some of the practices already adopted by HFEA and fertility clinics. It seeks to support medical research while respecting the dignity of human life and modern ethical values.

The Act extends the statutory storage period for embryos from five to ten years. If consent to storage and use of an embryo is withdrawn by one party, storage of the embryo will remain lawful for 12 months. This allows the parties time potentially to reach an agreement about the fate of the embryo after a relationship has broken down. Unfortunately, this will not resolve the type of problem that arose in the case of Natalie Evans where the parties were never able to reach an agreement. Sex-selection of an embryo for non-medical reasons is prohibited but is allowed in order to screen for gender specific diseases. The Act includes a 'saviour sibling' provision permitting the testing of embryos to establish whether the tissue from a child resulting from that embryo would be compatible for treating an existing sibling suffering from a serious medical condition.

The Act allows the creation of all three types of inter-species embryos: cybrids, human transgenic embryos and chimeras. They can be kept for a maximum of 14 days from the date of their creation. It is felt that this is both desirable and necessary for advanced medical research. A licence is necessary to carry out this type of research. Originally the Labour Government had planned to ban such activities but it was persuaded that the medical benefits outweighed any moral dilemma.

Other reforms in the Act aim to reflect changes in moral and social values. For instance, while the welfare of the child must be taken into account in cases of fertility treatment, the Act removes the reference to 'the need for a father' as a factor to be considered. Both partners in same-sex couples can be regarded as legal parents with parental responsibility, while in the past only the woman giving birth was regarded as the legal parent. The Act also introduces a new 'right to know' for children born as a result of fertility treatment who, on reaching majority, can apply for certain details of their biological origins.

Answering questions

1 **Does morality play an important role in the development of the law?**

A good start to this essay would be to define the meaning of morality – you could do this by contrasting moral rules with rules of law. Point out that, although morality is often talked of in connection with sexual issues, it is actually a much broader concept, covering many areas of law.

If you give morality this broad definition, you can argue that moral values have influenced most, if not all, areas of law, illustrating this point with areas of law you have studied in detail. For example, if you have studied contract law, you might consider the moral view which holds that some promises should be binding and others not; in criminal law, you could discuss the idea of *mens rea* as being indicative of moral fault, and the values behind some of the defences. You need to make this part of the essay quite detailed, giving specific examples from case and statute law which back up your points.

You might then go on to make the point that some areas of law seem to have an overtly moral content, but that here, again, morals are not absolute – the **Gillick** case is an example of a situation where the two sides each believed that their view represented morality.

Finally, you could discuss how far morality should influence the law, using the theoretical arguments of Devlin and Hart, and relating them to cases which you know, such as the case of **R v Brown** where criminal liability was imposed on homosexual sado-masochists.

2 **Is civil disobedience ever justified?**

In your introduction you could explain what is meant by civil disobedience and give recent examples of where the UK has seen such behaviour: for example, during the Poll Tax riots, the animal rights protests, the Greenham Common women and demonstrations against road developments in the interests of protecting the environment.

The material in the previous chapter under the heading 'The function of law' will be useful to answer this question. If you accept Marx's theory, the role of the law is to sustain the capitalist ideology and continue the oppression of the proletariat. If this is the case then civil disobedience would always seem to be justified as a means of ending that injustice and reaching the point when the law can 'wither away'. You could draw attention to the natural law theorists who mainly accept that laws failing to reach the standards of the higher, natural law are not laws at all and can, therefore, be disobeyed.

On the other hand, academics such as Durkheim and Weber would consider that obedience of the law is very important for the cohesion of society and the maintenance of order.

Finally you could consider some of the specific areas of our substantive law, such as the Criminal Justice and Public Order Act 1994 and the absence of an entrenched Bill of Rights and consider how far in the UK civil disobedience is justified.

3 **How far should the law enforce morality?**

This is a standard question on the relationship between law and morality and the central part of your essay would discuss the Hart–Devlin debate.

Summary of Chapter 13: Law and morals

Morals are beliefs and values which are shared by a society, or a section of a society; they tell those who share them what is right or wrong.

Law and morality
Both law and morals are normative; they specify what ought to be done, and aim to mark the boundaries between acceptable and unacceptable conduct. While moral rules tend not to be backed by the obvious sanctions which make some legal rules enforceable, they are often reinforced by pressures, such as the disapproval of family and friends.

Changes in law and morality
As we have observed, the moral values of a society tend to change over time; the same applies to its laws. In the UK, legal changes have tended to lag behind moral ones, coming only when the process of moral acceptance is well advanced. On the other hand, law can sometimes bring about changes in social morality.

Differences between law and morality
Although law and morality are clearly closely linked, there are certain ways in which they differ. Many types of behaviour exist which may be widely considered to be immoral, yet we would be very surprised to find laws against them: telling lies, for example. Equally, some forms of behaviour are illegal, but would not usually be described as immoral, such as parking on a yellow line. Then there are areas where the law shares morality's disapproval, but not so far as to prohibit the relevant behaviour.

Should law and morality be separate?
Making every immoral act also illegal seems both impossible and undesirable, yet law with no connection to morality might find it difficult to command much respect. There is still much debate as to how far law should reflect morality; the following are some of the key suggestions.

Natural law

Natural law theorists argue that law should strongly reflect morality. Though their specific theories differ, their shared premise is that there is a kind of higher law, known as the natural law, to which we can turn for a basic moral code.

Utilitarianism

One of the best-known exponents of this theory is John Stuart Mill (1859). He argued that, rather than society imposing morality on individuals, individuals should be free to choose their own conduct, so long as in doing so they did not harm others or, if they did, that the harm done did not outweigh the harm which would be done by interfering with individual liberty.

The Hart–Devlin debate

The issue of whether or not law should follow morality was hotly debated during the late 1950s, when there was public concern about what was perceived to be a decline in sexual morality. The Government of the day set up a commission to look at whether the laws on homosexuality and prostitution should be changed, and much debate was triggered by publication of the commission's findings, known as the Wolfenden Report (1957). Central to this debate were the writings of the leading judge, Lord Devlin, who opposed the report's findings, and Professor Hart who approved of them.

The Warnock Committee

The Warnock Committee was set up by the Government to consider issues relating to scientific advances concerning conception and pregnancy. Many of the Committee's conclusions became law in the Human Fertilisation and Embryology Act 1990. If we look at the reasoning behind the Committee's findings, we can see aspects of both Hart's utilitarian approach, and Devlin's upholding of common morality.

The Human Fertilisation and Embryology Authority

The Human Fertilisation and Embryology Act 1990 created the Human Fertilisation and Embryology Authority (HFEA). This body regulates scientific practice involving human genetics. The Human Fertilisation and Embryology Act 2008 has now replaced the provisions in the 1990 Act. It aims to update and rationalise the law in this field to reflect developments in research and recent case law.

Reading list

Aquinas, St T. (1942) *Summa Theologica.* London: Burns Oates & Washbourne.

Atiyah, P.S. (1979) *The Rise and Fall of Freedom of Contract.* Oxford: Clarendon.

Devlin, P. (1965) *The Enforcement of Morals.* Oxford: Oxford University Press.

Duster, T. (1970) *The Legislation of Morality.* New York: Free Press.

Fenton, A. and Dabell, F. (2007a) Time for change (1). *New Law Journal,* 157: 848.

    (2007b) Time for change (2). *New Law Journal,* 157: 964.

Fuller, L. (1969) *The Morality of Law.* London: Yale UP.

Hart, H.L.A. (1963) *Law, Liberty and Morality.* Oxford: Oxford University Press.

Lee, S. (1986) *Law and Morals.* Oxford: Oxford University Press.

Lukes, S. and Scull, A. (eds) (1983) *Durkheim and the Law.* Oxford: Robertson.

Mill, J.S. (1859) *On Liberty.* London: J.W. Parker.

Olivecrona, K. (1971) *Law as Fact*. London: Stevens.

Schur, E. (1965) *Crimes without Victims: Deviant Behaviour and Public Policy, Abortion, Homosexuality, Drug Addiction*. New York: Prentice-Hall.

Warnock, M. (1986) *Morality and the Law*. Cardiff: University College Cardiff.

Wolfenden, J. (1957) *Report of the Committee on Homosexual Offences and Prostitution*. Cm 2471. London: HMSO.

Young, J. (1971) *The Drugtakers: The Social Meaning of Drug Use*. London: Paladin.

On the internet

www   The website of the Human Fertilisation and Embryology Authority is:
http://www.hfea.gov.uk/

14

Law and justice

This chapter explores the concept of justice by looking at:

- the ideas of the Greek philosopher Aristotle;
- the theory of natural law;
- utilitarianism;
- the economic analysis of law;
- Professor John Rawls's theory of justice; and
- the communist views of Karl Marx.

Introduction

Achieving justice is often seen as one of the most basic aims of a legal system. When areas of that system go wrong, the result is often described as injustice: for example, when people are convicted of crimes they have not committed, as in the cases of the Tottenham Three and the Birmingham Six, we say that a miscarriage of justice has occurred. But what is justice, and what is its relationship with law? These questions have been addressed by writers throughout the centuries, and we will look at some of the most important views in this chapter.

Aristotle

The Greek philosopher Aristotle is responsible for some of the earliest thinking on justice, and his work is still influential today. He considered that a just law was one which would allow individuals to fulfil themselves in society, and distinguished between distributive justice and corrective justice.

Distributive justice was concerned with the allocation of assets such as wealth and honour between members of the community. Here the aim of justice was to achieve proportion, but this did not mean equal shares; Aristotle thought that individuals should receive benefits in proportion to their claim on those benefits.

Corrective justice, on the other hand, applies when a situation that is distributively just, is disturbed – for example, by wrongdoing. A judge should discover what damage has been done, and then try to restore equality by imposing penalties to confiscate any gain made by the offence, and compensate for any damage caused.

Natural law theories

Natural law theories assume that there is a higher order of law, and if the laws of society follow this order they will be just. Aristotle supported this view, and believed that the higher law could be discovered from nature; others, such as the medieval scholar St Thomas Aquinas, thought that the higher law derived from God.

For Aquinas, there were two ways in which law could be unjust. First, a law which was contrary to human good, whether in its form or in its result, was, according to Aquinas, not true law at all. However, such laws might still be obeyed if to do so would avoid causing social disorder. Secondly, a law which was against God's will, and therefore a violation of the natural law, should be disregarded.

Utilitarianism

The utilitarian movement, which includes such writers as Mill and Bentham, is based on the idea that society should work towards the greatest happiness for the greatest number, even if this means that some individuals lose out. Utilitarians assess the justice of rules (and therefore law) by looking at their consequences; in their view, if a rule maximised happiness or well-being or had some other desirable effect, for the majority, it was just. A law could therefore be just even if it created social inequalities, or benefited some at the expense of others, so long as the benefits to the many exceeded the loss to the minority.

The utilitarian approach can be criticised as focusing only on justice for the community as a whole, and leaving out justice for individuals.

The economic analysis of law

This approach has developed mainly in the US, and attempts to offer a more sophisticated alternative to utilitarianism. While the goal of utilitarianism was to promote the greatest happiness of the greatest number, it offered no reliable way of calculating the effect of a law or policy on this goal, or measuring the relative benefits.

The economic analysis takes the view that a thing has value for a person when that person values it; its value can therefore be measured by how much the person is prepared to pay for it, or what would be required to make them give it up. As we have seen, a conflict exists between the concerns of utilitarianism and individual justice, and the same conflict exists here. Take the example of an NHS doctor with a limited budget, faced with one person who needs a life-saving operation costing £100,000, and ten others who each need more minor operations costing £10,000 each. On the face of it, doing the ten operations clearly seems to produce benefit for a greater number at the same cost, and in this sense may be the best way to spend public money. But can we say that this solution offers the first person justice?

A common criticism of the economic analysis of law is that it favours a particular ideology, that of market capitalism. It is based on the idea that the prices at which goods and services are bought and sold are the direct result of the value placed on them by buyer and seller, and therefore the result of free will; it presumes that sellers cannot exploit buyers, because nobody would pay more for something than it was worth to them. Critics of this approach point out that, in practice, power in the marketplace is frequently unequal; a seller may have the monopoly on particular goods, or sellers may collude to keep prices high. Equally, the idea that a thing has value because a person wants it ignores the question of where the desire for that thing originates; expensive advertising campaigns may produce the desire for what they sell, but can we objectively say that such publicity gives them value? In the same way, people may take low-paid jobs, not because they agree with that valuation of their labour, but because there are no other jobs and they have no power in the labour market.

Rawls: *A Theory of Justice*

Professor John Rawls first presented his ideas in *A Theory of Justice* which was published in 1971, and amended them slightly in his later book, *Political Liberalism* (1972). He approaches the question of justice through an imaginary situation in which the members of a society are to decide on a set of principles designed to make their society just, and advance the good of all its members. He describes this initial debate as the original position. The individuals involved will hold their discussions without knowing what their own position in the society is to be – whether they will be rich or poor, of high or low social status, old or young, and what will be the economic or political situation in the society. This veil of ignorance is designed to ensure that the ideas put forward really are the best for all members of society, since nobody will be willing to disadvantage a section of the community if they might find themselves a member of it.

Rawls believes that the principles which would result from such a discussion would include an equal distribution of what he calls social primary goods: these are the things which individuals are assumed to want in order to get the most out of their own lives, including rights, powers and freedoms, and, in Rawls's later work, self-respect. In addition to this, there would be two basic principles. The first involves liberty: a set of basic liberties – including freedom of thought, conscience, speech and assembly – would be available to all. Each person's freedom would be restricted only where the restriction on them was balanced out by greater liberty for the community as a whole. So, for example, the liberty of a person suspected of crime could be restricted by police powers of arrest, since these would increase the freedom from crime of society as a whole. The second basic principle is based on equality. This covers both equality of opportunity – offices and positions within society should be open to all equally – and equality of distribution. Rawls envisages an equal distribution of wealth, with inequalities allowed only where necessary to help the most disadvantaged.

If a social order is just, or nearly just, according to these principles, Rawls argues that those who accept its benefits are bound to accept its rules as well, even if they may disapprove of some of them, provided that those rules do not impose heavy burdens unequally, nor violate the basic principles. Professor Rawls would support limited disobedience, where the basic principles are violated, other means of obtaining redress fail, and no harm is done to others.

Rawls's theory has been extensively criticised. The clearest problem is simply its artificiality, particularly that of the veil of ignorance. As Dworkin has pointed out, even if we accept the scenario Rawls creates, the fact that individuals accept certain principles when they do not know what their position in society will be does not necessarily mean they will continue to live by them if they find themselves in a position to maximise their own advantage at the expense of others. Rawls's theory appears to view human beings as rather more perfect than they have in fact shown themselves to be.

Nozick and the minimal state

Robert Nozick's provocative essay, *Anarchy, State and Utopia* argues that, for a truly just society, the state should have the minimum possible right to interfere in the affairs of individuals; its functions should be limited to the basic needs, such as protecting the individual against force, theft and fraud, and enforcing contracts. Published in 1975, the essay revives a claim traditionally associated with the seventeenth-century writer John Locke, and has strong links with eighteenth-century individualism, and nineteenth-century capitalism.

Nozick's theory emphasises the importance of individual rights and, in particular, rights to property. He argues that the right to hold property is based on the way in which that property is obtained, either by just acquisition (such as inheritance) or just transfer (such as purchase from another), or by rectification of an unjust acquisition (for example, returning stolen property to its owner). Provided individuals have obtained their property in a just manner, the distribution of property throughout society is just; attempts to redistribute wealth are unjust because they interfere with the individual's right to hold justly obtained property. The state should, therefore, have no role in adjusting the distribution of wealth. In fact, Nozick rejects the idea that there are any goods belonging to society; goods belong only to individuals and the state has no right to interfere with them. Nozick's theories have been criticised, but they do reflect a growing disenchantment in Western society with the idea of redistributing wealth – in Britain we can see this in the emphasis placed by recent Governments on lowering taxes and expecting individuals to look after themselves, rather than taking taxes from the rich to help the poor.

Karl Marx

Marx held that it was impossible for a capitalist society to be just: such a society was organised with the aim of upholding the interests of the ruling class, rather than securing justice for all. For Marx, a just society would distribute wealth 'from each according to his capacity, to each according to his needs'; individuals should contribute what they can to society, and receive what they need in return. Marx's views are still influential, but the main criticism made of them is that so far no country has been able to put them into practice with sufficient success to bring about the fair society Marx envisaged.

Kelsen and positivism

For positivists, law can be separated from what is just or morally right. Parts of law may be based on, or incorporate ideas of, morality or justice, but this is not a necessary component of law; a law is still a law and should be obeyed even if it is completely immoral.

One of the best-known positivists is Kelsen, whose theories were first published in 1911, and further developed in his *General Theory of Law and State,* first published in 1945. Kelsen tried to develop a pure theory of law, to explain what law is rather than suggesting what it ought to be. He saw justice as simply the expression of individual preferences and values and, therefore, as an irrational ideal. Because of this, argued Kelsen, it is not possible scientifically to define justice.

Justice in practice

One of the most important aspects of the British legal system is parliamentary supremacy, which essentially means that Parliament is the ultimate law-maker, and can make or unmake any law it wishes. In most other developed countries, a written constitution sets down basic principles with which law should conform, and judges can strike down any legislation which conflicts with them. That is not the case in the UK; our constitution is unwritten and judges must apply the law that Parliament makes, even if they believe it is unjust. If Parliament wanted to make laws condemning all blonde women to death, banning old men from keeping pet dogs, or obliging parents to sell their eldest child into slavery, there would probably be political obstacles to doing so, but there would be no legal ones and judges would be obliged to apply the laws.

Clearly, this situation conflicts with the natural law approach we discussed earlier, where unjust laws were considered not to be true law and, in some circumstances, not to require application by the courts or obedience by the citizen. Arguments for a Bill of Rights, a statement of basic principles against which courts could measure legislation and strike down any in conflict with them, have something in common with the natural law approach, since they assume that some values are fundamental and those given the power to make law in a society should be bound to follow them, rather than being free to make any law they want.

As with most developed legal systems, ours is based on the idea that, to achieve justice, like cases must be treated alike – thus if two people commit a crime in identical circumstances, they should be punished in a similar way. This aim requires fixed rules, so that decision-makers base their verdicts on the application of those rules to the case before them, and not on arbitrary factors such as their own mood or what they personally think of the defendant. However, the downside of this approach is that fixed rules can make it difficult to do justice in individual cases. Take the crime of murder, for example: to commit a murder, a defendant must have intended to kill or to cause serious injury; if this intention is present, the motive for killing is largely irrelevant. While this promotes the idea of like cases being treated alike, allowing judges to opt out of assessing the pros and cons of different motives, which must of necessity involve personal views, it presents problems in individual cases – can we say it is just for someone who kills a terminally ill relative to spare them from pain to be treated in the same way as someone who kills another so they can rob them? They both have intention but are they equally blameworthy? Fixed rules can sometimes promote justice in the majority of cases at the expense of justice in the individual, out-of-the-ordinary one.

The problem of fixed rules preventing justice in individual cases was one which our legal system faced early on in its life, when the common law was first becoming established. Then the answer was to develop a special branch of law, equity, with the specific aim of providing justice in cases where the ordinary rules of law failed to do so. Equity is no longer a separate branch of law, but equitable principles are still important in some areas of the civil law, and allow the courts to use their discretion in order to do justice in individual cases. In the criminal law (though not for the offence of murder) discretion over sentencing can fulfil a similar role. The challenge is to maintain a balance between too much discretion, leading to the possibility of arbitrary decisions, and too little, leading to harsh results in individual cases.

Answering questions

1 Various writers, such as Aristotle, Mill, Bentham, Rawls, Nozick, Marx and Kelsen, have advocated individual theories of justice. Explain, evaluate and analyse three of these. Which theory do you prefer? Explain why.

The question, in effect, sets out the structure of the answer for you. All that is required is to look in depth at theories that explain 'justice' as advocated by three of the above philosophers. You will need to know what each theory is, in detail, in order to be able to express your preference, and be able to evaluate their strengths and weaknesses before you can come to a view.

Summary of Chapter 14: Law and justice

Achieving justice is often seen as one of the most basic aims of a legal system. When areas of that system go wrong, the result is often described as injustice. But what is justice, and what is its relationship with law? These questions have been addressed by writers throughout the centuries.

Aristotle
Aristotle, the Greek philosopher, considered that a just law was one which would allow individuals to fulfil themselves in society, and distinguished between distributive justice and corrective justice.

Natural law theories
Natural law theories assume that there is a higher order of law, and if the laws of society follow this order they will be just.

Utilitarianism
The utilitarian movement is based on the idea that society should work towards the greatest happiness for the greatest number, even if this means that some individuals lose out. Utilitarians assess the justice of rules (and therefore law) by looking at their consequences; in their view, if a rule maximised happiness or well-being or had some other desirable effect, for the majority, it was just.

The economic analysis of law
The economic analysis takes the view that a thing has value for a person when that person values it; its value can therefore be measured by how much the person is prepared to pay for it, or what would be required to make them give it up.

Rawls: *A Theory of Justice*
Professor John Rawls approaches the question of justice through an imaginary situation in which the members of a society are to decide on a set of principles designed to make their society just, and advance the good of all its members. He describes this initial debate as the original position. Rawls believes that the principles which would result would include

an equal distribution of what he calls social primary goods. In addition to this, there would be two basic principles: liberty and equality.

Nozick and the minimal state

Robert Nozick argues that, for a truly just society, the state should have the minimum possible right to interfere in the affairs of individuals; its functions should be limited to the basic needs, such as protecting the individual against force, theft and fraud, and enforcing contracts.

Karl Marx

Marx held that it was impossible for a capitalist society to be just: such a society was organised with the aim of upholding the interests of the ruling class, rather than securing justice for all. For Marx, a just society would distribute wealth 'from each according to his capacity, to each according to his needs'; individuals should contribute what they can to society, and receive what they need in return.

Kelsen and positivism

For positivists, law can be separated from what is just or morally right. Parts of law may be based on, or incorporate ideas of, morality or justice, but this is not a necessary component of law; a law is still a law and should be obeyed even if it is completely immoral.

Reading list

Hayek, F. (1982) *Law, Legislation and Liberty: A New Statement of the Liberal Principles of Justice and Political Economy*. London: Routledge.

Kelsen, H. (1945) *General Theory of Law and State*. Cambridge, MA: Harvard UP.

Locke, J. (1967) *Two Treatises of Government*. London: Cambridge University Press.

Nozick, R. (1975) *Anarchy, State, and Utopia*. Oxford: Blackwell.

Rawls, J. (1971) *A Theory of Justice*. Oxford: Oxford University Press.

(1972) *Political Liberalism, John Dewey Essays in Philosophy*. NY: Columbia University Press.